Bloom's Modern Critical Views

Bloom's Modern Critical Views

Bloom's Modern Critical Views

EUDORA WELTY
Updated Edition

Edited and with an introduction by
Harold Bloom
Sterling Professor of the Humanities
Yale University

CHELSEA HOUSE
P U B L I S H E R S
An imprint of Infobase Publishing

Bloom's Modern Critical Views: Eudora Welty, Updated Edition

©2007 Infobase Publishing

Introduction © 2007 by Harold Bloom

Chelsea House
An imprint of Infobase Publishing
132 West 31st Street
New York NY 10001

Library of Congress Cataloging-in-Publication Data
Eudora Welty / Harold Bloom, editor. — Updated ed.
    p. cm. — (Bloom's modern critical views)
  Includes bibliographical references and index.
  ISBN 0-7910-9311-5 (hardcover)
  1. Welty, Eudora, 1909-2001—Criticism and interpretation. 2. Women and literature—Southern States—History—20th century. I. Bloom, Harold. II. Title. III. Series.
  PS3545.E6Z58 2006
  813'.52—dc22   2006020207

Contributing Editor: Amy Sickels
Cover designed by Takeshi Takahashi
Cover photo © MPI/Hulton Archive/Getty Images

Printed in the United States of America
Bang EJB 10 9 8 7 6 5 4 3 2 1

This book is printed on acid-free paper.

Contents

Editor's Note

My Introduction centers upon two of Eudora Welty's storytelling masterpieces, "A Still Moment" and "The Burning," each of which achieves sublimity. I recall commending the stories to Ms. Welty, when we both spoke at a memorial service for Robert Penn Warren in New York City, in 1989. She smiled gently, and observed only that they had been so long composed that they abode in her consciousness as a kind of inner music. Reading them again, now in 2006, they renew the power they always have held over me.

Peggy Whitman Prenshaw sensitively attempts to unify Welty's profound inwardness and her personal political convictions, while Kenneth Bearden brings together Welty's 1981 foreword to Virginia Woolf's *To the Lighthouse* and the much earlier Welty story, "Powerhouse," where the protagonist is the great jazz singer, Fats Waller.

The extraordinary Welty story, "A Worn Path," is interpreted by Dean Bethea as a properly radical assault against white Evangelical racism, after which Charles E. May considers Welty's widely anthologized story, "Why I Live at the P.O."

The great poet-novelist Robert Penn Warren eloquently traces the development of Welty's storytelling art from *A Curtain of Green* through *The Wide Net*.

Warren French celebrates *The Robber Bridegroom* as a triumph of civilized wisdom, while Suzanne Marrs illuminates the humane achievement of *Delta Wedding*.

The Golden Apples received an appropriate tribute from Elizabeth Bowen, one of Welty's handful of contemporary peers, after which Marilyn Arnold analyzes the loneliness of Edna Earle Ponder in *The Ponder Heart*.

The lyrical narratives of *The Bride of the Innisfallen* are aptly compared to John Keats's poetry by Ruth M. Vande Kieft, while Sally Wolff describes the erotic intensities of *Losing Battles*.

Reynolds Price, himself a distinguished novelist, reads *The Optimist's Daughter* with verve and intensity, after which Franziska Gygax gives the novella a more feminist interpretation.

In this volume's final essay, the noted Irish critic Denis Donoghue gives a thoughtful account of the spirit of place in Eudora Welty's art of fiction.

HAROLD BLOOM

Introduction

I

Eudora Welty divides her remarkable brief autobiography, *One Writer's Beginnings*, into three parts: "Listening," "Learning to See," "Finding A Voice." Gentle yet admonitory, these titles instruct us in how to read her stories and novels, a reading that necessarily involves further growth in our sense of inwardness. Certain of her stories never cease their process of journeying deep into interior regions we generally reserve only for personal and experiential memories. Doubtless they differ from reader to reader; for me they include "A Still Moment" and "The Burning."

Mark Twain has had so varied a progeny among American writers that we hardly feel surprise when we reflect that Welty and Hemingway both emerge from *Huckleberry Finn*. All that Welty and Hemingway share as storytellers is Twain's example. Their obsessive American concern is Huck's: the freedom of a solitary joy, intimately allied to a superstitious fear of solitude. Welty's people, like Hemingway's, and like the self-representations of our major poets—Whitman, Dickinson, Stevens, Frost, Eliot, Hart Crane, R. P. Warren, Roethke, Elizabeth Bishop, Ashbery, Merrill, and Ammons—all secretly believe themselves to be no part of the creation and all feel free only when they are quite alone.

In *One Writer's Beginnings*, Welty comments upon "A Still Moment":

> "A Still Moment"—another early story—was a fantasy, in which
> the separate interior visions guiding three highly individual and
> widely differing men marvelously meet and converge upon the
> same single exterior object. All my characters were actual persons
> who had lived at the same time, who would have been strangers
> to one another, but whose lives had actually taken them at some
> point to the same neighborhood. The scene was in the
> Mississippi wilderness in the historic year 1811—"*anno mirabilis*,"
> the year the stars fell on Alabama and lemmings, or squirrels
> perhaps, rushed straight down the continent and plunged into the
> Gulf of Mexico, and an earthquake made the Mississippi River
> run backwards and New Madrid, Missouri, tumbled in and
> disappeared. My real characters were Lorenzo Dow the New
> England evangelist, Murrell the outlaw bandit and murderer on
> the Natchez Trace, and Audubon the painter; and the exterior
> object on which they all at the same moment set their eyes is a
> small heron, feeding.

Welty's choices—Lorenzo Dow, James Murrell, Audubon—are all
obsessed solitaries. Dow, the circuit rider, presumably ought to be the least
solipsistic of the three, yet his fierce cry as he rides on at top speed—"I must
have souls! And souls I must have!"—is evidence of an emptiness that never
can be filled:

> It was the hour of sunset. All the souls that he had saved and all
> those he had not took dusky shapes in the mist that hung between
> the high banks, and seemed by their great number and density to
> block his way, and showed no signs of melting or changing back
> into mist, so that he feared his passage was to be difficult forever.
> The poor souls that were not saved were darker and more pitiful
> than those that were, and still there was not any of the radiance
> he would have hoped to see in such a congregation.

As Dow himself observes, his eyes are in a "failing proportion to my
loving heart always," which makes us doubt his heart. He loves his wife,
Peggy, effortlessly since she is in Massachusetts and he is galloping along on
the Old Natchez Trace. Indeed, their love can be altogether effortless,
consisting as it does of a marriage proposal, accepted as his first words to her,
a few hours of union, and his rapid departure south for evangelical purposes,

pursued by her first letter declaring that she, like her husband, fears only death, but never mere separation.

This remarkable hunter of souls, intrepid at evading rapacious Indians or Irish Catholics, can be regarded as a sublime lunatic, or merely as a pure product of America:

> Soon night would descend, and a camp-meeting ground ahead would fill with its sinners like the sky with its stars. How he hungered for them! He looked in prescience with a longing of love over the throng that waited while the flames of the torches threw change, change, change over their faces. How could he bring them enough, if it were not divine love and sufficient warning of all that could threaten them? He rode on faster. He was a filler of appointments, and he filled more and more, until his journeys up and down creation were nothing but a shuttle, driving back and forth upon the rich expanse of his vision. He was homeless by his own choice, he must be everywhere at some time, and somewhere soon. There hastening in the wilderness on his flying horse he gave the night's torch-lit crowd a premature benediction, he could not wait. He spread his arms out, one at a time for safety, and he wished, when they would all be gathered in by his tin horn blasts and the inspired words would go out over their heads, to brood above the entire and passionate life of the wide world, to become its rightful part.
>
> He peered ahead. "Inhabitants of Time! The wilderness is your souls on earth!" he shouted ahead into the treetops. "Look about you, if you would view the conditions of your spirit, put here by the good Lord to show you and afright you. These wild places and these trails of awesome loneliness lie nowhere, nowhere, but in your heart."

Dow is his own congregation, and his heart indeed contains the wild places and awesomely lonesome trails through which he endlessly rushes. His antithesis is provided by the murderous James Murrell, who suddenly rides at Dow's side, without bothering to look at him. If Dow is a mad angel, Murrell is a scarcely sane devil, talking to slow the evangelist down, without realizing that the sublimely crazy Lorenzo listens only to the voice of God:

> Murrell riding along with his victim-to-be, Murrell, riding, was Murrell talking. He told away at his long tales, with always a distance and a long length of time flowing through them, and all

centered about a silent man. In each the silent man would have done a piece of evil, a robbery or a murder, in a place of long ago, and it was all made for the revelation in the end that the silent man was Murrell himself, and the long story had happened yesterday, and the place *here*—the Natchez Trace. It would only take one dawning look for the victim to see that all of this was another story and he himself had listened his way into it, and that he too was about to recede in time (to where the dread was forgotten) for some listener and to live for a listener in the long ago. Destroy the present!—that must have been the first thing that was whispered in Murrell's heart—the living moment and the man that lives in it must die before you can go on. It was his habit to bring the journey—which might even take days—to a close with a kind of ceremony. Turning his face at last into the face of the victim, for he had never seen him before now, he would tower up with the sudden height of a man no longer the tale teller but the speechless protagonist, silent at last, one degree nearer the hero. Then he would murder the man.

Since Murrell is capable of observing nothing whatsoever, he does not know what the reader knows, which is that Lorenzo is not a potential victim for this self-dramatizing Satanist. Whatever the confrontation between angel and devil might have brought (and one's surmise is that Murrell might not have survived), the crucial moment is disturbed by the arrival of a third, the even weirder Audubon:

Audubon said nothing because he had gone without speaking a word for days. He did not regard his thoughts for the birds and animals as susceptible, in their first change, to words. His long playing on the flute was not in its origin a talking to himself. Rather than speak to order or describe, he would always draw a deer with a stroke across it to communicate his need of venison to an Indian. He had only found words when he discovered that there is much otherwise lost that can be noted down each item in its own day, and he wrote often now in a journal, not wanting anything to be lost the way it had been, all the past, and he would write about a day, "Only sorry that the Sun Sets."

These three extraordinarily diverse obsessives share a still moment, in which "a solitary snowy heron flew down not far away and began to feed beside the marsh water." To Lorenzo, the heron's epiphany is God's love become visible. To Murrell, it is "only whiteness ensconced in darkness," a prophecy of the slave, brigand, and outcast rebellion he hopes to lead in the Natchez country. To Audubon it is precisely what it is, a white heron he must slay if he is to be able to paint, a model that must die in order to become a model. Welty gives us no preference among these three:

> What each of them had wanted was simply *all*. To save all souls, to destroy all men, to see and record all life that filled this world—all, all—but now a single frail yearning seemed to go out of the three of them for a moment and to stretch toward this one snowy, shy bird in the marshes. It was as if three whirlwinds had drawn together at some center, to find there feeding in peace a snowy heron. Its own slow spiral of flight could take it away in its own time, but for a little it held them still, it laid quiet over them, and they stood for a moment unburdened....

To quest for *all* is to know anything but peace, and "a still moment" is only shared by these three questers in a phantasmagoria. When the moment ends with Audubon's killing of the bird, only Lorenzo's horrified reaction is of deep import or interest. Murrell is content to lie back in ambush and await travelers more innocent, who will suit his satanic destiny as Lorenzo and Audubon could not. Audubon is also content to go on, to fulfill his vast design. But Lorenzo's epiphany has turned into a negative moment and though he will go on to gather in the multitudes, he has been darkened:

> In the woods that echoed yet in his ears, Lorenzo riding slowly looked back. The hair rose on his head and his hands began to shake with cold, and suddenly it seemed to him that God Himself, just now, thought of the Idea of Separateness. For surely He had never thought of it before, when the little white heron was flying down to feed. He could understand God's giving Separateness first and then giving Love to follow and heal in its wonder; but God had reversed this, and given Love first and then Separateness, as though it did not matter to Him which came first. Perhaps it was that God never counted the moments of Time; Lorenzo did that, among his tasks of love. Time did not occur to God. Therefore—did He even know of it? How to explain Time and Separateness back to God, Who had never

thought of them, Who could let the whole world come to grief in
a scattering moment?

This is a meditation on the verge of heresy, presumably Gnostic, rather
than on the border of unbelief. Robert Penn Warren, in a classical early essay
on "Love and Separateness in Eudora Welty" (1944), reads the dialectic of
Love and Separateness here as the perhaps Blakean contraries of Innocence
and Experience. On this reading, Welty is an ironist of limits and of
contamination, for whom knowledge destroys love, almost as though love
could survive only upon enchanted ground. That may underestimate both
Lorenzo and Welty. Pragmatically, Lorenzo has been unchanged by the still
moment of love and its shattering into separateness; indeed he is as
unchanged as Murrell or Audubon. But only Lorenzo remains haunted by a
vision, by a particular beauty greater than he can account for, and yet never
can deny. He will change some day, though Welty does not pursue that
change.

II

The truth of Welty's fictive cosmos, for all her preternatural
gentleness, is that love always does come first, and always does yield to an
irreparable separateness. Like her true mentor, Twain, she triumphs in
comedy because her deepest awareness is of a nihilistic "unground" beyond
consciousness or metaphysics, and comedy is the only graceful defense
against that cosmological emptiness. Unlike Faulkner and Flannery
O'Connor, she is, by design, a genial writer, but the design is a subtler
version of Twain's more urgent desperation. "A Still Moment," despite its
implications, remains a fantasy of the continuities of quest. Rather than
discuss one of her many masterpieces of humorous storytelling, I choose
instead "The Burning," which flamboyantly displays her gift for a certain
grim sublimity, and which represents her upon her heights, as a stylist and
narrator who can rival Hemingway in representing the discontinuities of war
and disaster.

"The Burning" belongs to the dark genre of Southern Gothic, akin to
Faulkner's "A Rose for Emily" and O'Connor's "A Good Man Is Hard to
Find." Welty, as historical a storyteller as Robert Penn Warren, imagines an
incident from Sherman's destructive march through Georgia. The imagining
is almost irrealistic in its complexity of tone and indirect representation, so
that "The Burning" is perhaps the most formidable of all Welty's stories,
with the kind of rhetorical and allusive difficulties we expect to encounter
more frequently in modern poetry than in modern short stories. Writing on

form in D. H. Lawrence's stories, Welty remarked on "the unmitigated shapelessness of Lawrence's narrative" and sharply noted that his characters would only appear deranged if they began to speak on the streets as they do in the stories:

> For the truth seems to be that Lawrence's characters don't really speak their words—not conversationally, not to one another— they are not speaking on the street, but are playing like fountains or radiating like the moon or storming like the sea, or their silence is the silence of wicked rocks. It is borne home to us that Lawrence is writing of our human relationships on earth in terms of eternity, and these terms set Lawrence's form. The author himself appears in authorship in places like the moon, and sometimes smites us while we stand there under him.

The characters of Welty's "The Burning" fit her description of Lawrence's men and women; their silence too is the silence of wicked rocks. Essentially they are only three: two mad sisters, Miss Theo and Miss Myra, and their slave, called Florabel in the story's first published version (*Harper's Bazaar*, March, 1951). The two demented high-born ladies are very different; Miss Theo is deep-voiced and domineering, Miss Myra gentler and dependent. But little of the story is seen through their eyes or refracted through either's consciousness. Florabel, an immensely passive being, sees and reacts, in a mode not summarized until nearly the end of the story, in its first printed form:

> Florabel, with no last name, was a slave. By the time of that moment on the hill, her kind had been slaves in a dozen countries and that of their origin for thousands of years. She let everything be itself according to its nature—the animate, the inanimate, the symbol. She did not move to alter any of it, not unless she was told to and shown how. And so she saw what happened, the creation and the destruction. She waited on either one and served it, not expecting anything of it but what she got; only sooner or later she would seek protection somewhere. Herself was an unknown, like a queen, somebody she had heard called, even cried for. As a slave she was earth's most detached visitor. The world had not touched her—only possessed and hurt her, like a man; taken away from her, like a man; turned another way from her and left her, like a man. Her vision was clear. She saw what was there and had not sought it, did not seek it yet. (It

was *her* eyes that were in the back of her head, her vision that met itself coming the long way back, unimpeded, like the light of stars.) The command to loot was one more fading memory. Many commands had been given her, some even held over from before she was born; delayed and miscarried and interrupted, they could yet be fulfilled, though it was safer for one once a slave to hear things a second time, a third, fourth, hundredth, thousandth, if they were to be carried out to the letter. In that noon quiet after conflict there might have been only the two triumphant, the mirror which was a symbol in the world and Florabel who was standing there; it was the rest that had died of it.

The mirror, "a symbol in the world," is in this first version of "The Burning" a synecdoche for the fragmented vision of both mad sisters and their slave. In rewriting the story, Welty uses the mirror more subtly. Delilah (as Florabel is now named) sees Sherman's soldiers and their apocalyptic white horse directly as they enter the house, and she runs to tell Miss Theo and Miss Myra. They deign to look up and observe the intruders in the mirror over the fireplace. Throughout the rest of the catastrophic narrative, the sisters behold everything that transpires as though in a mirror. Clearly they have spent their lives estranging reality as though looking in a mirror, and they move to their self-destruction as though they saw themselves only as images. The violence that prepares for the burning is thus rendered as phantasmagoria:

The sisters showed no surprise to see soldiers and Negroes alike (old Ophelia in the way, talking, talking) strike into and out of the doors of the house, the front now the same as the back, to carry off beds, tables, candlesticks, washstands, cedar buckets, china pitchers, with their backs bent double; or the horses ready to go; or the food of the kitchen bolted down— and so much of it thrown away, this must be a second dinner; or the unsilenceable dogs, the old pack mixed with the strangers and fighting with all their hearts over bones. The last skinny sacks were thrown on the wagons—the last flour, the last scraping and clearing from Ophelia's shelves, even her pepper-grinder. The silver Delilah could count was counted on strange blankets and then, knocking against the teapot, rolled together, tied up like a bag of bones. A drummer boy with his drum around his neck caught both Miss Theo's peacocks,

Marco and Polo, and wrung their necks in the yard. Nobody could look at those bird-corpses; nobody did.

The strangling of the peacocks is a presage of the weirdest sequence in "The Burning," in which Miss Theo and Miss Myra hang themselves from a tree, with Delilah assisting as ordered. It is only when the sisters are dead that we begin to understand that "The Burning" is more Delilah's story than it ever could have been theirs. A baby, Phinny, who had been allowed to perish in the fire (Welty does not allow us to know why), turns out to have been begotten by Miss Theo's and Miss Myra's brother Benton upon Delilah:

> The mirror's cloudy bottom sent up minnows of light to the brim where now a face pure as a water-lily shadow was floating. Almost too small and deep down to see, they were quivering, leaping to life, fighting, aping old things Delilah had seen done in this world already, sometimes what men had done to Miss Theo and Miss Myra and the peacocks and to slaves, and sometimes what a slave had done and what anybody now could do to anybody. Under the flicker of the sun's licks, then under its whole blow and blare, like an unheard scream, like an act of mercy gone, as the wall-less light and July blaze struck through from the opened sky, the mirror felled her flat.
>
> She put her arms over her head and waited, for they would all be coming again, gathering under her and above her, bees saddled like horses out of the air, butterflies harnessed to one another, bats with masks on, birds together, all with their weapons bared. She listened for the blows, and dreaded that whole army of wings—of flies, birds, serpents, their glowing enemy faces and bright kings' dresses, that banner of colors forked out, all this world that was flying, striking, stricken, falling, gilded or blackened, mortally splitting and falling apart, proud turbans unwinding, turning like the spotted dying leaves of fall, spiraling down to bottomless ash; she dreaded the fury of all the butterflies and dragonflies in the world riding, blades unconcealed and at point—descending, and rising again from the waters below, down under, one whale made of his own grave, opening his mouth to swallow Jonah one more time.
>
> Jonah!—a homely face to her, that could still look back from the red lane he'd gone down, even if it was too late to speak. He was her Jonah, her Phinny, her black monkey; she worshiped

him still, though it was long ago he was taken from her the first time.

Delilah, hysterical with fear, shock, and anguish, has fallen into the mirror world of the mad sisters, her self-slain mistresses. She is restored to some sense of reality by her search for Phinny's bones. Carrying them, and what she can save of the sisters' finery, she marches on to what is presented ambiguously either as her own freedom, or her death, or perhaps both together:

> Following the smell of horses and fire, to men, she kept in the wheel tracks till they broke down at the river. In the shade underneath the burned and fallen bridge she sat on a stump and chewed for a while, without dreams, the comb of a dirtdauber. Then once more kneeling, she took a drink from the Big Black, and pulled the shoes off her feet and waded in.
> Submerged to the waist, to the breast, stretching her throat like a sunflower stalk above the river's opaque skin, she kept on, her treasure stacked on the roof of her head, hands laced upon it. She had forgotten how or when she knew, and she did not know what day this was, but she knew—it would not rain, the river would not rise, until Saturday.

This extraordinary prose rises to an American sublime that is neither grotesque nor ironic. Welty, in her *On Short Stories*, asked the question: "Where does beauty come from, in the short story?" and answered only that beauty was a result:

> It *comes*. We are lucky when beauty comes, for often we try and it should come, it could, we think, but then when the virtues of our story are counted, beauty is standing behind the door.

I do not propose to count the virtues of "The Burning," or even of "A Still Moment." Both narratives are as thoroughly written through, fully composed, as the best poems of Wallace Stevens or of Hart Crane, or the strongest of Hemingway's stories, or Faulkner's *As I Lay Dying*. American writing in the twentieth century touches the sublime mode only in scattered instances, and always by reaching the frontier where the phantasmagoric, and the realism of violence, are separated only by ghostlier demarcations, keener sounds. Welty's high distinction is that in her, the demarcations are as ghostly, the sounds as keen, as they are in her greatest narrative contemporaries, Faulkner and Hemingway.

PEGGY WHITMAN PRENSHAW

Welty's Transformations of the Public, the Private, and the Political

For some years I have been interested to read Eudora Welty for the many ways she suggests in her fiction, essays, and interviews that the personal *is* political, though to use this familiar feminist phrase is not Welty's way. The outpouring of enlightening critical studies of Welty over the past two decades has not only enriched my understanding of the essential feminism informing Welty's work but has corroborated my long-held view that she gives us a fictional world that profoundly challenges the roles men and women have been given to play in Western culture—that is, that questions conventional systems of sexual politics.[1]

What I wish to do here, however, is not so much to revisit topics well explored by recent critics who have written knowledgeably and expansively of Welty's feminism. Instead, I intend to employ a conventional definition of "politics" as the means by which a society governs itself, or to discuss what one might call simply "public affairs," in an exploration of Welty's views of the public, the private, and the political spheres of human activity. In particular, I want to inquire into Welty's practice of relocating, or displacing, the public and the political spheres to private and moral ones—and to ask why she so deeply distrusts "politics" in fiction and in life.

Providing a point of departure is a recollection of an interview with Eudora Welty that Albert Devlin and I undertook in 1986 in her home in

From *Eudora Welty and Politics: Did the Writer Crusade?* Harriet Pollack and Suzanne Marrs, eds. © 2001 by Louisiana State University Press.

Jackson, Mississippi. For several hours we engaged in a lively but relaxed conversation, mostly concerning other writers, but toward the end of the visit the discussion became quite intense. The change in tone occurred as Welty replied to a question about her political assessment of the nation and the times, the mid-1980s. Her response is notable in several respects, most especially in revealing the negative connotations she associates with the word *politics*, linked as it was in her mind with demagogic leaders and racism.

As recorded in the published interview, Devlin begins the sequence of questions by noting that he became interested in politics in the early 1960s, inspired by President Kennedy and civil rights legislation, which he said had given him "a sense of unity ... and also a national purpose." By contrast, he had come two decades later to have "no idea where we are, either nationally or individually." Then he asks, "You've seen this over a longer period of time, do you have a sense of perplexity too?"

"I do, I feel that the perplexity is all over the nation," Welty answered. "And I also loved John F. Kennedy; I thought something wonderful was going to happen in the world when he was elected. And that really vanished with his assassination."

Turning from the national scene to consider her own local experience of "politics," she voiced not so much grief as deep frustration. "When I was growing up here, politics was everywhere, but there was not any kind of glorification of politics in my family on either of my parents' sides." Distancing herself from immoderate politics by claiming a familial disposition for reasonable moderation, she remembers Mississippians "like Bilbo and Vardaman who were almost unbelievable. And that is the kind of thinking that a lot of Jackson who were on the wrong side of Civil Rights hark back to: 'What we need is somebody like ...!' So that's where their ideals led them, an idiotic return to something that was not any good in the first place."

Welty sharply dismissed such politics, registering her exasperation, and then made in quick succession a series of assertions that summarize the main points I want to pursue in this analysis of her "political" thought. Of the ideals of those who canonize Bilbo and Vardaman, she said, "Well, that's not anything to place too much confidence in. I can't talk. Such a tremendous—I do feel that private relationships between blacks and white have always been the steadying thing. I believe in private human relations anyway, for understanding. And I've always had faith that they would resolve problems."[2]

Here we find Welty silencing herself as she attempts to speak about "politics," a silencing that she accomplishes, one notices, with passion and resignation. Her hope for a better society lies not with "political ideals," compromised as they are for her by group conformity and racism, but rather in the individual heart, which is most effectively reached through private relations or art, not politics. The distinction between the domains of art and of politics (which she refers to variously as crusading, propagandizing, exhorting, etc.) is one Welty returns to again and again in essays and interviews. Steadfastly skeptical of politics, she does not pin hopes for individual rights or social justice upon a linking of the personal and the political. Instead, she makes a case for the superior efficacy of the separate, personal sphere as the venue where understanding of the Other takes place, where self-knowledge occurs, and where one's political beliefs may therefore take humane shape. "I don't think literature—I'm talking about fiction now—I don't think it can exhort. Or it loses every bit of its reality and value. I think it speaks to what is more deeply within, that is, the personal, and conveys its meaning that way. And then one hopes that a person made alert or aroused to be more sensitive to other human beings would go on to look at things on a larger scale by himself. I wouldn't like to read a work of fiction that I thought had an ulterior motive, to persuade me politically. I automatically react the other way." A little later she concluded her rather lengthy commentary on politics and fiction with a reassertion of her separateness from group affiliations, even literary ones, such as Bloomsbury. "I'm just interested in people as individuals ... caring for individuals so much."[3]

Welty's frequently stated aversion to the politicizing of fiction and her fictional practice of steering well clear of overtly political topics, except in a few exceptional cases,[4] have made it commonplace throughout the nearly sixty years of her literary career for reviewers and critics to think and write of her fiction as nonpolitical. Diana Trilling's reviews of *The Wide Net* and *Delta Wedding* spoke of a fictional vision that was like a ballet—stylized, elegant, too often precious, and lacking in a realistic engagement with the South as it actually existed in a social, political manifestation. "Cloud Cuckoo Land" was the label given by a *Time* magazine reviewer to Welty's portrait of the 1923 Mississippi Delta, the nod to Aristophanes serving to indict what the reviewer regarded as the novel's political naïveté. A generation later, in his 1980 study of the Southern Renaissance, Richard King made the problematical assertion, often rebutted in the intervening years, that Welty, along with other southern women writers (excepting Lillian Smith), was "not concerned with the larger cultural, racial, and political themes" that he was focusing upon. According to King, Welty and the others "did not place the region at the center of their imaginative visions."[5]

For many years there have also been rumors of repeated Nobel Prize nominations that have met resistance because of judges' perception of a lack of social-political consciousness in Welty. And Welty herself has, of course, somewhat exacerbated her reputation for apoliticality by such pieces as "Must the Novelist Crusade?" Published in the *Atlantic* in October 1965, the essay pointedly differentiates the arena of the novelist from that of the social or political crusader. "The writing of a novel is taking life as it already exists," Welty writes, "not to report it but to make an object, toward the end that the finished work might contain this life inside it, and offer it to the reader.... What distinguishes it above all from the raw material, and what distinguishes it from journalism, is that inherent in the novel is the possibility of a shared act of the imagination between its writer and its reader." For Welty, a crusading novelist is damned from the start by the deadening effects for fiction of totalizing generalities. These generalities, the pronouncements the crusader is trying to drive home, "make too much noise," as Welty personifies them, "for us to hear what people might be trying to say." By contrast, she says, "there is absolutely everything in great fiction but a clear answer."[6]

In interviews she has frequently spoken dismissively of efforts by social activists to engage her in causes. Jonathan Yardley reported in 1973 that, "as a Southerner and a woman," Welty was "constantly pressed for her opinions on race and Women's Liberation." She told Yardley, "I've never had any prejudice shown to me, so I have no bone to pick. I do think women should be paid as much as men, which I don't suppose anyone would disagree with. I don't see why, just because I write stories, that should give me the authority about, say, what should happen about abortion. Maybe I'm shirking responsibility, but I don't think so. Everything I feel is in my stories."[7]

Without engaging here the question of Welty's construction of "prejudice," I should like to inquire into her assumptions about what constitutes public space and political action, as distinguished from the private domain, and how these assumptions are related to the South in which she grew up and began seriously to write about in the 1930s.

The space in which Welty places what one might call acts of political behavior—listening, talking, debating, evaluating argument, coming to evaluative positions regarding competing arguments about the society's good—that is, a free political arena—is only infrequently located in town halls, state capitols, political campaign sites, or union halls. Nonetheless, I would argue that the fiction displays a persistent regard for political negotiations but displaces such negotiations from political sites to what she regards as—and indeed, what has traditionally been regarded as—the private sphere, private, perhaps, because these sites are so often the domain of women. Welty's first collection of short stories, *A Curtain of Green* (1941), later included in *The Collected Stories of Eudora Welty*, opens with "Lily Daw and the Three Ladies," a story centered upon the question of what constitutes the good life for Lily Daw, a young woman who is effectively the ward of the town. Is her welfare best served by the protection offered by the state in the form of the Ellisville Institute for the Feeble-Minded of Mississippi? Or should she be mainstreamed into marriage with a traveling xylophone player and thus into the society of bourgeois individualism? The debate, held by three main female personages of Victory, Mississippi, is intense, impersonal, and conducted in the civic space of the post office, the street, the foot of the water tank, Lily's house, and the train station. But the political import of the story is oblique, camouflaged from most readers by Welty's humor, her genial but subversive mockery of the three ladies' exaggerated self importance, and a general readiness to read female outcomes as private, domestic matters rather than political ones.

When Welty depicts a condition or site where debate freely occurs, which engages persons of equal standing in speech and action—and which leads to a consequence of persuasion, rather than despotic enforcement of will—she is usually describing what is conventionally regarded as a private, rather than public, realm. She presents, however, a display of political negotiation, one that resembles Hannah Arendt's description in *The Human Condition* of the Greek polis, wherein the quality of debate differs from that of the private household. In the Greek world, the household was subject to the absolute rule of the household head, whereas the polis offered a site for contesting speech and action. "The *polis*," writes Arendt, "was distinguished from the household in that it knew only 'equals,' whereas the household was the center of the strictest inequality. To be free meant both not to be subject to the necessity of life or to the command of another *and* not to be in command oneself."[8] For the Greeks it was the public realm, not the private, that constituted the sphere of freedom and individuality. Arendt goes on to discuss the blurring of the public and private in the modern period, which has produced a social sphere she sees as constraining individual action and producing an ever-increasing conformity. That Welty's ladies of Victory debating the best life choice for Lily Daw are operating in the political realm, however, rather than the social, is evidenced by the existence of opposing conceptions of right action that are debated and enacted in an extrafamilial civic space. What is anomalous for Welty's Victory in comparison with the Greek polis is that the matter subjected to public debate (Lily's future) seems trivial and particular, rather than serious and communal.

Many critics have written that the *Curtain of Green* fiction reflects a modernist vision, that the seventeen stories are populated with an array of psychically wounded, self-conscious, cut-off-from-the-world characters.[9] Tom Harris in "The Hitch-Hikers," the stranger in "The Key" who tries to bridge a chasm between a deaf-mute couple and his world, Howard in

"Flowers for Marjorie," who is both starved and surfeited by the gaudy, empty commercial world he can't escape—these and others are rather familiar wanderers, lost souls who have neither physical nor spiritual security. The stories are also responses in a specific historical context to one particular time and place, as Welty notes in her introduction to *The Collected Stories of Eudora Welty*. They depict an impoverished, poorly educated, agrarian, small-town populace of 1930s Mississippi, a cast that steps almost directly from the photographs and articles of Welty's WPA work as a "junior publicity agent" traveling all eighty-two counties of the state. As snapshots of Mississippi people and places and as constructions of literary modernism, the world of these stories is mostly one in which political talk and action rarely occur. Sister in "Why I Live at the P.O." inquires into the operative conditions for justice—fairness, impartiality, reciprocity—but her auditor is wordless and no debate ensues. "Lily Daw" and "Petrified Man" are rather exceptions in the *Curtain of Green* collection, posing as they do public discussions (on the street and in the beauty shop) of what constitutes right action. More typical are "The Whistle," in which a desperate farm couple try to save their tomato crop by covering the tender plants with their very nightclothes, and "Death of a Traveling Salesman," Welty's first published story (1936), in which R. J. Bowman's lonely death and the nearly silent presence of the backwoods couple mark the Mississippi hill country as utterly remote from political life.

With a few exceptions already noted, Welty rarely entertains the possibility of political discourse in these early stories. Emancipatory strategies of speech possession and empowerment are revealed as available in a potential or chrysalis stage, as Patricia Yaeger observes of the character Ruby Fisher in her commentary on "A Piece of News," or even in a realized, albeit monologic, stage such as Dawn Trouard persuasively argues for Ruby Fisher,[10] but sustaining, confirming, negotiating, contestatory speech is far less present in most of these stories than is a muted spirit of endurance (Phoenix Jackson), a display of performative speech (Powerhouse), or utter self-silencing (Clytie).

And yet when Welty comes a generation later in her full maturity to the writing of *Losing Battles* (1970), returning to a hill-country farm similar to the one she first wrote about in "Death of a Traveling Salesman," she creates a parliament of vigorous voices, freely speaking, debating issues of authority, and legitimacy, and the boundaries between self, the nuclear family, and the larger group, debating, that is, the nature of justice and the knowledge most worth knowing. In fact, the novel is remarkably classical in its affirmation of the possibility of sustaining and renewing group life through the agency of human speech. If one is to appreciate fully the connection—and contrast—

between the Welty of "Death of a Traveling Salesman" and the Welty of *Losing Battles*, one must gain an understanding of her views of the South—her views of politics, race, religion, and poverty, for example—as well as an understanding of the influence of literary modernism upon her writing.

Born in 1909, Welty grew up in a Mississippi dominated by a political and governmental system organized upon racial segregation. Open public debate exhibiting differing views about what constitutes, say, fair and equal treatment, or political legitimacy, or—more radically—racial justice, was not audible in the civic life of Jackson. The racism was, of course, exacerbated by the poverty, which Welty saw at close hand during her travels in the 1930s. She told Jonathan Yardley, and has often repeated in interviews, that the experience was pivotal in her growth as a writer. "It was a matter of getting to see something of the state.... I went to every county seat.... It was a—I almost said "heart-opener"—a real eye-opener. My feelings were engaged by the outside world, I think for the first time.... I never had really understood what was going on in the world until I saw it by myself. I'd always been sheltered, traveling with my father. I was shown the Grand Canyon, but that's not the same as seeing one family, living by the side of the road. That was when I really started writing stories."[11]

What she saw was often wrenching poverty and what she heard from Mississippi political leaders as Roosevelt's New Deal programs began to take effect was often complaint that the national relief programs were subverting the going wage for farm laborers and disturbing the political-social-racial system.[12] Ironically, even as they complained, the politically powerful planters in the Delta became the major beneficiaries of the New Deal in Mississippi. In fact, as historian James C. Cobb notes, the New Deal gave a tremendous boost to the state's economy, bringing to "the poorest state in the Union" its major source of income in 1934. Writing of the Delta region in the Depression era, Cobb observes that some "slender benefits" of federal aid did trickle down to the African American farm laborers, but that it was the planters to whom the federal funds mainly flowed. They received government crop subsidies, protection against risk, and assistance with machinery purchases, while enjoying the advantage of a cheap labor pool that federal aid helped support.[13]

In the 1940 story "Keela, the Outcast Indian Maiden," first submitted for publication in 1938, Welty portrays an onlooker, Steve, who has witnessed an act of oppression, carried to the point of torture and enslavement, visited upon a black man, small of stature and crippled, who is "saved" by a tall white man from Texas.[14] The restorative act is private and personal. Its outcome is neither monument nor legislation but rather Steve's anguished remembering and confessing his sense of guilt to Little Lee Roy, the victim, and to the impassive Max, Steve's guide in Cane Springs, Mississippi.

Instructively, in this story Welty substitutes the evangelical site of personal confession of sins for a public or political space of redress of civil grievance. Indeed, the story points up conditions of political life in the South that Welty came to know during these early years: a contaminated political space that allowed for little or no free discussion of societal relations; a religious space congenial to fundamentalist belief; private responsibility for one's salvation; and confessionals that occurred in dramatic moments of strong emotion or duress, such as one might experience in revival meetings or, as Welty describes in *One Writer's Beginnings*, religious gatherings held in the city auditorium, led by celebrated evangelists like Gypsy Smith or Billy Sunday. Although in the story of Keela Welty does not explicitly attribute Steve's motive for expiation to a religious conversion, there is ample evidence among historical studies of southern culture that religious belief contributed extensively to public ethical practice. Feelings of remorse for one's own guilt and for society's sins against another was an acknowledged, even familiar, motivation for political reform. Morton Sosna is one of many historians who has observed, for example, the importance of evangelicalism to southern liberalism. "Religion played a dominant role in the career of many," he writes, "and one is struck by the number of white Southern liberals who pointed to simple Christian pieties as the essential element of their thinking." Southern religion scholar Samuel S. Hill finds a marked "religious momentum" in the region's culture beginning in the 1870s and 1880s, although he notes that evangelical Protestantism had achieved dominance by 1830. Hill writes that evangelicalism was "relatively inert for half a century" but from the late nineteenth century to the present "it has been busy and aggressive, converting the lost, purifying an imperfect church, and going forth to transform the world."[15]

Since the church and the courthouse were perhaps the two most public sites available for adult social exchange in Mississippi, it would be useful here to look briefly at the relation of religion to politics in the decade of the thirties and in the preceding period, the years of Welty's childhood. Of particular interest is the role of the Methodist Church in efforts to improve the work and living conditions of the poor and needy, specifically, the home missions effort of Methodist women. Welty herself grew up going to the Methodist church, as she tells Patricia Wheatley in a 1986 interview taped for a BBC documentary, although hers was not, she notes, a particularly religious household. "My mother was brought up in the Methodist church, and my father, too. His father led the choir in the Methodist church in Ohio in his little town. And I was brought up going to the Methodist Sunday School, for which I'm glad, and learned the Bible, which I love to read."[16]

As one learns from John Patrick McDowell's *The Social Gospel in the South*, the women's home mission movement provided the most accessible avenue for southern Methodist women to participate in public social action. Their starting point, as McDowell notes, was the home and the family, their "desire to see stable, moral homes among the poor as well as the rich, and among the unchurched as well as the churched" their major motivation. The women involved in home mission work came, as Methodists, from "a religious tradition that emphasized the importance of ethical activity and the possibility of human improvement." McDowell cautions that one should not view the Methodist women's home mission work as overturning the widespread view that southern religion "focused primarily on individual salvation and personal morality," but he argues for an acknowledgment of their contribution to political and social reform in the South.[17]

Among the reform activists from Mississippi during this period were two women who did indeed get their start in politics in Methodist home missions: Nellie Nugent Somerville and Ellen Woodward. Both women furnish instructive examples of how socially constructed gender roles framed the "political sphere" for women, even for such activists as Somerville and Woodward. Implicit in much of their work and in their statements about their motivation for public service is the assumption that the purpose of political action is the establishment of justice in the personal, familial, and domestic realms, a view anticipating and closely paralleling Welty's political thought.

Born in 1863, Somerville, a devout Methodist, organized and served as president of a church home mission group when she was thirty-three. Later, despite what historian Anne Firor Scott describes as the obstacle of Mississippi's being "probably the most unpromising state in the country for a suffrage organizer," Somerville became an active suffragist leader and, later, in 1923, the first woman to be elected to the Mississippi legislature.[18] Ellen Woodward was active at the federal level in the Roosevelt administration, directing women's work relief under three successive New Deal agencies from 1933 to 1938, then joining the Social Security Board, and retiring as director of a division of the Federal Security Agency in 1953. According to her biographer, Martha Swain, Woodward's social conscience "in all probability" developed from her experience in the Methodist church and from the influence of knowing and working with Nellie Somerville, though as Swain also notes, "What is remarkable about Woodward is that her advancement was based almost entirely on her own self-education in public affairs."[19] Both women justified much of their political activity as a defense of women and the family, which was, as already noted, a traditional stance for women and also consistent with their religious belief and church work. One must acknowledge, however, that even allowing for their political origins in home and church, these two political figures were surely "exotic plants" among southern women, to use Scott's apt phrase describing Somerville.

Despite the evidence that some religious organizations did offer access to public involvement and that a few exceptional political figures—female as well as male—did question the social arrangements of a segregated, paternalistic society and status quo politics, one must still conclude that the possibilities for public exchange of open speech and action in socially conservative Mississippi were to a great extent constrained, if not truncated or vitiated, for white women and, especially, for African American men and women.[20] Welty's *Curtain of Green* stories largely reflect this time and place through mute presences or monologic voices. As her experience and literary power grew during the 1940s, '50s, and '60s, she suggested in her fiction that public venues were not only deformed spaces but were remote and beyond one's power to affect or even were empty, inconsequential spaces. To an extent she seems to be anticipating the postmodern, postcolonial configuration that has come increasingly to characterize the political thought of the 1990s, that is, that the world is moving toward a two-tier system comprising the global and the local.

Especially during the years of World War II, precisely the period during which Welty was trying to launch her literary career, the public consciousness was focused upon global warfare. As a woman whose brothers and friends were engaged in the life-threatening, heroic enterprise of combat, Welty took in the war as a deeply personal experience but at a remove from any direct agency she might bring to it. For her, the unity of the nation in support of the conflict placed it beyond politics. In a 1980 interview she told Charles Ruas that "everybody honestly believed we were trying to save the world from Nazism.... It was a very pure kind of wish to accomplish this victory, and we were in it heart and soul." A little later she added, "It was a terrible time to live through. I couldn't write about it, not at the time—it was too personal. I *could* write or translate things into domestic or other dimensions in my writing, with the same things in mind."[21] The domain she had knowledge of and dominion over—and thus could employ as a venue for investigating "the same things" (e.g., the terror of warfare)—is the domestic sphere. World War II was personally close, via her connection to military men, and mythically remote. This "public world" upon which the world's eyes were focused was not an available, viable "public world" for her.

In the last several decades much feminist critical attention, including Welty criticism, has been given to the many ways in which society genders human action, usually in a hierarchy that privileges male values. A recent formulation of such a gendering of "necessary oppositions" within the world and within the self is given by the European intellectual Tzvetan Todorov in *Facing the Extreme*, an examination of moral values manifest in the camps of Nazi victims. Todorov writes of Europe's disposition over the centuries to create gendered separate spheres to embody traits necessary to society's well-being. "To men, then, the world of work, politics and public affairs, heroic virtues, and the morality of principles; to women, the domain of human relations, the private sphere, ordinary virtues, and the morality of sympathy." Todorov sees and names the pernicious effect of such division and calls for a different paradigm. The complete moral being may not be the individual, he notes, but, metaphorically, the couple. So as not to be misunderstood, Todorov adds the disclaimer, "Needless to say, when I speak of the couple I am not speaking of the heterosexual paradigm only or of a relationship that is necessarily stable or permanent."[22]

Welty well understood the damage to the psyche of rigid gender roles and stereotyping, as she shows in fiction that we are increasingly coming to read for its radical transformations of notions of "masculine" and "feminine" as well as "public" and "private." Peter Schmidt and Rebecca Mark, among many, have shown in recent studies of Welty how forcefully she challenges conventional patterns of gender relations, especially as these are manifest in Western heroic-quest narratives, and how insistently she exposes negative stereotypes that operate upon women, suggesting new definitions of heroism as feminine. Similarly, Ann Romines, Gail Mortimer, and others have instructively inquired into the consequence for the developing writer of a childhood and young adulthood that was experienced within a highly gendered society.[23]

Among many useful examinations of Welty's approaches to the displacement of stereotypical male fields of action upon female fields is Albert Devlin's recent study of the relation of *Delta Wedding* to the wartime context in which it was written. Devlin argues that Welty's choice of the "benign year" of 1923 as the novel's temporal setting served not only to distance the action from the savagery of the war but to echo "in its own refined way ... Welty's considered response to the bristling historic present." Drawing upon many sources, most notably Welty's letters to her literary agent Diarmuid Russell, quoted by Michael Kreyling in *Author and Agent*, and the text of the novel itself, Devlin persuasively argues that *Delta Wedding* and the drawing of the character Ellen Fairchild in particular embody a response to World War II that is directed not toward the world's political stage but toward "the solitary human heart," the venue offering the "only hope of correction." Acknowledging that Welty largely omits a contextualizing sociopolitical history of the Mississippi Delta in the 1920s, Devlin writes: "History itself is diminished as a primary category of experience, and fiction too is relieved of any need to act '*as a means*' (as G. E. Moore put it).... To test the efficacy of 'human understanding' against the present 'outrage' is the urgent mission that Welty gave to Ellen Fairchild, and it allowed neither of them any unbridled wandering in the field of Delta history."[24] In tracing the course of the composition of *Delta Wedding*, the progression of thought that gave it form, Devlin points up Welty's disposition to see politics as most vitally—and effectively—conducted at the site of the local and particular, the environs of the free individual engaging the immediate surround.

A number of critical analyses of *Delta Wedding* have enlarged our reading of the novel as an interrogation of cultural definitions of "public" and "private" and of "what counts" in our cultural valuing of the "heroic" and the "domestic."[25] Most recently, Susan Donaldson has discussed Welty's placing the ostensible hero, George Fairchild, on the back stage of the action while giving over the narrative consciousness to the women who surround him. Effectively, the foreground figure and the background players swap places, a reversal, notes Donaldson, that "highlights and problematizes the relationship between public and private, the world of historical action and the world of domesticity—or, one might say, the frontlines and the homefront."[26]

One infers from the portrayal of George Fairchild and many other "vaunting" heroes of Welty's fiction that she somewhat suspects public heroism to be tainted by a kind of theatricality that necessarily accompanies it. This is, of course, precisely the view held in *The Optimist's Daughter* by Laurel Hand, who objects to the community's effort to aggrandize her father as a public hero during the ceremonies attendant upon his death. The image of the public sphere that is projected again and again by the fiction is one that partakes of hyperbole and, often, insincerity or even sham.

Welty's photographs likewise expose the ineffectuality of "official" public speech to communicate much of anything trustworthy or meaningful to the public. In an image entitled "Political Speaking" in *One Time, One Place*, the speaker is entirely absent from the scene and the audience is revealed as inattentive, even bored. Centering the photograph is a parked car, site of the only animated conversation seeming to take place, that of a standing woman speaking to the driver of the car. In an adjacent photograph, "Political Speech," the viewer's eye is directed to the sleeping figure of a young girl, whose whole body is turned away from the speaker. Again, Welty frames the image so as to cut the political speaker entirely from view. Indeed, as Harriet Pollack has pointed out, in these images and in another from *Photographs* entitled "Political Speech, Tupelo, 1930s," one finds group scenes that withhold or deny any sense of a focal center.[27] Welty's visual messages unmistakably deconstruct the grandiose claims of political speech.

Welty's stated reservations about the claims of public politics do not preclude our acknowledgment of her sharply aware consciousness of public life—what I would call a political consciousness—although perhaps they do help explain why that consciousness is manifested so obliquely in her work. She has frequently voiced her wariness about the enervating effect of the political when in works of fiction it is allowed to encroach upon the quieter workings of more private terrains. A reading of the two volumes of collected interviews, however, reveals that she has long regarded herself as a liberal Democrat and spoken of herself as an admirer of Adlai Stevenson, a foe of Nixon's politics, and a possessor of Michael Dukakis and Clinton–Gore bumper stickers.[28] She was an unflagging supporter in the 1980s of Mississippi's progressive governor, William Winter, who was also one of the members of the task force on race relations named by President Clinton in 1997. She is a careful news watcher, an avid follower of the PBS *Jim Lehrer News Hour* (formerly McNeil-Lehrer). Her interest in such overt political activity notwithstanding, one must infer from her essays and interviews that she regards her citizen's voice as singular, slight, and largely ineffectual in setting or effecting social policy. But increasingly it would seem that she has come to think of that ineffectuality as no great loss, that finally the private and local sphere, which is also (as she has repeatedly said the habitation of fiction, is the place where informed and persuasive deliberation occurs, where speech legitimated by authority of experience and identity can be spoken and heard—the site, finally, where meaningful action can occur.

In her article "Women's History and Political Theory: Toward a Feminist Approach to Public Life," Sara M. Evans has traced changing conceptions of "public life" in the United States over the past two centuries, discussing many of the points I have been dealing with here. In her call for a feminist reconception of public life, she says attention must be paid first of all to the relationship between public and private. She notes that liberal theory of the nineteenth century, which amplified the public sector of governance to include the private sector of civil society, still was predicated, as in classical theory, upon an assumption of domestic life, the sphere of women, where life's essential needs were to be provided for. In her thought-provoking article, Evans suggests infinite ways in which the private and personal *are* political, and she insists that political history be redefined to represent "the dynamic relation between public and private life.[29] Evans focuses on women's organizations—voluntary associations, missionary societies such as the Methodist home missions discussed earlier, and reformist crusades growing from commitments to a social gospel—but I take her point also to elucidate Welty's defense of the local, the private sphere, as a site of "political" consequence.

Let me briefly reiterate my points about the evolution of Welty's political views. In the 1920s and 1930s authentic public political exchange was largely unavailable to Mississippians, especially to white women and blacks who were constrained by their "place" in the societal hierarchy, and the effect was usually cooptation or isolation of the individual, a condition Welty frequently represents in her early stories. Her witnessing a World War in the 1940s, McCarthyism in the 1950s, and the violent resistance to the civil rights movement in the early 1960s all greatly lessened whatever trust she had had in the political macrocosm and bolstered her belief in the microcosm as the only efficacious, viable sphere of human understanding and negotiation. As she worked on the writing of *Losing Battles* over fifteen years, from "a long story about the country" completed by spring 1955 to the publication of the novel in 1970,[30] Welty came to see in the rural story a possibility of—and human habitation for—active debate and discussion of topics that were in the last analysis not merely private needs but also political issues.

When Judge Moody's black Buick breaks in upon the family scene in *Losing Battles*, its wreck calling upon everyone to take notice and try to "save" the assaulting vehicle, the Bannerites do not retreat into some quiet Promethean myth of heroism and renewal, as do the young farmer Sonny and his pregnant wife in "Death of a Traveling Salesman" in their response to R. J. Bowman's similar intrusion upon a rural family scene. Indeed, the vehicles and the accidents are nearly duplicates—Bowman's car, like Judge Moody's, hangs "on the edge of a ravine that fell away, a red erosion." In the novel the Beecham-Renfro clan vigorously dispute the standing of the judge in the court of the Banner front porch, charging him, a Ludlowite, with a barbarian's ignorance of the rightful claims of justice in Banner. In fact, *Losing Battles*, Welty's longest work, embodies an intricately detailed inquiry into the nature of justice, that ubiquitous, time-honored topic of political discourse.

One of the numerous family members attending the reunion celebrating Granny Vaughn's birthday and grandson Jack's release from Parchman penitentiary is Aunt Cleo, recently married into the family and endlessly curious about their history. "What I mainly want to hear," she announces early in the novel, "is what they sent Jack to the pen for."[31] The ensuing replies pose an opposition of two modes of justice: that grounded in constitutional law, which in the novel has been administered by Judge Moody from his courthouse in Ludlow, and that grounded in mediational law, which takes account of the specific conditions and context in which wrongdoers, victims, and crimes are considered in their singularity, an application of law considered by the family to be fair and just.

There have been many differing approaches to naming and understanding the opposing sides Welty has created in this novel. Michael Kreyling has written of myth versus history, with attention especially to the role of the schoolteacher Julia Mortimer. James Boatwright has analyzed speech versus silence, and Susan Donaldson has examined opposing modes of discourse, the spoken and the written, an opposition I have also discussed in addressing the contest between orality and literacy in *Losing Battles*.[32] Despite a tendency to admire Miss Julia's societal meliorism, readers generally acknowledge Welty's balancing of claims by the Julia/Judge side and the Beecham/Renfros, finding the family's arguments for justice fully as commanding as those of its educated, progressive adversaries. Indeed, the family's hero, Jack, seemingly constrained by poverty and political powerlessness, is arguably the most humane and caring character in *Losing Battles*.

Ruth Weston has argued that Welty's portrayal of Jack gives evidence of a "gender role reversal" that extends even further the novel's reversing and balancing of a traditionally valued public or "heroic" sphere with that of a devalued private or "ordinary" sphere.[33] Noting the depiction of Jack as a "wonderful little mother," Weston observes that Welty deflates Jack's "masculine vaunting and blind optimism" but not his "feminine" nurturing traits. Weston's commentary here calls to mind Todorov's metaphor of the couple as an image of the linking of "necessary opposites" within human society. "As elsewhere," she writes, "Welty emphasizes human limitations by pairing two 'halves' that together constitute one whole human character— here, Jack and Gloria, a nurturing, family-oriented father and an independent, authoritative mother."[34] The hierarchical pattern of public over private and male over female is thus dramatically reversed.

Similarly, the judge's secure, publicly powerful position as objective dispenser of justice, removed from contingent and extenuating circumstances, gives way under the pressure of his own vulnerability to time and chance. With his car wrecked and perched precariously on an embankment in Banner territory, he has to turn to a "human chain" for rescue. Although he rejects the family's insistence upon *understanding* (mediation) as a basis for justice, he nonetheless accepts their forgiveness for his transgression against Jack. The family likewise makes concessions: they admit him to the reunion as an equal and listen to what he has to say.

In this late novel of her career, Welty turns outward to the world and explores its multiple displays of human needs and possibilities. Unlike *The Optimist's Daughter*, which represents more of a journey inward for Welty, this lengthy dialogic novel brings the moral-private realm of society into direct contention with the political-public realm. Embattled, the family not only hold their own against Judge Moody and his Ludlow courthouse, but stand their ground against the accumulated power of Julia Mortimer, the correspondingly embattled teacher, adversary of ignorance, righteous reformer-crusader committed to bringing in a modern social gospel, or, perhaps more properly, a secular humanism for the purpose of improving her country charges' minds and lives. What Welty manages to do with extraordinary skill in *Losing Battles* is dramatize an almost idealized political occasion on which the stump speakers—whether young or old, male or female—have knowledge of the subjects debated and full standing in the forum of exchange. Indeed, as Suzan Harrison observes, the voices are principally female.[35] The speakers, who have differing conceptions of rights, responsibilities, boundaries, and justice, each possess the rhetorical ability to express themselves with force, the memory to call upon relevant precedent, and, most significantly, the freedom to speak. It is a polis in action.

For Welty, legitimate political speech, as distinguished from propaganda, demagoguery, fatuous display, intimidating threats, inspired revelation, or guilt-ridden confession, reflects the complexity and relatedness of human action. For her, the site where such speech is most likely to occur is a local, even private, habitation, and in this it is like fiction. Political debate subjected to the testing and tempering of a home place may thus achieve validity and persuasiveness in much the same way that Welty describes as the way of art in "Place in Fiction:" "the art that speaks most clearly, explicitly, directly and passionately from its place of origin will remain the longest understood."[36]

In a 1978 interview, Jan Gretlund asks Welty a series of questions about her political interests, to which she responds with a discussion of her enthusiasm for the candidacy of Adlai Stevenson in the 1950s and of her efforts to stay informed about political issues and to vote. But she adamantly reiterates her disapproval of a writer's undertaking to crusade in fiction. "I think it's wrong when somebody like Steinbeck crusades in his fiction. That's why Steinbeck bores me so. The real crusader doesn't need to crusade; he writes about human beings in the sense Chekhov did. He tries to see a human being whole with all his wrong-headedness and all his right-headedness. To blind yourself to one thing for the sake of your prejudice is limiting. I think it is a mistake." Welty then adds a quick afterword that points up her self-exclusion from those who would "write politics": "There's so much room in the world for crusading, but it is for the editorial writers, the speech-maker, the politician, and the *man* in public life to do [emphasis mine], not for the writer of fiction." I think we see in Welty's response here her equation of "political" thought and action with a kind of rigidity, a blindness to all but one's own position, a firmness of purpose that is a prejudice and is self-limiting—the conditions she characterizes as "crusading." By contrast, an arena where open discussion occurs, where multiple options for action are considered, where the complexity of knowing the good and acting upon it is fully revealed is, for her, not a "political" arena. Distrusting the arena of politics as a location for ascertaining justice and right action, she looks rather to the "moral" arena for an understanding of life as it is—and as it should be. Replying in a mid-1970s interview to a question posed by Bill Ferris, "Do you feel the artist has a political role to play in a society?" she demonstrates a wariness about what she regards as the intellectual and psychological narrowness of politics, as well as the propensity of politics to turn all too readily into propaganda:

> I don't believe that a work of art in itself has any cause to be political unless it would have been otherwise. I think there are places for political outspokenness, but in my mind, it should be done editorially, and in essays and things that are exactly what they seem. But I think a work of art, a poem or a story, is properly something that reflects what life is exactly at that time. That is, to try to reveal it. Not to be a mirror image, but to be something that goes beneath the surface of the outside and tries to reveal the way it really is, good and bad. Which in itself is moral. I think a work of art must be moral. The artist must have a moral consciousness about his vision of life and what he tries to write. But to write propaganda I think is a weakening thing to art.[37]

Welty's assumptions about what constitutes political action—that is, what the word "politics" denotes for her—are perhaps most clearly illustrated in the 1966 story "The Demonstrators." The main figure of the story, Dr. Richard Strickland, attends a dying young black woman, Ruby Gaddy, who has been stabbed by her jealous common-law husband, Dove Collins, himself wounded in turn by her and also dying. On the night of the story the physician moves among the black and white citizens of Holden, Mississippi, sensitively registering all the human connections that make moral—and political—decisions so difficult. He thinks of a young civil rights worker who in a newspaper piece has forcefully made a case against white oppression, but with clarity bought at the cost of truth telling:

> "Speaking of who can you trust," [he had said to the young man,] "what's this I read in your own paper, Philip? It said some of your outfit over in the next county were forced at gunpoint to go into the fields at hundred-degree temperature and pick cotton. Well, that didn't happen—there isn't any cotton in June."
>
> "I asked myself the same question you do. But I told myself, 'Well, they won't know the difference where the paper is read.'"
>
> "It's lying, though."
>
> "We are dramatizing your hostility," the young bearded man had corrected him. "It's a way of reaching people. Don't forget—what they *might* have done to us is even worse."[38]

In this story Welty dramatizes the complicity of everyone in what is a familiar human drama of self-serving and self-protection, of violence, betrayal, grief, bitterness, just old recalcitrant human perversity. Holden's county newspaper runs the Gaddy-Collins murder on the back page, with the subhead "No Racial Content Espied," advertising white innocence while indulging in titillating gossip: "TWO DEAD, ONE ICE PICK, FREAK EPISODE AT NEGRO CHURCH." Both the civil rights paper and the county paper are stating and defending their political positions, unwittingly demonstrating the narrowness of each point of view. And even the kindly Dr. Strickland's sense of connectedness with the black household he attends is exposed as inextricably linked to the privileged affluence of his family in this segregated southern town. Hand-me-down dresses of his mother's, sister's, wife's fly out from Ruby Gaddy's front porch, where they hang, starched, reflecting the moonlight like ghostly presences.

Nonetheless, it is clear in this story, as in *Losing Battles*, that the moral position Welty endorses is a respectful listening to the position of the other and a willingness to engage it empathetically. Jack Renfro is the hero of *Losing Battles* because, unlike his wife Gloria, who wants to withdraw to a private sphere and concentrate on her nuclear family's self-interest, he is willing to listen to all the others' stories—cases, if you will—and to put forward his own. What he counsels is a reasoning and sympathetic arena for Banner.

In "Must the Novelist Crusade?" Welty quotes E. M. Forster's "Only connect," calling the phrase "ever wise and gentle and daring words [that] could be said to us in our homeland quite literally at this moment." The homeland about which Welty writes in both the essay and "The

Demonstrators"—Mississippi in the 1960s—was not congenial to the kind of piety of human connection she espoused. And it is telling that, several paragraphs later, it is the relation of a writer to Czarist Russia that comes to mind when she speaks of the role the artist can properly play in the support of such piety: "We are told that Turgenev's nostalgic, profoundly reflective, sensuously alive stories that grew out of his memories of early years reached the Czar and were given some credit by him when he felt moved to free the serfs in Russia. Had Turgenev set out to write inflammatory tracts instead of the sum of all he knew, could express, of life learned at firsthand, how much less of his mind and heart with their commitments, all implicit, would have filled his stories! But he might be one of us now, so directly are we touched."[39]

Welty suggests that the act of identification may give rise to civic virtue, and that such identification may be prompted by fiction. Following a long line of intellectual predecessors, she grounds right political action in moral virtue, and she then links these to the aesthetic, ever insisting upon the aesthetic realm as the legitimate home precinct of the writer. For her, being a writer is prepolitical, postpolitical, always and already political. In this view, she is quite close to Todorov, who pointedly discusses the relation of the political to the aesthetic in his 1996 review of J. M. Coetzee's collection of essays *Giving Offense: Essays on Censorship*. Toward the end of the review, Todorov remonstrates against what he regards as Coetzee's too-narrow understanding of the "political" and gives a spirited endorsement of the position that I have argued likewise constitutes Welty's political thought:

> Everything in this book reads as though Coetzee were defending himself against the charge of not having written more politically engaged work. His argument consists of saying that all engagement is futile, because the struggle against an adversary makes one like the adversary. This argument is wrong. But it is also, happily, unnecessary: Coetzee's position as a writer is above reproach. For the writer has no obligation, as a writer, to engage in political struggles. By means of his writing, he is already engaged, since his works help humanity to find meaning in existence, and no struggle is greater than the struggle for meaning. All true works of art create values, and in so doing they are political.[40]

Perhaps Welty, southern daughter of a bristling traditional society struggling to maintain itself, and Todorov, Bulgarian son of a truculent but dying Soviet Union totalitarianism, are similarly suspicious of defining politics as ideology and wary of political thought that codifies forces of necessity and coercion. In her writings and interviews, Welty shows unmistakably that what she regards as the politics of substance and courage, politics that is truly public, civil, and communal, is the human connection between freely operating individuals who confront issues that directly affect their lives. The domain where such connection occurs for Welty the writer, and also, I think, for Welty the human being, is typically personal, private, and interior. One thus finds no discrepancy between the title of "Must the Novelist Crusade?"—the writing that offers perhaps her most emphatic defense of the writer as a political (but not propagandizing) being—and the title affixed earlier to the same essay: "The Interior Affair."[41]

NOTES

1. An early reading of gender roles in Welty's fiction was my "Woman's World, Man's Place: The Fiction of Eudora Welty," in *Eudora Welty: A Form of Thanks*, ed. Louis Dollarhide and Ann J. Abadie (Jackson: University Press of Mississippi, 1979), 46–77. The present essay is a revised and extended version of a paper appearing in *Mississippi Quarterly* 50 (1997): 617–30.

2. Albert J. Devlin and Peggy Whitman Prenshaw, "A Conversation with Eudora Welty," in *More Conversations with Eudora Welty*, ed. Peggy Whitman Prenshaw (Jackson: University Press of Mississippi, 1996), 114.

3. Ibid., 118–9.

4. The two final stories in *The Collected Stories of Eudora Welty* (New York: Harcourt Brace, 1980), "Where Is the Voice Coming From?" (1963) and "The Demonstrators" (1966), portray contrasting responses of white southerners to events that resulted from the civil rights movement of the 1960s. In a 1978 interview with Tom Royals and John Little, Welty spoke of "The Demonstrators" as "a reflection of society at the time" and not primarily a civil rights story. She also mentioned in the interview her intention to publish a collection of stories that "reflect the way we were deeply troubled in that society and within ourselves at what was going on in the sixties." To date no such book has been published. See Royals and Little, "A Conversation with Eudora Welty" in *Conversations with Eudora Welty*, ed. Peggy Whitman Prenshaw (Jackson: University Press of Mississippi, 1984), 259.

5. "Fiction in Review," *Nation*, 2 October 1943, 386–7, and 11 May 1946, 578; "Cloud-Cuckoo Symphony," *Time*, 22 April 1946, 104ff.; Richard H. King, *A Southern Renaissance: The Cultural Awakening of the American South, 1930–1955* (New York: Oxford University Press, 1980), 9. Representative of the many well-argued rebuttals to King's assertion are those of Susan V. Donaldson, "Gender and the Profession of Letters in the South," in *Rewriting the South: History and Fiction*, ed. Lothar Honnighausen and Valeria Gennaro Lerda (Tubingen: Francke, 1993), 35–46, and Carol S. Manning, With Ears *Opening Like Morning Glories: Eudora Welty and the Love of Storytelling* (Westport, Conn.: Greenwood Press, 1985), 70ff.

6. Eudora Welty, "Must the Novelist Crusade?" in *The Eye of the Story: Selected Essays and Reviews* (New York: Random House, 1978), 147–9.

7. "A Quiet Lady in the Limelight," in *More Conversations with Eudora Welty*, ed. Prenshaw, 11.

8. Hannah Arendt, *The Human Condition* (1958; rpt. Garden City, N.Y.: Doubleday Anchor, 1959), 30. In chap. 2, "The Public and the Private Realm," Arendt offers a full discussion of the Greek concept of the division between the polis and the household.

9. See, for example, Daniele Pitavy-Souques, "A Blazing Butterfly: The Modernity of Eudora Welty," *Mississippi Quarterly* 39 (1986): 537–60; Michael Kreyling, *Eudora Welty's Achievement of Order* (Baton Rouge: Louisiana State University Press, 1980), 3–15; Kreyling, "Modernism in Welty's *A Curtain of Green and Other Stories*," *Southern Quarterly* 20 (1982): 40–53; Barbara Fialkowski, "Psychic Distances in *A Curtain of Green*: Artistic Success and Personal Failures," in *A Still Moment: Essays on the Art of Eudora Welty*, ed. John F. Desmond (Metuchen, N.J.: Scarecrow Press, 1978), 63–70.

10. See Yaeger, *Honey-Mad Women: Emancipatory Strategies in Women's Writing* (New York: Columbia University Press, 1988), 114–23, and Trouard, "Diverting Swine: The Magical Relevancies of Eudora Welty's Ruby Fisher and Circe," in *The Critical Response to Eudora Welty's Fiction*, ed. Laurie Champion (Westport, Conn.: Greenwood Press, 1994), 335–55. Trouard writes that "Welty creates men who function as props in Ruby's little theater, and the reader's pleasure, as well as Ruby's, emanates from her ability to determine her own pleasure, the delight of self-absorption" (344).

11. In *More Conversations with Eudora Welty*, 6.

12. For a succinct overview of economic and political conditions in Mississippi and the South, see *Mississippi: Conflict and Change*, ed. James W. Loewen and Charles Sallis (New York: Pantheon Books, 1974), 236ff. A much more detailed discussion of general economic conditions may be found in Gavin Wright, *Old South, New South: Revolutions in the Southern Economy since the Civil War* (New York: Basic Books, 1986; rpt. Baton Rouge: Louisiana State University Press, 1996), 198 ff., and a more detailed social history in Jack Temple Kirby, *Rural Worlds Lost; The American South, 1920–1960* (Baton Rouge: Louisiana State University Press, 1987). For an excellent treatment of the conditions of life of black tenant families during the years 1890–1940, see Neil R. McMillen, *Dark Journey: Black Mississippians in the Age of Jim Crow* (Urbana: University of Illinois Press, 1989), especially chap. 4, "Farmers without Land." Also consult vol. 2 of *A History of Mississippi*, ed. Richard Aubrey McLemore (Jackson: University Press of Mississippi, 1973), for relevant and wide-ranging topical essays. Undoubtedly among the most authoritative and interesting sources of information about the Mississippi Welty came to know during her years of work with the WPA and afterwards are the author's own collection of photographs in *One Time, One Place* (New York: Random House, 1971), and the WPA guidebook, *Mississippi: A Guide to the Magnolia State* (New York: Viking Press, 1938). An excellent scholarly source of information about Welty's Mississippi is Albert J. Devlin's *Eudora Welty's Chronicle: A Story of Mississippi Life* (Jackson: University Press of Mississippi, 1983); see especially the opening chapter.

13. James C. Cobb, *The Most Southern Place on Earth: The Mississippi Delta and the Roots of Regional Identity* (New York: Oxford University Press, 1992), 196–7.

14. See Noel Polk, *Eudora Welty: A Bibliography of Her Work* (Jackson: University Press of Mississippi, 1994), 366–7, for information about the publishing history of "Keela."

15. Eudora Welty, *One Writer's Beginnings* (Cambridge: Harvard University Press, 1984), 32–3; Morton Sosna, *In Search of the Silent South: Southern Liberals and the Race Issue* (New York: Columbia University Press, 1977), 173; Samuel S. Hill, ed., *Varieties of Southern Religious Experience* (Baton Rouge: Louisiana State University Press, 1988), especially "Conclusion," 226.

16. Patricia Wheatley, "Eudora Welty: A Writer's Beginnings," in *More Conversations with Eudora Welty*, ed. Prenshaw, 130.

17. John Patrick McDowell, *The Social Gospel in the South: The Woman's Home Mission Movement in the Methodist Episcopal Church, South, 1886–1939* (Baton Rouge: Louisiana State University Press, 1982), 144–8.

18. Anne Firor Scott, *Making the Invisible Woman Visible* (Urbana: University of Illinois Press, 1984), 169–70. See also Marjorie Spruill Wheeler, *New Women of the New South: The Leaders of the Woman Suffrage Movement in the Southern States* (New York: Oxford University Press, 1993), 53ff.

19. Martha H. Swain, *Ellen S. Woodward: New Deal Advocate for Women* (Jackson: University Press of Mississippi, 1995), 10, x.

20. For discussions of implicit and explicit manifestations of the repression of white women in southern society, see discussions by Anne Firor Scott, *The Southern Lady* (Chicago: University of Chicago Press, 1970); Anne Goodwyn Jones, *Tomorrow Is Another Day: The Woman Writer in the South, 1859–1936* (Baton Rouge: Louisiana State University Press, 1981), especially chap. 1; and Louise Westling, *Sacred Groves and Ravaged Gardens: The Fiction of Eudora Welty, Carson McCullers, and Flannery O'Connor* (Athens: University of Georgia Press, 1985), especially "The Blight of Southern Womanhood," 8–35.

21. Charles Ruas, "Eudora Welty," in *More Conversations with Eudora Welty*, ed. Prenshaw, 66.

22. Tzvetan Todorov, *Facing the Extreme*, trans. Arthur Denner and Abigail Pollak (New York: Holt-Metropolitan Books, 1996), 293–4. Among many critics who precede Todorov in analyzing gendered cultural conventions, see especially the responses of twentieth-century female artists to such conventions: Teresa de Lauretis, *Alice Doesn't: Feminism, Semiotics, Cinema* (Bloomington: Indiana University Press, 1984), and Rachel Blau DuPlessis, *Writing Beyond the Ending: Narrative Strategies of Twentieth-Century Women Writers* (Bloomington: Indiana University Press, 1985).

23. Rebecca Mark, *The Dragon's Blood: Feminist Intertextuality in Eudora Welty's "The Golden Apples"* (Jackson: University Press of Mississippi, 1994), especially 3–30; Peter Schmidt, *The Heart of the Story: Eudora Welty's Short Fiction* (Jackson: University Press of Mississippi, 1991), 53ff.; Ann Romines, *The Home Plot: Women, Writing, and Domestic Ritual* (Amherst: University of Massachusetts Press, 1992), especially 192ff.; Gail L. Mortimer, *Daughter of the Swan: Love and Knowledge in Eudora Welty's Fiction* (Athens: University of Georgia Press, 1994), especially 1–42. For an examination of the influence upon Welty of a regionally gendered South and North, see Peggy Whitman Prenshaw, "The Construction of Confluence: The Female South and Eudora Welty's Art," in *The Late Novels of Eudora Welty*, ed. Jan Nordby Gretlund and Karl-Heinz Westarp (Columbia: University of South Carolina Press, 1998), 176–94.

24. Albert J. Devlin, "The Making of *Delta Wedding*, or Doing 'Something Diarmuid Thought I Could Do,'" in *Biographies of Books: The Compositional Histories of Notable American Writings*, ed. James Barbour and Tom Quirk (Columbia: University of Missouri Press, 1996), 252, 260.

25. See especially Louise Westling's "The Enchanted Maternal Garden of *Delta Wedding*," in *Sacred Groves and Ravaged Gardens*, 65–93; Ann Romines, *Home Plot*, 211 ff.; and Suzan Harrison, *Eudora Welty and Virginia Woolf: Gender, Genre, and Influence* (Baton Rouge: Louisiana State University Press, 1997), 22–47.

26. Susan V. Donaldson, "Gender and History in Eudora Welty's *Delta Wedding*," *South Central Review*, 14 (1997), 5.

27. Eudora Welty, *One Time, One Place*, 66–7; *Eudora Welty Photographs* (Jackson: University Press of Mississippi, 1989), no. 62; Harriet Pollack, "Photographic Convention and Story Composition: Eudora Welty's Uses of Detail, Plot, Genre, and Expectation

from 'A Worn Path' through *The Bride of the Innisfallen*," *South Central Review* 14 (1997): 29.

28. For a quick guide to Welty's discussion of these subjects, one may consult the indexes to *Conversations with Eudora Welty* and *More Conversations with Eudora Welty*.

29. Sarah M. Evans, "Women's History and Political Theory: Toward a Feminist Approach to Public Life," in *Visible Women: New Essays on American Activism*, ed. Nancy A. Hewitt and Suzanne Lebsock (Urbana: University of Illinois Press, 1993), 119ff., 126–7.

30. See Polk, *Welty: A Bibliography*, 122–4, for a summary of the composition history of *Losing Battles*. See also Suzanne Marrs, *The Welty Collection: A Guide to the Eudora Welty Manuscripts and Documents at the Mississippi Department of Archives and History* (Jackson: University Press of Mississippi, 1988), 40ff., for an annotated listing of draft manuscripts of the novel.

31. Eudora Welty, *Losing Battles* (New York: Random House, 1970), 21.

32. See Kreyling, *Eudora Welty's Achievement of Order*, 140ff.; James Boatwright, "Speech and Silence in *Losing Battles*," *Shenandoah* 25 (1974): 3–14; Susan V. Donaldson, "'Contradictors, Interferers, and Prevaricators': Opposing Modes of Discourse in *Losing Battles*," in *Eudora Welty: Eye of the Storyteller*, ed. Dawn Trouard (Kent, Ohio: Kent State University Press, 1989), 32–43; Peggy Whitman Prenshaw, "The Harmonies of *Losing Battles*," in *Modern American Fiction: Form and Function*, ed. Thomas Daniel Young Baton Rouge: Louisiana State University Press, 1989, 184–97.

33. For an enlightening discussion of the "heroic" and the "ordinary" as contrasted, gendered virtues, see Todorov, *Facing the Extreme*, 107 ff.

34. Ruth D. Weston, Gothic *Traditions and Narrative Techniques in the Fiction of Eudora Welty* (Baton Rouge: Louisiana State University Press, 1994), 152.

35. Harrison, *Eudora Welty and Virginia Woolf*, 108.

36. Eudora Welty, "Place in Fiction" (first published in 1955), in *Eye of the Story*, 132.

37. Jan Gretlund, "Seeing Real Things: An Interview with Eudora Welty," rpt. in *Conversations with Eudora Welty*, ed. Prenshaw, 226; Bill Ferris, "A Visit with Eudora Welty," ibid., 165.

38. Eudora Welty, "The Demonstrators," in *Collected Stories of Eudora Welty*, 617.

39. In *Eye of the Story*, 156.

40. Tzvetan Todorov, "Tyranny's Last Word," *New Republic*, 18 November 1996, 33.

41. Noel Polk, *Welty: A Bibliography*, 381, notes that the Russell and Volkening file card for the essay bears the deleted title "The Interior Affair."

KENNETH BEARDEN

Monkeying Around:
Welty's "Powerhouse," Blues-Jazz,
and the Signifying Connection

> *To The Lighthouse* is at once ethereal and firm, as perhaps only a
> vision can be. A presiding presence with streaming hair and
> muscles stretched, the novel's conception has the strength of a
> Blake angel. It is an exertion, a vaunting, a triumph of wonder, of
> imaginative speculation and defiance; it is that bolt of lightning
> Virginia Woolf began with, an instantaneous burst of coherence
> over chaos and the dark. She has shown us the shape of the
> human spirit. (Foreword xii)

So ends Eudora Welty's 1981 foreword to Virginia Woolf's 1927 novel, a
work which Welty claims "once and forever opened the door of imaginative
fiction" for her (vii). Employing phrases such as "perpetually changing"
"unpredictable," "tricky," and "illusory," Welty emphasizes a most
interesting quality of the work, a "rhythm" which forms "a pattern of waking
and sleeping, presence and absence, living and living no longer, between
clamorous memory and lapses of mind" (ix). What makes such comments
intriguing is that we find in many of Welty's own works—especially *Delta
Wedding* (1946) and *The Optimist's Daughter* (1972)—that very same essence
of rhythm between extremes, that very same essence of liminality and
ambiguity.[1]

From *Southern Literary Journal* 31, no. 2 (Spring 1999): 65–79. © 1999 by the University of
North Carolina Press.

What I find even more intriguing though is the connection between Welty's 1981 foreword and a short work she produced more than forty years earlier. First published in *The Atlantic Monthly* in June of 1941 and later included in *A Curtain of Green and Other Stories*, "Powerhouse" has to be one of Welty's most unusual works in terms of both style and subject matter. Indeed, the short story appears to share little with most of her other texts. But we can say that early explorations in ambiguity and narrative technique are obvious, and these experiments are refined later in her other works. The words that Loretta M. Lampkin chooses to describe Welty's narrative style in "Powerhouse"—"slowly, antiphonally, disjunctively, rhythmically"— sound strikingly similar to Welty's words above (27).

Despite the story's unusual style and ambiguous elements, however, critics have been able to arrive at a fairly congruent reading of the text, a reading which highlights both Welty's incorporation of a jazz style and the protagonist's attempt to end his feelings of alienation by connecting with his audience. Yet, while previous discussions of "Powerhouse" are valid, they either fail to recognize or fail to discuss in depth an extremely crucial aspect of the work: the blues-jazz aesthetic.[2] I assert that Welty's use of blues-jazz elements goes much deeper than most critics have fathomed, drawing upon three qualities inherent in the musical art form itself: improvisation, ambiguity, and signifying. A close reading of the work with these aspects in mind leads us to an interpretation significantly different from those previously put forth.

It has been well-documented by now that Welty composed "Powerhouse" almost immediately after seeing a performance by Fats Waller, the jazz pianist made famous—and infamous—during the twenties and thirties. Recalling the performance in a 1981 interview, Welty states: "I had no idea I was going to write anything when I went to that ... But I was so excited by the evening that I wrote ["Powerhouse"], after I got home" (Jones 328). This excitement Welty felt after hearing and watching Waller perform live is what she attempted to translate into her writing. "Of course" she states, "what I was trying to do was to express something about the music in the story. I wanted to express what I thought of as improvisation" (328).

Indeed, improvisation is at the heart of jazz and blues; it is at the very heart of the black oral tradition itself. In his autobiographical *Black Boy*, Richard Wright describes the verbal practices of young, black males, how the talk would "weave, roll, surge, spurt, veer, swell, having no specific aim or direction, touching vast areas of life, expressing the tentative impulses of childhood" (95).[3] Powerhouse and his band perform in very much the same way: "Improvising" the narrator describes him, "coming upon a very light and childish melody, smooch—he loves it with his mouth" ("Powerhouse"

707).[4] The narrator later uses phrases like "skating," "rowing," "starting up," and "pouring it out" to describe Powerhouse's style.

However, the narrator also notices a sense of ironic isolation about the performer: "Powerhouse seems to abandon them all; he himself seems lost— down in the song—yelling up like somebody in a whirlpool—not guiding them, hailing them only. But he knows, really. He cries out, but he must know exactly" (708). This paradox of "seeming lost" yet "knowing exactly" is best explained by Ralph Ellison: "because jazz finds its very life in an endless improvisation upon traditional materials, the jazzman must lose his identity even as he finds it" (qtd in Gates vii). Throughout Welty's story we find Powerhouse himself creating the very life of his music, and hence his own life, through improvisation, the fabrication of the story of his wife's death.[5] It is this creation of life through a story of death that presents one of the clearest ambiguities in the story. But like improvisation, ambiguity lies at the very heart of jazz and blues. Ellison explains that the blues is "an impulse to keep the painful details and episodes of a brutal experience alive in one's aching consciousness, to finger its jagged grain, and to transcend it, not by the consolation of philosophy but by squeezing from it a near-tragic, near-comic lyricism" (78). The attraction of the blues, he says later, is that "they at once express both the agony of life and the possibility, of conquering it through sheer toughness of spirit" (94).

It is with Ellison's notions in mind that most critics turn toward their interpretation of the story, an interpretation which hinges on the concluding lines taken from a 1930s jazz tune: "Somebody loves me—I wonder who! ... Maybe— ... Maybe— ... —Maybe it's you!" Indeed, these lines appear to indicate a search on Powerhouse's part for some form of acceptance and an escape from the alienation which seems implied throughout the story. Smith Kirkpatrick sees Powerhouse's plea as a "challenge" but claims that the performer "knows love is there if [the audience] will only dare" to give it to him (108).[6] There are several problems with these interpretations, however. For one, we must not forget that we are receiving the story's closing scene, as well as the first two scenes, from a white audience member's perspective. Hence, we must ask questions. Why is it that of the "twelve or fourteen choruses" that Powerhouse piles up with "Somebody Loves Me" we only receive the last lines? There are continual indications throughout the story, as we'll see, that the narrator and fellow audience members fail to even understand what it is they hear. And if Powerhouse is indeed seeking a loving acceptance from the audience, why is he described in terms that denote anger and rage: "His mouth gets to be nothing but a *volcano* when he gets to the end;" and "A vast, *impersonal*, and yet *furious grimace* transfigures his wet face" ("Powerhouse" 713; emphasis added). While the narrator fails to understand much of what Powerhouse says throughout the performance, she is able to pick up on his anger and rage.

The crushing blow, perhaps, to this notion of Powerhouse attempting to gain an acceptance from the audience and thus escape his isolation comes with the realization that the conclusion we receive with published texts of the story is not the conclusion Welty originally composed. Her original manuscript, which concluded with lines from the famous (infamous) jazz tune "Hold Tight" was returned to her with a request that she change the ending (the reason why will be discussed later). When we consider the original ending, we must then reconsider everything that has come before. Surely, with as great a writer as Welty, endings cannot be tossed around without altering the meaning of texts. Welty herself has stated how "Powerhouse" in particular defied revision: "I did have the sense to know that there was no use in me trying to correct or revise or anything. It was that or nothing, because it had to be written at that moment, or not at all" (Jones 328). It is difficult, if not impossible, to retain the same interpretation once we consider a different ending. What are we to then make of Welty's unusual story?

The key is understanding the full extent to which Welty is representing Fats Waller and the blues aesthetic. While we cannot be certain that the story is about Waller himself, there are indeed staggering similarities in the descriptions of the performers—physical appearance, stylistic preferences, personality traits, even musical repertoire? All one has to do in order to see these similarities is to view a picture of Waller himself performing. And how can one separate the performance of an artist—especially that of a blues or jazz artist—from the performer himself? Welty certainly knew Waller's music, she undoubtedly knew about the man, and she undoubtedly drew upon this knowledge to add depth to the story. This is obvious when we highlight a few facts concerning Waller, especially his connection with Welty's South.

Sporting the nickname "Filthy" Fats Waller was known, and even ironically admired, for his bawdy reputation: "Waller, by an ironic twist of events, owed much of his fame to the brutality with which he burlesqued and lampooned the more banal of the songs he was asked to perform" (Fox 47). Even when Waller was able to tone his exuberance down in order to play a tune "very delicately" there still remained "mockery lurking behind the reticence" (48). His fast-paced style often left less experienced musicians, especially ones "assigned" to play with him, behind. A performance in England, for example, was described thus in a 1938 issue of *Melody Maker*: "He had to rely on the pit orchestra, and very little support did he get. Not only was the accompaniment so loud as to drown most of Fats' vocalisms, but it actually dragged one beat behind for a whole chorus until Fats played a miraculous nine-beat break to put it right" (Fox 60). Such frustrations—dealing with white musicians who didn't understand his style of blues and jazz—were the least of Waller's worries. At home in the states, Waller, like most early blues and jazz performers who were black, had to contend with financial concerns. Racial attitudes often prevented them from gaining recognition for their work, and many of their songs were "sold" to white artists who then claimed them as their own. While Waller didn't speak out openly and directly about his anger, he did express it in his own way, inserting semiangry outbursts during radio broadcasts (Vance 78). And he surely supplemented his more explicit outbursts with his more implicit, bawdy style.

Welty herself could not have remained totally ignorant of Waller and the debates surrounding him.[7] She herself acknowledges her love of Waller's music, and she must have certainly followed his career to at least some extent, especially since he was a celebrity. In addition, she would have certainly picked up news of him during her years with the WPA, traveling in urban and rural black communities. And she most likely would have known about or at least anticipated the troubles Waller faced during his southern tours. Joel Vance describes what Waller encountered:

> On a date in Mississippi, where the band was booked at a backwoods affair, local white apes slashed the tires of Waller's car and poured sand in the gas tank. Hotel accommodations for the band were simply not possible down South, so the musicians had to be put up in private homes. They were denied meals in restaurants, and gas stations refused to service "Old Methusela" as the bus was nicknamed .... [M]ost of his work on the road consisted of grueling and infuriating one-nighters, usually promoted by quick-buck local sharpies who sometimes refused to pay the band after the performance and then called in the law to run it out of town. (128)

Without a doubt, Waller knew the meaning of what Du Bois considered the black man's "double-consciousness." Du Bois's classic statement deserves quoting in its entirety here:

> It is a peculiar sensation, this double-consciousness, this sense of always looking at one's self through the eyes of others, of measuring one's soul by the tape of a world that looks on in amused contempt and pity. One ever feels his twoness—an

American, a Negro; two souls, two thoughts, two unreconciled strivings; two warring ideals in one dark body, whose dogged strength alone keeps it from being torn asunder. (3)

Aspects of Waller's life and experiences, especially those aspects noted above, certainly impacted Welty's story. Even if we were to grant the fact that Welty had not heard any of these details, Waller himself carried those details of his life in with him that night in Jackson, and they undoubtedly affected his performance. Being the artist she is, the observer she is, Welty would have picked up on the tension.[8] And we indeed see that tension displayed throughout the story. In describing Powerhouse, Welty employs the word "obscene" numerous times and makes use of other words such as "monstrous," "derogatory," and "dirty" to describe his style. When he performs a requested song, he does so with "the greatest delight and brutality" (708). And Powerhouse even exhibits anger toward the white audience he is performing for: he displays "such a leer for everybody" (708), and he "roars" an order to "Come on!" when he and the band leave the white dance hall for intermission (709).[9] And of course the anger he displays at the end of the evening has been pointed out.

These displays of anger are not without cause. Like Waller, Powerhouse and the band are there, after all, for a one-night-only gig: "They can't stay" the narrator tells us. "They'll be somewhere else this time tomorrow" (707). And undoubtedly Powerhouse, again like Waller, knows Du Bois's "double-consciousness" knows the attitudes of his audience members, people who think of him as something entertainingly nonhuman: "You can't tell what he is. He looks Asiatic, monkey, Babylonian, Peruvian, fanatic, devil.... And his mouth is going every minute, like a monkey's when it looks for fleas" (707). When intermission arrives, it is surely the same racial policies Waller encountered which force Powerhouse and his fellow performers to go "across the tracks" to the "World Care" in order to get some drinks (710).

What is even more intriguing and startling, perhaps, is how Welty incorporates a traditional African American folktale figure into the story, a figure that not too many of her contemporary white readers would know. Powerhouse is referred to once as a "monkey" his mouth is like that of a "monkey"; and his "long yellow-sectioned strong fingers" are the size of "bananas" (707). When we also consider that he is often "obscene," he "beats down piano and seat," he is "monstrous," he speaks "in another language" and he "has as much as possible done by signals," we cannot help but make the connection between Powerhouse and the Signifying Monkey, that trickster figure who is capable of causing calamity (specifically to the Lion) through his mastery of language. In the Signifying Monkey tales, Henry Louis Gates explains,

> the Signifying Monkey invariably repeats to his friend, the Lion, some insult purportedly generated by their mutual friend, the Elephant. The Monkey, however, speaks figuratively. The Lion, indignant and outraged, demands an apology of the Elephant, who refuses and then trounces the Lion. The Lion, realizing that his mistake was to take the Monkey literally, returns to trounce the Monkey. (55)[10]

Again, it is highly probable that Welty ran across this African American trickster legend while working with the WPA in black communities.[11]

Like his monkey counterpart, Powerhouse continually speaks in an ambiguous, figurative fashion. When he asks his band if they are ready to begin, he queries, "You-all ready to do some serious walking?" ("Powerhouse" 708). When he wants the drum player to join in, he prompts, "Where that skin-beater?" (708). And his tendency to improvisationally "brutalize" songs in a Walleresque manner has already been noted. The audience revels in this "primitive" display.

Yet Powerhouse's improvisation also serves as a double-edged sword. In the Signifying Monkey tales, as Gates points out, the success of the Monkey's trick hinges upon such improvisation, a manipulation of (monkeying around with) language: "It is [the] relationship between the literal and the figurative, and the dire consequences of their confusion, which is the most striking repeated element of these tales. The Monkey's trick depends on the Lion's inability to mediate between those two poles of signification, of meaning" (55). In Welty's story, it is the white audience who is unable to accomplish this mediation: "Powerhouse is so monstrous he sends everybody into oblivion.... Watch them carefully; hear the least word, especially what they say to one another, in another language; don't let them escape you" ("Powerhouse" 707). The narrator is admitting early the audience's inability to understand the band's "foreign language"—their figurative language—their signifying. The word "escape" even suggests the audience's (society's) desire to pin down and fix Powerhouse's identity. The performer's popularity with the white audience immediately places him in a liminal position: while he is a black individual, he is yet admired for his performative ability. This unique position—on the border between white and black worlds—permits Powerhouse to manipulate the very words the white audience loves to hear, thus creating multiple meanings which are only visible when one adopts a different perspective. "A chief value of parody" explains Jeanne Rosier Smith, "is in exposing any one perspective, or any one language, as necessarily limited. Tricksters can parody languages, and therefore worldviews, because of their liminal cultural position."[12] Therefore, as a performer, Powerhouse refuses to be "limited" refuses to be, as Keith Byerman would state, "categorized and thus brought into the system."[5] In his attempts to "escape" this "categorization" Powerhouse finds it helpful to adopt roles, a very significant tool of resistance according to Byerman: "Role playing denies ... permanence and external control, in part by suggesting that the fixed identity, like the system that produces it, is only one among several possibilities."[5] We almost hear, then, Welty herself speaking, warning us that what she is about to present is multilayered; we have to remember that her performer is a role player; we have to remember that "Powerhouse has as much as possible done by *signals*" (707; emphasis added). Yet, despite this warning, much of what Welty does is lost to readers, at least to readers who also write about her work.

Perhaps the best example of Powerhouse's brilliance in language manipulation is the brutalized, improvised "Pagan Love Song" Powerhouse's mastery is so great that, when he and the band continue their improvisation at the World Cafe, he is even able to fool the black waitress.[12] The improvisational, jazz-like style of his story creation has received a great deal of attention. And it is not at all surprising that scholars have noted the mythological and folkloric implications in Welty's choice of the name "Uranus Knockwood"; notions of Uranus the star are implied in the story itself, and both the mythological god Uranus and the folkloric belief of "knocking on wood" readily come to mind, especially considering Welty's love of mythology.[13] How is it, however, that the most obvious reading of the name, the phonetic one, if you will—"your anus knock wood"—remains largely undiscussed?

Perhaps the lack of consideration of this bawdy, bodily interpretation is due to scholars' prior inability to make any sense of it. Perhaps it seems more logical that Welty would privilege scholarly elements like mythology over bawdy, childish, phonetic games. But again, Welty has warned us of Powerhouse's obscene style and love of "childish melod[ies]" (707). And how likely is it that Welty would have imbued this black jazz performer with a working knowledge of Western mythology and folklore? It is only when we recognize the Signifying Monkey trope and recall the details of the folktale, that we realize what Welty is having Powerhouse do. The ultimate, dire consequence of the Monkey's figurative remarks to the Lion is the latter's return, saying, in essence, "I am going to knock your ass (anus) down." It is not unusual that the Monkey remains in a tree (wood) and that all of this takes place in the jungle (wood). Undoubtedly, if the Monkey wishes to stay alive, he had better knock on wood for good luck. If all of this seems far-fetched, let us consider characters themselves.

In Welty's story, we have two Signifying Monkeys. One is Powerhouse's Mr. Uranus Knockwood, the one who debunks Powerhouse's authority as the "man-of-words" by sending the figurative note announcing the death of Powerhouse's wife.[14] All the band members recognize him immediately because he is indeed the Monkey trickster figure: he represents all those who mess up their lives. Byerman notes that the blues performer "provides a personal version of a common condition and this linking of the individual and the community makes him effective" (8). Powerhouse's "story" prompts all to signify upon their own troubles, "spelling" Knockwood's name "all the ways it could be spelled" ("Powerhouse" 713). This signification, itself such a vital part of not only the blues and jazz tradition but black oral performance in general, allows Powerhouse and his band members to "transcend" their troubles, at least momentarily, by creatively finding Ellison's "near-tragic, near-comic lyricism." Knockwood is an ironic Monkey trope, however, because some of those he represents are not black but white.[15] Welty has Powerhouse complain: "That no-good pussy-footed crooning creeper, that creeper that follows around after me, coming up like weeds behind me, following around after me everything I do and messing around on the trail I leave. Bets my numbers, sings my songs, gets close to my agent like a betsybug—when I going out he just coming in" (711). Here, Powerhouse is the Lion, having been victimized by the tricks of the Knockwoods he has known. We can't help but think of Waller's songs stolen by white artists and his need to perform one-night gigs in areas where blacks were treated like animals. But rather than knocking Knockwood's anus, Powerhouse decides to usurp the Monkey position, figuratively to regain the ground he held at the beginning of the performance—the master of words.

We see our other Signifying Monkey in Powerhouse himself (he was the original Monkey). In a final reaction to Knockwood's figurative message, Powerhouse responds: "Take a telegram! ... Here's the answer. Here it is right here. 'What in the hell you talking about? Don't make any difference: I gotcha.' Name signed: Powerhouse" (713). Once Powerhouse "signs" (reasserts) his name, Knockwood's name literally disappears from the story. When Valentine questions, "That going to reach him, Powerhouse?" the response is quite appropriate: "Reach him and come out the other side" (713). The play upon language ("Uranus' anus") is again obvious, and the humor reaches a high point The improvisation upon Uranus Knockwood comes to an end.

The ultimate significance of Powerhouse as Signifying Monkey now becomes clearer; while his performance of the requested "Pagan Love Song" is on one level a form of entertainment for the white audience, it is, at a deeper level, a form of entertainment for Powerhouse and the band. The joy they get is not from merely performing, although performing is a source of release; they also enjoy laughing at the audience's expense. The signifying which goes on with the rendition of "Pagan Love Song" totally escapes the white audience's comprehension. What also totally escapes their attention is the "paganly" sexual gestures Powerhouse compliments his "love song" with: "Powerhouse's head rolls and sinks ... He groans ... with wandering fingers ... His mouth gathers and forms a barbarous O, while his fingers walk up straight, unwillingly, three octaves" (708–709). The narrative voice misses the juxtaposition of the sacred (Love) and the profane (Pagan), and she mistakenly remarks, "It is a sad song" (708).

Powerhouse's role as the Signifying Monkey is driven home once we consider Welty's original conclusion to the story:

> Well, we [the white audience] requested Hold Tight, and he's already done twelve or fourteen choruses, one in Fu Manchu talk. It will be a wonder if he ever gets through. His mouth gets to be nothing but a volcano. "When I come home late at night I want my favorite dish—FISH. Hold tight—Fix me some that old Babylonian seafood, Mama—Yeahhh!" He does scare you. He really does. He has a mysterious face. (qtd in Schmidt 270)

Whether or not we consider them to be controversial, these lyrics, in the late 1930s, were in fact deemed sexually suggestive. What is even more ironic, however, and what lends even more significance to Welty's use of them, is that white audiences could not hear the song often enough, apparently remaining ignorant of the vulgar innuendos. The April 24, 1939 issue of *Time* magazine attempted to inform its readers of this scandal:

> Eye-rolling Harlemites have long chuckled over the way the usually prissy white folks' radio has been going to town for a month on Hold Tight. In Harlem Hold Tight's fishy lyrics are considered no ordinary clambake stuff, but a reasonable duplication of the queer lingo some Harlem bucks use in one form of sex perversion. Harlemites chuckled even more last week when, taking a hint from Broadway columnists, radiomen hastily demanded that Hold Tight's lyrics be bowdlerized.

> Hold Tight was originally conjured up in Harlem's "Congo" district where a black and elemental breed of cats drink cheap King Kong liquor, puff reefers and shout a frank and sexy jive talk all their own. (44)[16]

Those who performed this song either knowing the controversy over the lyrics or believing the lyrics to be sexually suggestive, and realizing the naivete of their white audience, were clearly assuming the role of the Signifying Monkey. The "eye-rolling Harlemites" and the "black and elemental breed of cats" surely take on Monkey roles. Fats Waller himself, we must make note, was born and raised in Harlem, was known for his "eye-rolling" style, and, as Welty herself notes in an interview, was known to have performed the bawdy "Hold Tight": "You know the lyrics," she tells Jane Reid Petty, "with Fats Waller singing 'fooly racky sacky want some seafood, Mama!'" (Petty 209). And once the song had been popularized, according to the *Time* article, by the supposedly naive white audience, "it was being innocently squalled all over the land" (44).

It is highly unlikely that Welty was unaware of the controversy surrounding this song, despite her implicit claims to the contrary.[17] Having her narrator comment that Powerhouse is "not a show-off like the Harlem boys—not drunk, not crazy, I think" (707), at once suggests that Welty was even aware of the specifics of the controversy. The ultimate irony, however, is that, regardless of her knowledge or ignorance, the original text of "Powerhouse," like the song she concluded it with, was bowdlerized. Lest we view Welty as incapable of pushing the delicate boundaries of literary decorum, it was approximately one year after "Powerhouse" that Welty's manuscript of *The Robber Bridegroom* was sent back to her for revision; it was also bowdlerized due to the many passages thought to be too sexually suggestive.[18] Certainly; Welty could not argue the censorship if she, as a young, up-and-coming artist, wished to be published; her literary reputation, after all, had not yet been established.

We find ironic humor in both cases, however. No one doubts the bawdiness that we still find in *The Robber Bridegroom*, even after the censorship. And as it should be clear by now, bawdiness remains even in the bowdlerized text of "Powerhouse" Welty herself has become the Signifying Monkey, playing with language and motifs with such mastery that the significance of her words even escapes the probing intellects of most literary scholars, scholars who have continually attempted to identify "truly artistic" elements associated with the Western literary tradition. And just as the Monkey takes pride in pushing his own luck, in "going out on a limb" Welty sees risk as a vital part of truly artistic, truly enjoyable creation: "When we think in terms of the spirit" she states, "which are the terms of writing, is there a conception more stupefying than that of security? ... No art ever came out of not risking your neck. And risk—experiment—is a considerable part of the joy of doing" (qtd in Vande Kieft 193).

NOTES

1. Liminal elements can be found in works such as *Delta Wedding* and *The Optimist's Daughter*, where houses themselves reflect liminal aspects of characters. The influence of Woolf is striking. Such liminal elements can also be seen in Welty's shorter works. The importance of such elements to the interpretation of Welty's works indeed deserves more critical attention.

2. Many critics who examine the jazz style in "Powerhouse" do so either without discussion of the blues elements or do so using theories applicable to more modern jazz. While there is more of a distinction made today between blues and jazz art forms, the two were more closely linked in the past in terms of styles, lyrics, roots, etc. I will therefore take some minor liberties in applying quotes made about one of the forms or the other, and I will often refer to them collectively as the "blues-jazz art form." Such liberties may be qualified somewhat by the fact that Fats Waller himself, who influenced the story, often blended the forms.

3. Much has also been said about Wright and the impact of the blues and jazz art forms upon his works. Some articles include Bruce Dick's "Richard Wright and the Blues Connection" in *Mississippi Quarterly* 42 (1989), 393–408; Ralph Ellison's "Richard Wright's Blues" in *Antioch Review* 50:1–2 (Winter 1992), 61–74 (reprint of 1945 article), also included in Ellison's *Shadow and Act* (1953); and Edward Watson's "Bessie's Blues" in *New Letters* 38 (1971), 64–70. Welty herself, however, has not mentioned much about Wright's texts.

4. For reasons that will be made clear later, I have chosen to cite from the earliest published text, that from *Atlantic Monthly*. I will, however, alter Welty's use of single and double quotations both to conform to modern practice and to avoid confusion.

5. I find it difficult to believe that many critics still debate over the fictitious nature of Powerhouse's story. Welty herself clarifies the issue in her interview with Jones: "I wanted to express what I thought of as improvisation, which I was watching [Fats Waller and his band] do, by making [Powerhouse] improvise this crazy story, which I just made up as I went along" (328). Another reason—more textually centered—to acknowledge the fictitious nature of Powerhouse's story is given later in the essay.

6. I have come across very few articles which do not see these concluding lines as expressing his anxiety at and desire to escape from his isolation.

7. Welty has been ambiguous in this matter; she told Linda Kuehl in 1972, "I tried to write my idea of the life of the traveling artist and performer—not Fats Waller himself, but any artist" (85), yet she reminded Jane Reid Petty in 1977, "It was a story about Fats Waller, you know" (209).

8. One cannot help but think of a quote from Welty's *One Writer's Beginnings*. Referring to her childhood habit of listening to her parents talk privately, Welty explains: "A conscious act grew out of this by the time I began to write stories: getting my distance, a prerequisite of my understanding of human events, is the way I begin to work. Just as, of course, it was an initial step when, in my first journalism job, I stumbled into making pictures with a camera. Frame, proportion, perspective, the values of light and shade, all are determined by the distance of the observing eye" (21).

9. I also find the following passage interesting: "'It going to be intermission,' Powerhouse declares, lifting up his finger with the signet ring" (709). Since it would be somewhat awkward to actually indicate a chorus number with the ring finger, it is quite possible Welty was implying the use of another finger. Since many performers wear multiple rings, it is quite possible that the finger Powerhouse raises is the middle one, hence displaying more than a mere sign of the chorus number. The fact that he has a "signet" (signifying) ring on the finger he raises perhaps adds to the plausibility. This would also be an additional sign of anger, one the audience would mistake for a mere performance gesture. All of my attempts to find a picture of Fats Waller wearing rings, however, have failed.

10. While the citation of a Signifying Monkey variant would be helpful, most are too long to be included here. Daryl Dance provides two variants on pages 197–198 of her *Shuckin' and Jivin'* (Bloomington: Indiana UP, 1978). While I draw connections between them, much more could be made of the social and cultural implications implied in the tales, Waller's life, and Welty's story.

11. Since no one, to my knowledge, has noticed the Signifying Monkey trope in any of Welty's works, and since no one, to my knowledge, has ever asked her about her knowledge of African American folklore, I am not able to verify her knowledge of the tale. Her early love of mythology, though, could have inspired her to find out about African American folklore when the opportunity arose. It is also worth noting that even if someone were to question Welty on this matter, there is no guarantee that she would "give away" a secret. One has only to remember her elusive response to the question concerning whether Phoenix Jackson's grandson was alive or dead: "I could only reply that it doesn't make any difference. I could also say that I did not make him up in order to let him play a trick on Phoenix. But my best answer would be: 'Phoenix is alive.'" Also see notes seven and seventeen.

12. One way to explain the waitress' gullibility is to say that perhaps she is playing along as well, pretending to be foolish. However, the black verbal bantering tradition was and still is largely, although not exclusively, practiced by males. How much of this was actually known to Welty, though, remains questionable.

13. Various critics have taken these mythological allusions to varying extremes. Smith Kirkpatrick states that "both names [Uranus and Knockwood] represent formalizations of the mysteries of life" (105). I find a footnote given by William B. Stone to be so potentially insightful that I quote it at length: "The implications of the use of the name of the god 'Uranus' are complex, but it may be noted that the terrible Furies were created from his blood, and that Aphrodite, a representative of beauty emerging 'from the monstrous element' (Walter F. Otto, *The Homeric Gods* [Boston: Beacon Press, 1964], p. 93), was born, according to Hesiod, from the sea foam around Uranus's severed genitals (95). Unfortunately, Stone makes nothing of it at all." Ironically, though, Appel states a page later, "Powerhouses creation of 'that creeper' Knockwood may be a folk image of the devil" (229).

14. Roger Abrahams has coined the phrase "man-of-words" in his discussions of "respectable" and "nonsense" speech. Much of his work has provided a theoretical basis for this work.

15. The Monkey, in the performance/telling of the tale, is almost always associated with the black man, the Lion and the Elephant (the victims of the trickster) representing the whites. An intriguing exception, however, may be found in Wright's *Black Boy*, where the black narrator and his friend end up the victims of a white man's signifying (see Mechling, 87–88, for a discussion of this incident).

16. The article gives at least one version of the lyrics, which are as follows: Hold tight, hold tight, / Hold-tight-hold-tight / Foo-ra-de-ack-a-sa-ki / Want some Sea food, Mama / Steamers and sauce / And then of course / I like oysters, lobsters, too, / And I like my tasty butterfish. / When I come home from work at night / I get my favorite dish, Fish! / Hold tight, hold tight, / Hold-tight-hold-tight / Foo-ra-de-ack-a-sa-ki / Want some Sea food, Mama / Shrimpers and rice, they're very nice!

17. Welty comments upon the news she received in an interview: "They [*Atlantic Monthly*] censored my selection of a song that ended the story. It was 'Hold Tight, I Want Some Seafood, Mama' a wonderful record. They wrote me that *The Atlantic Monthly* cannot publish those lyrics. I never knew why" (Petty 209). We must question whether or not Welty is playing innocent here. While I do not know exactly when Welty attended Waller's performance and subsequently wrote the story, there are striking similarities between elements in the story and what the *Time* magazine article states. Additionally, she has contradicted herself somewhat in other matters (see notes seven and eleven).

18. A good, albeit short discussion of this can be found in W.U. McDonald, Jr.'s "Miss Eudora's 'Dirty' Book: Bowdlerizing *The Robber Bridegroom*" (*Eudora Welty Newsletter* 11 [1987]: 4–5).

WORKS CITED

Abrahams, Roger D. "The Training of the Man of Words in Talking Sweet." *Verbal Art As Performance*. Ed. Richard Bauman. Prospect Heights, IL: Waveland P, 1977. 117–132.

Byerman, Keith E. *Fingering the Jagged Grain: Tradition and Form in Recent Black Fiction*. Athens, GA: U Georgia P, 1985.

Du Bois, W.E.B. *The Souls of Black Folk*. Chicago: A.C. McClurg, 1903.

Ellison, Ralph. *Shadow and Act*. New York: Random House, 1953.

Fox, Charles. *Kings of Jazz: Fats Waller*. New York: A.S. Barnes, 1961.

Gates, Henry Louis, Jr. *The Signifying Monkey: A Theory of Afro-American Literacy Criticism*. New York: Oxford UP, 1988.

"Hold Barred." *Time* 33 (24 April, 1939): 44.

Jones, John Griffin. "Eudora Welty" (1981 Interview). *Conversations with Eudora Welty*. Ed. Peggy Whitman Prenshaw. Jackson: UP of Mississippi, 1984. 316–341.

Kirkpatrick, Smith. "The Anointed Powerhouse." *Sewanee Review* 77 (1969): 94–108.

Kuehl, Linda. "The Art of Fiction XLVII: Eudora Welty" (1972 Interview). *Conversations with Eudora Welty*. Ed. Peggy Whitman Prenshaw. Jackson: UP of Mississippi, 1984. 74–91.

Lampkin, Loretta M. "Musical Movement and Harmony in Eudora Welty's 'Powerhouse.'" *CEA Critic* 45 (1982): 24–28.

Mechling, Jay. "The Failure of Folklore in Richard Wright's *Black Boy*." *Journal of American Folklore* 104 (1991): 275–294.

Petty, Jane Reid. "The Town and the Writer: An Interview with Eudora Welty" (1977). *Conversations with Eudora Welty*. Ed. Peggy Whitman Prenshaw. Jackson: UP of Mississippi, 1984. 200–210.

Schmidt, Peter. *The Heart of the Story: Eudora Welty's Short Fiction*. Jackson: UP of Mississippi, 1991.

Smith, Jeanne Rosier. *Writing Tricksters: Mythic Gambols in American Ethnic Literature*. Berkeley: U of California P, 1997.

Vance, Joel. *Fats Waller: His Life and Time*. Chicago: Contemporary Books, 1977.

Vande Kieft, Ruth M. *Eudora Welty*. New York: Twayne Publishers, 1962.

Welty, Eudora. Foreword to *To The Lighthouse*. New York: Harcourt Brace, 1981. vii–xii.

———. *One Writer's Beginnings*. Cambridge, MA: Harvard UP, 1995.

———. "Powerhouse." *Atlantic Monthly* 167 (June 1941): 707–713.

Wright, Richard. *Black Boy*. New York: HarperCollins, 1993.

DEAN BETHEA

Phoenix Has No Coat:
Historicity, Eschatology, and Sins of Omission
in Eudora Welty's "A Worn Path"

Unsurprisingly, Eudora Welty's short story "A Worn Path" has inspired many interpretations. Most critics, including Elaine Orr, James Walter, Peter Schmidt, and James Robert Saunders, assert the work as an optimistic depiction of its protagonist, Phoenix Jackson.[1] However, no previous study has discerned what I believe to be the work's primary purpose: to attack the debased Bible Belt Christianity that does not eradicate but instead accommodates racism through sins of both commission and omission. Even the many poststructuralist readings of "A Worn Path" have exhibited a shared, essentially formalist strategy: a tendency to divorce the "text" from the vitally important historical conditions and social relationships so carefully limned therein. But an understanding of the history from which the story's action emerges is required if we are to grasp Welty's larger concerns. Through the profound implications of its setting during the Christmas season in and around Natchez, Mississippi, in the twentieth century's early decades, and through its delineation of the protagonist's selflessness and courage, "A Worn Path" calls for the implementation of a theology that would make Phoenix's dangerous—and possibly fatal—journey unnecessary. In my view, Welty's primary intent is not to console, inspire, or edify her readers; nor does she want them merely to take heart from Phoenix's example. Rather, the story is a call to action against the "Christian" world

From *The International Fiction Review* 28, nos. 1 and 2 (2001): 32–41. © 2001 by International Fiction Association, Fredericton, N.B.

that oppresses the protagonist. Phoenix's arduous, life-threatening trek is not solely reflective of the human spirit's capacity to triumph over circumstantial difficulties but revelatory of a society in which very different, patently unjust standards exist.

"A Worn Path" illuminates crucial distinctions between apocalyptic and ethical eschatology in Christian theology. Apocalyptic eschatology refers to the conventional belief that a last judgment will be meted out by a deus ex machina, and allows, indeed encourages, disinterest in and disdain for the events and realities of the mundane world. In contrast, ethical eschatology argues for an apocalypse in that quotidian realm, for an "end time" in the here and now achieved by humans who seek to transmogrify the mores of a corrupt social realm. This interpretation of apocalypse forms the basis of Liberation Theology, a phenomenon whose origins can be traced back to the Civil Rights Movement in the United States: "in the 1950s [Martin Luther King, Jr.] was the pioneer, the forerunner, of all the other liberation theologies that began only in the 1960s and 1970s."[2] If a Christian framework is to be imposed on "A Worn Path" at all, this radical eschatology seems the best choice, since it stems from the same racist experiences as those Phoenix endures. Attempting to read the story through the lens of a quietist eschatology recalls James H. Cone's cogent assertion that American theology has "failed miserably in relating its work to the oppressed in society by refusing to confront this nation with the evils of racism.... Most of the time American theology has simply remained silent, ignoring the condition of the victims of this racist society."[3] I wish to argue that Welty has sought at the fictional level what Cone demands at the theological: through the acute historical consciousness and moral vision that infuses "A Worn Path," she confronts her nation with the lasting effects of its troubled history.

Readers of the story must decipher a subtle prose puzzle, one whose carefully chosen components—including tone, plot structure, setting, the juxtaposition of characters, the racist misinterpretations of Phoenix—only cohere when they are closely examined in light of the story's sociohistorical bases, revealing the rage churning beneath its deceptively placid surface. First, Welty filters her assault through her objective tone, a task she accomplishes perhaps too skillfully, as her concealed authorial presence may have fostered the consensual view of "A Worn Path" as a story concerned primarily with spiritual triumph. Second, the work's cunning structure invokes and apparently valorizes racist stereotypes while withholding crucial information until a final, revelatory reversal. Third, deep and furious irony is expressed through the title itself and its physical and seasonal settings. While the latter has been interpreted as an optimistic framework for the plot, this setting shows instead that the spiritual rebirth which the Christmas holiday symbolizes has not occurred in the heart of the so-called Bible Belt. Welty is also quite specific about where in the Bible Belt Phoenix is journeying to: Natchez—one of the South's most grandiose architectural gems and a bleak monument to the slave economy that built it. The setting's precise geography is thus complemented by its historical associations. The story's picaresque plot also augments Welty's fourth tactic, the juxtaposition of the other characters' material wealth and self-concern with Phoenix's poverty and selflessness, a contrast intensified by their interactions with, and misunderstanding of, her.

Taken together, these four components recall Christ's directive as stated in the Gospel of Matthew that "if anyone wants to sue you and take your coat, give your cloak as well. And if anyone forces you to go one mile, go also the second mile. Give to everyone who begs from you, and do not refuse anyone who wants to borrow from you."[4] Welty's careful description of her protagonist's clothing reveals that Phoenix has no coat, and despite the freezing weather, none of the several people she meets offer her one. It seems probable that Welty, a product of the Bible Belt herself, had this precise verse in mind when she wrote the story. Christ demands that humans give more than what is asked of them and indicts the passive acceptance of another's suffering as an active form of evil, as a sin of omission. Yet no one in the story offers to "walk" even a mere yard with Phoenix, neither on the specific and perilous trip at hand nor on the larger "journey" that is her life. All of the work's white characters, because they do nothing in any real sense to improve Phoenix's plight, are revealed through their apathy as active sinners by the standards of their espoused religion's namesake. Welty invites us to castigate them not merely for their racist actions, but also for their callous inaction. She also implies that if they will not help Phoenix even now, during Christianity's most sacred season, they certainly will not do so during "ordinary times" either. Finally, after examining these four primary issues, we can turn to the story's open-ended conclusion, which should strike us as ominous and foreboding that the road's end for Phoenix will be the complete loss of her faculties or simply death—a fate that the work implies is near at hand.

The exclusion of such important factors from interpretations of "A Worn Path" diminishes its powerful range of meanings and recalls Walter Benjamin's assertion that "nothing that has ever happened should be regarded as lost for history."[5] By pursuing what Benjamin calls the "fullness of the past" through the restoration of the story's historical and social contexts, we discern not a benign and bland Christian allegory, but instead an impassioned and comprehensive indictment of the American South and, by extension, of the larger republic to which it belongs.[6] Phoenix does not live "primarily" as "a text ... beyond the boundaries drawn by her social superiors."[7] Nor does she exist merely "within the world created by her own interior monologue," but rather as an individual trapped within the very real boundaries of a historically defined, deeply racist society.[8] These boundaries create monumental barriers to her expressive love, barriers that would have been confronted only by an illiterate, impoverished, isolated, and elderly African-American woman in the Deep South.

"A Worn Path" inveigles readers by invoking and apparently endorsing a host of "Aunt Jemima" or "Mammy" stereotypes regarding Phoenix's appearance and behavior. This entrapment begins with the story's first two paragraphs: "Far out in the country there was an old Negro woman with her head tied in a red rag.... She wore a dark striped dress reaching down to her shoe tops, and an equally long apron of bleached sugar sacks, with a full pocket."[9] Her makeshift cane and clothing accord perfectly with racist cliches of the time, as do her untied shoes, which many mid-century readers would have seen as corroborative of their specious belief in African-Americans' "innate" laziness and lack of self-regard. More importantly, Welty indicates that her readers must be acutely aware not only of those details she mentions but also of those that she does not. We must notice that Phoenix has no coat, for this fact greatly magnifies the callousness of the white people she encounters, none of whom could have failed to remark her inadequate clothing, and none of whom bother to remedy it.

The invocation of racist stereotypes in describing Phoenix's appearance is immediately augmented by her behavior, as she begins conversing with both her surroundings and herself. In the next several paragraphs she continues to "talk loudly to herself" as well as to trees and to a thorn bush in which she becomes tangled, to a boy who brings her a slice of cake in a moment of hallucination, and then to a "ghost" that she finally realizes is only a scarecrow, around whom she subsequently dances a jig of relief (143). Phoenix's appearance is "comical," her behavior "childish" and "superstitious." Welty augments this apparent valorization of racist cliches by withholding the true reason for Phoenix's journey until the story's concluding paragraphs. Readers are tempted to agree with the white hunter Phoenix encounters who claims "I know you old colored people! Wouldn't miss going to town to see Santa Claus!"(145).

James Walter argues that "the red rag [Phoenix] wears on her head, then, is, in one perspective, her tiara, signifying her sovereignty over the creatures in her domain."[10] Similarly, Elaine Orr sees this passage as exemplifying a dominant concern with inscribing "contradictions" in the story: "For example, Welty describes her protagonist as 'neat and tidy' and yet Phoenix walks all the way to town with her shoes untied ... but no careful reader will believe Phoenix could not tie her own shoes."[11] "Careful readers" ought to realize that Phoenix has untied laces not because she is lazy or unconcerned about her appearance but rather because her advanced age— the white hunter claims she "must be a hundred years old"—prevents her from tying them (146). That she is so wizened by time, yet so determined to complete her life-threatening quest, is a detail meant to deepen our admiration of and empathy for Phoenix. Walter's claim that the red rag she wears is a "tiara" signifying her dominance of a world that so clearly dominates her seems inaccurate, especially since such notions of sovereignty are quickly dismissed when she is knocked into a ditch by a dog and jeered at by the white hunter who discovers her there. The rag signifies the cause-and-effect relationship between Phoenix's indigence and her slave heritage: such scraps of fabric were the most common regalia of slave women in the South, the closest thing to a hat that they were often allowed, or could afford. Finally, her apron made of sugar sacks not only comments movingly on her privation but also alludes to the terrible legacy of the Jim Crow laws, which in many Southern towns prohibited most black men from wearing white shirts during the week and required all black women to wear aprons in public as humiliating signs of their continued oppression.

Neil Isaacs focuses on the symbolic dimensions of the Christmas setting, which for him inspires hope and provides a transcendental, timeless framework within which the text's specific details should be subsumed.[12] Yet the rebirth implied in Phoenix's name not only pertains to her repeated journeys in search of medicine, but also reveals the complete absence here of the spiritual rebirth that the Christmas holiday represents: the arrival of a new god, one whose love extends to all people regardless of skin color and whose main dictum to humanity is to love their neighbors as themselves. Phoenix's plight, and the indifference she faces, indicate that this spiritual rebirth has not occurred in her world. Welty's description as Phoenix first arrives in Natchez is deceptively innocuous: "Bells were ringing. Phoenix walked on. In the paved city it was Christmas time. There were red and green electric lights strung and crisscrossed everywhere and turned on in the daytime.... A lady came along in the crowd, carrying an armful of red-, green-, and silver-wrapped presents" (146–47). The spirit of Christmas, however, is nowhere to be found as Natchez exhibits all of the season's trappings but none of its true meanings. While the city can afford not only to pay for decorative lights but also to burn them in the daytime, Phoenix is forced to live in a primitive house so cold that her grandson awaits her return wrapped up in "a little patch quilt" (148). Moreover, the contrast between Phoenix's makeshift clothing and the woman who approaches her bearing an armful of gifts only deepens the scene's irony.

Having Phoenix arrive in Natchez sets a host of negative historical associations reverberating throughout the story. Mississippi's first capital, Natchez was once the apotheosis of the King Cotton, slave-built South, a territorial hub where by 1850 two-thirds of the nation's millionaires lived and where at least forty mansions had been erected by 1860.[13] Moreover, the town marked the southern terminus of the Natchez Trace, the Mississippi River route that provided cheap and quick transportation for cotton—and for the newly arrived slaves who would be shipped to regional plantations, making the Trace forever a "Trail of Tears" for all African-Americans. After 1812, the rapid expansion of the Cotton Empire in the Southwest made Natchez and Algiers, Louisiana, the busiest slave markets in the nation. Natchez records for an "unknown part of the year 1833" show that thirty-two non-resident slave traders made the then staggering sum of $238,879, a figure that does not include the earnings of resident slavers, who conducted a much greater portion of the sales. Natchez's thriving economy is further evidenced by the presence of the regional offices of Franklin, Armfield and Company, the nation's major slave-trading firm. Moreover, slave prices in the city quadrupled over the course of sixty years primarily because of the "increasing significance of chattel ownership as a symbol in the frenzied quest for status among the middle and upper class whites."[14]

Finally, unlike similarly magnificent cities in the eastern Deep South such as Savannah and Charleston, which had been long established before the cotton gin's invention in 1793 and the ensuing explosive rise of King Cotton, Mississippi as a whole and Natchez in particular owed their very existence—and certainly their wealth—to Whitney's technological innovation. Beginning with Mississippi, Alabama, and western Tennessee, and finally extending into northern Louisiana, Arkansas, and parts of Texas, the slave-based cotton industry itself impelled the westward expansion of the American South, as the demand for more and more suitable land drove new settlement. When Phoenix enters the streets of Natchez, we should be struck not only by the obvious contrast between her material poverty and the wealth that surrounds her, but as well by the deeper irony that she is walking through the midst of a material opulence she once labored to build, against her will. Her story is a living testament to the dismal origins of the city's spurious grandeur; her understanding of, connection to, and exclusion from the "splendors" of Natchez is immediate and personal, rendering the racist condescension the city's white residents subject her to even more intolerable and maddening.

If Phoenix is a symbolic figure, then she has arrived in a kind of "Anti-Bethlehem," a spiritual necropolis whose white denizens cling to the wreckage of an ideology that is the antithesis of the egalitarian and unifying philosophy attributed to Christ in the Gospels. In this city festooned with and illuminated by seasonal decorations, Phoenix is the only true "Christmas light," so to speak, but that small flame does nothing to mitigate the emotional darkness enveloping Natchez, as her experiences there will prove. Natchez, built largely through what Benjamin has labeled the "anonymous toil" of people like Phoenix, perfectly exemplifies his characterization of "cultural treasures" as composites of both barbarism and civilization.[15] Using the city as a setting deepens the necessity of examining the historical wreckage that "A Worn Path" subtly delineates and indicts.

The interactions between Phoenix and the story's other characters augment its setting's multiple ironies. The first person Phoenix encounters is a white hunter, who pulls her out of a ditch into which a dog has just knocked her. Isaacs asserts this man as "a Santa Claus figure himself (he carries a big sack over his shoulder, he is always laughing, he brings Phoenix a gift of a nickel)."[16] Similarly, Saunders asserts that "there is enough of an understanding between the hunter and the woman for him to be genuinely concerned; he had helped her off her back and shared a word or two."[17] Isaacs and Saunders fail to mention, however, that "Santa" finds the frail Phoenix in the ditch, that his initial laughter occurs when he sees her lying helpless, that this outburst is not followed by an apology, that his subsequent laughter is derisive of her, and that he refers to her by the racist term "Granny," which he would never use for an elderly woman if she were white. Moreover, Isaacs's "Santa" does not intend to give Phoenix a nickel but drops it just before claiming that he would give her a dime if he had any money. He then points his gun at her only to see if she will react in terror, which she does not. Finally, the hunter abandons Phoenix miles from town, without offering her a coat or helping her reach her destination.

Other important contrasts are created in this scene as well: the hunter, in addition to the money he claims not to have, carries a string of dead quail on his belt, an abundance of food that Phoenix is not likely to experience. His claim that he understands "colored people" only typifies the repellant thinking of those who equate racist stereotypes with knowledge. The hunter's reaction upon learning of her destination further reveals his complete misunderstanding of her: "Why that's too far! That's as far as I walk when I come out myself, and I get something for my trouble" (145). This encounter ends with his attempt to terrify Phoenix by threatening her with his gun. Phoenix believes he is aiming the rifle at her because she has been caught "stealing" his dropped nickel, although he does not realize that he has lost the coin. She has seen "plenty" of other African-Americans getting shot, at closer range and for less than the crime she believes she might have committed: stealing five cents (145). Her resigned tone evidences the absolute lack of both justice and safety for blacks in her world, as if being shot now would be the next "logical" consequence in a world founded on injustice.

The story's ironies continue in the apparently benign encounter between Phoenix and the white lady in Natchez. This scene initiates a series of important reversals of the racist stereotypes invoked earlier: Phoenix asks someone to tie her shoes as soon as she arrives in town. Far from being slovenly, she is quite concerned with her appearance, and has not tied her laces only because her aged fingers lack the dexterity to do so. The white woman must set her armload of presents down beside Phoenix's untied and worn shoes, after asking "What do you want, Grandma?," using, as did the hunter, the patronizing terminology sanctioned by a racist world (147). That Phoenix asks a favor of the "lady"—a title then reserved for white women— alludes again to Christ's commandment in Matthew, yet the woman, despite being confronted with an elderly, coatless woman on a day earlier described as "frozen," only grudgingly fulfills the request and then abandons her (142).

The next passage contains the story's crowning misinterpretation of Phoenix by the white people she meets. Having finally reached a doctor's office, she simply asserts "Here I be." The office attendant immediately assesses Phoenix, whom she calls "Grandma," as "a charity case" because she is elderly, black, and poorly dressed. Perhaps flustered by this snideness, Phoenix seems to forget temporarily why she has come, but the attendant's response is not concern but consternation: "'Are you deaf?' cried the attendant." Her shouts cause a nurse to come in, who reveals "that's just old Aunt Phoenix.... She doesn't come for herself—she has a little grandson. She makes these trips as regular as clockwork. She lives away back off the Old Natchez Trace" (147).

At this juncture Welty's carefully laid trap is sprung as she annihilates the racist stereotypes she seemed to endorse. In Phoenix's poignant recollection of the reason for her pilgrimage, we learn that we have not really "known" her at all and that she is the only truly humane character in the work: "I'm an old woman without an education. It was my memory fail me. My little grandson, he is just the same and I forgot it in the coming.... Every little while his throat begin to close up again, and he not able to swallow. He not get his breath. He not able to help himself. So the time come around and I go on another trip for the soothing medicine ..." (148). Phoenix is uneducated, of course, because she was denied schooling due to her race. In the world depicted in the story, she and her grandson are the "only two left in the world" who care about each other. By the explicitly Christian standards invoked in the story, they are its "only two" truly humane characters. No one else exhibits more than a slightly vexed interest in them, a reality underscored by the nurse's two responses to Phoenix's speech: "'All right. The doctor said as long as you came to get it, you could have it.... But it's an obstinate case....' The nurse was trying to hush her now. She brought her a bottle of medicine. 'Charity,' she said, making a check mark in a book" (148). The grudgingly donated medicine does not constitute charity in the sense demanded by Christ, an irony that is only deepened by the seasonal setting. Moreover, Phoenix's forgetfulness, coupled with her earlier hallucinations, augurs ominous developments. Rather than being a confident assertion, her claim that "I not going to forget him again, no, the whole enduring time" functions as a kind of desperate incantation, as a magic spell she wields against the increasing desperation of her plight and the inexorable advance of time. But people of her age and condition, especially those with no access to proper care, will not get better (148). When Phoenix does lose her grasp of reality, no one else in her world—as this scene makes abundantly clear—will step in to help her grandson.

And Phoenix's utter isolation in this deeply racist world is borne out by the story's most ironic passage: "'It's Christmas time, Grandma,' said the attendant. 'Could I give you a few pennies out of my purse?'" (148). This statement culminates Welty's incremental attack on the Bible Belt's self-serving definition of Christian duty: moral sanctity purchased for a few pennies, not through any real, substantive concern for other humans. Appropriately, even the typically unflappable protagonist approaches curtness in her response: "'Five pennies is a nickel,' Phoenix said stiffly" (149). Besides constituting a final reference to Christ's directive in Matthew, this passage is the crowning denouncement of the miserable inhumanity exemplified throughout the story. It is imperative to note that every white character—the hunter who terrifies her, the white lady, the snide attendant, and the dismissive nurse—is revealed as someone who views Phoenix through the dehumanizing perspective of racism.

Phoenix then combines her charitably acquired nickel with the one from the hunter, and instead of spending it on something for herself, she states her intention to buy her grandson a little paper windmill. We must remember that, despite her long journey to Natchez and the return trip she now faces, Phoenix has not eaten at all; her earlier hallucination of a boy offering her a piece of cake is just that, a dream of sustenance in an uncharitable world. This passage recalls the white woman and her armful of brightly wrapped presents, in stark contrast to Phoenix's grandson's reality, for whom a simple paper windmill promises to be an unexpected gift. Such an obvious allusion to the journey of the magi in the Gospels only intensifies Welty's ironic rendering of the South's racist Christianity. The story's final sentence also augments this anger, as Phoenix leaves the office: "Then her slow step began on the stairs, going down" (149). The participial phrase symbolizes a bleak future for her and her grandson—and for the society that perpetuates inhumanity. That symbolic foreshadowing is augmented by the conclusion's lack of closure, which impels readers to wonder if Phoenix, unfed, coatless, having already suffered a hallucination and a memory blackout, will be able to make the trip safely.

At this juncture the story's title demands further consideration: at one level "A Worn Path" stakes a claim for the deep humanity, fortitude, and courage of black women, the most oppressed of all the oppressed in the American South. At another level, the title is an indictment of the social world that causes Phoenix's suffering, a call to Welty's readers to exit the "worn path" of human relations constructed by a racist society, one in which an elderly woman must imperil her life to gain begrudged medical treatment for her grandson. Through this story, Welty attempts to make her readers relinquish the established road of social interaction, to break new ground in their treatment of each other, to effect at one level the kind of rebirth signified by the story's Christmas setting.

As the final work in *A Curtain of Green and Other Stories*, "A Worn Path" functions as a sort of last testament on the Southern world presented in that collection. The story is as radical an assault on racism for its time as Faulkner's story "The Bear." Both authors came, of course, from white Mississippi families and both deftly delineate the dimensions and lasting effects of the South's racist heritage, with Faulkner asserting the "mongrel" Sam Fathers as the true role model for Ike McCaslin, and Welty according the same status to Phoenix Jackson for all of her readers.

NOTES

1. See Orr, "Unsettling Every Definition of Otherness: Another Reading of Eudora Welty's 'A Worn Path,'" *South Atlantic Review* 57 (1992); Walter, "Love's Habit of Vision in Welty's Phoenix Jackson," *Journal of the Short Story in English* 7 (1986): 78; Schmidt, *The Heart of the Story: Eudora Welty's Short Fiction* (Jackson: University Press of Mississippi, 1991); and Saunders, "'A Worn Path': The Eternal Quest of Welty's Phoenix Jackson," *Southern Literary Journal* 25 (1992): 71.

2. Alfred T. Hennelly, *Liberation Theologies: The Global Pursuit of Justice* (Mystic, CT: Twenty-Third Publications, 1995) 122.

3. James H. Cone, *A Black Theology of Liberation* (Philadelphia: Lippincott, 1970) 46.

4. *The New Oxford Annotated Bible: New Revised Standard Version* (New York: Oxford University Press, 1991) Matt. 5:40–42.

5. Walter Benjamin, *Illuminations*, ed. Hannah Arendt (New York: Harcourt Brace, 1968) 254.

6. Benjamin 254.

7. Orr 66.

8. Schmidt 39.

9. Eudora Welty, "A Worn Path," in *The Collected Stories of Eudora Welty* (New York: Harcourt Brace Jovanovich, 1980) 142. Subsequent references are to this edition and are cited parenthetically in the text.

10. Walter 82.

11. Orr 63.

12. Neil Isaacs, "Life for Phoenix," *Sewanee Review* 71 (1963): 40.

13. Clayton D. James, *Antebellum Natchez* (Baton Rouge: Louisiana State University Press, 1968) 144.

14. James 197–98.

15. Benjamin 256.

16. Isaacs 40.

17. Saunders 71.

CHARLES E. MAY

Why Sister Lives at the P.O.

Often in literary studies a well-known artist will turn critic briefly and make an offhand comment about the work of a fellow writer that becomes solidified into dogma and thus creates a critical or interpretative dead end. Such seems to be the case with the one-liner that Katherine Anne Porter tossed off over thirty years ago about Eudora Welty's popular little family comedy, "Why I Live at the P.O." Porter's classifying of the story as a "terrifying case of dementia praecox" seems so "right" that no one has ever bothered to examine or challenge her judgment. If the story is a case study, albeit an hilarious one, of paranoia in action, then little is left for the critic to do except nod his head with a knowing smile.

However, this alone does not account for the lack of discussion of one of the most anthologized stories of a writer whose other stories are discussed widely. Another reason for critical silence on the work is that it is comic. No interpretation can fully account for what makes it so funny, and no one wants the thankless task of explaining a joke. One could point out, as Ruth M. Vande Kieft has, that the narrator of the story nicely illustrates Bergson's notion that mechanical rigidity in human beings is laughable. There is certainly nothing flexible about Sister's persecution obsession. One could suggest, as Sean O'Faolain has, that the story, like most good humor, is a very mixed affair and thus hides a groan somewhere behind the joke. Again, it

From *Short Stories for Students*, Vol. 10. Originally published in *The Critical Response to Eudora Welty's Fiction*, Laurie Champion, ed. © 1994 Greenwood Press.

seems clear that if we laugh because the characters of the story seem so obsessed with trivia, we also despair to think that people *can* be so obsessed with trivia. After making these general comments, critics have found little else to say about the humor of the story except to admire Welty's ability to capture a particular humorous verbal idiom. Everyone agrees that the story is a *tour de force*.

An additional problem that faces Welty critics who would interpret "Why I Live at the P.O." is the fact that its tone and technique seem radically different from Welty's usual fictional milieu. Best known and most discussed for stories that take place in a "Season of Dreams" where reality is transformed into fantasy and fable, and, as R. P. Warren has noted in a famous essay, the logic of things is not the logic of ordinary daylight life, Welty, in this, one of her most widely-read stories, creates a season that is not one of dream at all; the reality of things seems to remain stubbornly, almost militantly, real. Warren has suggested that the dream-like effect of the typical Welty story seems to result from her ability to squeeze meaning from the most trivial details. However, here in a story that depends on the triviality of things, there is no dream-like effect; the trivial details are comically allowed to remain trivial. They are never transformed into hierophanic entities the way they are in such typical Welty fables as "First Love," "Livvie," "Death of a Traveling Salesman," or "A Worn Path." No one has dared to try to show how Sister's green-tomato pickle or Stella-Rondo's flesh-colored kimono are transformed from the profane into the sacred.

For these reasons the story seems almost impervious to critical analysis. Aside from Robert Drake's interesting but inconclusive analysis of the story as a "cater-cornered epic" several years ago in *The Mississippi Quarterly*, the only comments that have been made about the form of the story are the suggestions made by several readers that it is a monologue similar to Ring Lardner's "Haircut," for Sister reveals more about her moral status than she intends to or is aware of. Drake never makes clear just what the nature of the "cater-cornered epic" genre is. He suggests that it involves the exalting of the everyday and the familiar to the level of the heroic and epic; yet the result is not mock-heroic, but rather something harder to define than that. Somehow, the cater-cornered nature of the story is related to a multiple point of view in which sister seems inwardly aware of the absurdity of her position in the P.O., but must justify her position anyway. Because Drake does not make the connection between Sister's psyche and the story's structure clear, I am left unsure about how the work is epical, cater-cornered, butt-ended, parallel-parked, or otherwise geometrically arranged.

I have reviewed these desultory comments about Welty's little story at such length because they illustrate certain basic interpretative problems about the work. The problem of calling Sister a schizophrenic is the resulting temptation to leave the issue there and thus ignore both the structural implications the phenomenon has for the story and the phenomenological implications it has for the characters. The problem of making such general comments about the story's monologue genre, its insane logic, its geometrical design, or its trivia-saturated detail is that all these remarks seem to be critical dead ends. None lead to a unified interpretation of the story or an appreciation of the complexity of its human content and artistic structure. R. P. Warren says that Welty's typical fictional character is, in one way or another, isolated from the world. Around this character, Warren further suggests, Eudora Welty creates either the drama of the isolated person's attempt to escape into the real world, or the drama of the discovery, either by the isolated character or by the reader, of the nature of the particular predicament. Of these two types, "Why I Live at the P.O." seems clearly to belong to the latter. Moreover, it seems equally clear that since Sister is less interested in discovering than justifying her situation, the drama of the story resides in the reader's gradual discovery of just exactly why Sister does live at the P.O. Consequently, although the story, by its very nature, seems to resist interpretation, by its very nature also it requires interpretation. The drama of the story exists as the drama of the reader's analysis of sister's basic situation as she herself describes it.

To make this discovery, I suggest the reader play the role of phenomenologist rather than psychoanalyst. To say that Sister's motives, actions, and intentions are other than those she proclaims is to indulge in the obvious and get nowhere. To attempt to analyze Sister's phenomenological situation in relation to her family, particularly her relation to her sister, Stella-Rondo, is to participate in the drama of discovery that Welty's story demands. R. D. Laing rather than Freud seems to be the best guide here. If Sister is indeed a schizophrenic, whatever that means, her predicament should not be analyzed *in vacuo*, but within the family nexus itself. I don't pretend that the method developed by R. D. Laing and Aaron Esterson in *Sanity, Madness and the Family* for analyzing families of schizophrenics can be adopted whole cloth to apply to the situation of "Why I Live at the P.O." After all, we do only have Sister's word on evening that happens, and, as everyone agrees, she is not to be trusted. Moreover, we are dealing here with the static, closed form of the art work, not the open, dynamic situation of existential reality. Yet, to use Laing's Sartrean terminology, we cannot make "intelligible" what the basic situation of the story is until we very carefully retrace the steps from what is going on (the "process") to who is doing what (the "praxis"). If the action of the story, or Sister's recounting of it, is "cater-cornered," circular, "one-sided," or "cut on the bias," then we must determine the existential source of both Sister's logic and the story's geometry.

A close look at the events of Sister's momentous Fourth of July indicates that she is an example of what Laing has termed the "unembodied self." She does nothing directly, but rather observes and criticizes what the body experiences and does. More specifically, in this story, Sister is one who does things subjectively rather than objectively. Welty dramatizes Sister's divided self by splitting her quite nearly into a subjective side, Sister herself, and an objective side, Stella-Rondo, who is "exactly twelve months to the day younger." Stella-Rondo acts out everything that Sister subjectively thinks or feels. In this sense Sister is right when she insists throughout the story that she does nothing, that everything is Stella-Rondo's fault. Yet the reader is also right in suspecting that everything that happens is Sister's doing. It is Sister who first dates Mr. Whitaker, but it is Stella-Rondo who marries him and moves away from the family; both are desires which Sister harbors but cannot act out. Stella-Rondo did not break up Sister and Mr. Whitaker by telling him that she was "one-sided," or as Sister says, "bigger on one side than the other." Rather, Stella-Rondo's action dramatizes that the one side which is sister is the subjective side that cannot act.

According to Sister, Stella-Rondo turns the other members against her one by one. However, what Stella-Rondo really does throughout the story is act out Sister's subjective feelings. First, Sister says that Shirley-T is the "spit-image of Papa-Daddy if he'd cut off his beard." A bit later at the table, Stella-Rondo turns Papa-Daddy against Sister by telling him, "Sister says she fails to understand why you don't cut off your beard." Although Sister's defense—"I did not say any such of a thing, the idea!"—is literally true; that is, she did not say these exact words, it is obvious that "the idea" was indeed hers. Next, when Uncle Rondo appears in Stella-Rondo's flesh-colored kimono, Sister says he looks like a "half-wit" in it. Later, Stella-Rondo echoes Sister by saying that Uncle Rondo "looks like a fool." At supper, Stella-Rondo thus articulates Sister's feelings when she tells Uncle Rondo that Sister said he looked like a fool in the pink kimono. Again, although Sister did not use these exact words, she thought what Stella-Rondo voices. When Sister asks the imaginary listener, "Do you remember who it was really said that?" the listener should remember all too well.

Sister communicates everything in this oblique, cater-cornered way; she does not express her feelings directly, but rather diagonally through Stella-Rondo. Consequently, she can cause a great many events to occur, yet disclaim responsibility for any of them. She can sit in the post office, proclaiming, "I didn't do anything," and thereby believe that she preserves her freedom, her individuality, her blamelessness, and her inviolate self.

R.D. Laing's description of the schizoid individual indicates the nature and result of Sister's self justification: she tries to preserve the self by withdrawing into a central citadel and writing off everything else except the self. The tragic paradox of this situation, says Laing, is that the more the schizoid person tries thusly to defend the self, the more he or she destroys it. The real danger stems not from the "enemies" outside, but rather from the destructive defensive maneuvers inside.

Once we see that Stella-Rondo is the objective side of Sister's subjective self, the inevitability of Sister's being driven out of the house precisely because she urges the exile of Stella-Rondo becomes clear. If Stella-Rondo is a female version of the prodigal son returned, then like the good and faithful son who stayed home, Sister resents the fact that Stella-Rondo has failed in the prodigality of the venture that Sister's subjective side has sent her out on. M. H. Abrams, in his study, *Natural Supernaturalism*, has reminded us that the prodigal son story is a figure for life as a circular rather than a linear journey. The leaving of home is a fall from unity into self-dividedness; the return is the circularity of the return to union. It is precisely this union of subjectivity and objectivity that Sister does not want.

Sister now desires to remain safe at home where she can manipulate the family from her position as dutiful daughter. However, given her subjective/objective split, the very existence of this desire means that Stella-Rondo will become the favorite while Sister becomes the exile. The psychological mechanism here is similar to that which Edgar Allan Poe describes as the "perverse"—that "radical, primitive, irreducible sentiment" often overlooked by moralists and psychologists alike.

Thus, in a very complex way the story illustrates the schizoid self-deception of the unembodied self. Moreover, it also dramatizes the results of a complete failure of communication when people not only refuse to listen to each other, but refuse to listen to themselves as well. The basic irony of the story is that although Sister spends the whole tale explaining why she lives at the P.O., she really does not know why. Although she talks, talks, talks, no one listens to what she says, not even herself. In fact, no one listens to anyone else in the story; the motif is constant throughout. When Sister denies that she said Papa-Daddy should shave off his beard, Stella-Rondo says, "Anybody in the world could have heard you, that had ears." And the more Sister protests, the less Papa-Daddy listens; "he acts like he just don't hear me," says Sister. "Papa-Daddy must of gone stone deaf." When Sister warns Uncle Rondo not to go near Papa-Daddy, he ignores her and goes on "zigzagging right on out to the hammock" anyway.

Sister, of course, is the character most guilty of not listening in the story, even though she is always accusing others of this. She tells Mama that if it had been her that had run away to Illinois and returned, Mama would not have been so overjoyed to see her. When Mama insists that she would have, Sister says, "she couldn't convince me though she talked till she was blue in the face." The last words of the story further emphasize Sister's refusal to listen, and sum up her situation: "And if Stella-Rondo should come to me this minute, on bended knees, and *attempt* to explain the incidents of her life with Mr. Whitaker, I'd simply put my fingers in both my ears and refuse to listen." The fact is, Sister has been telling the whole story with her fingers figuratively in both ears. She will not listen to Stella-Rondo because she will not listen to herself. Consequently, she will go to her grave denying the facts of life, as she claims Stella-Rondo will do. Our response to Sister as we read the story might best be expressed in the Southern colloquialism, "I just wish you could hear yourself talk." It is precisely the point of the story that Sister cannot.

A speech to a listener that the speaker cannot actually hear, a speech in which the speaker reveals herself unawares, is, of course, the kind of utterance that we often attribute to the dramatic monologue form. However, Welty's story poses an important difference. The monologue speakers in Robert Browning's poems, for example, have dramatized listeners to whom they speak, with definite strategies in mind. Andrea del Sarto, Fra Lippo Lippi, the infamous Duke, all either have certain aims in speaking as they do to their listeners, or else they speak as a way to discover just what their situation is. A closer analogue to "Why I Live at the P.O." is Browning's "Soliloquy of the Spanish Cloister." The poem is not a soliloquy in the sense that it is a set speech, a delivery of feelings or ideas previously arrived at by the speaker, but rather a soliloquy in the sense that it is spoken to no one. The particular ironic nature of the "Soliloquy of the Spanish Cloister" which makes it closer to "Why I Live at the P.O." than the work with which it is usually compared, Ring Lardner's "Haircut," is that the speaker in Browning's poem is "guilty" precisely of those sins which he attributes to Brother Lawrence. Consequently, he damns himself even as he believes he is damning Brother Lawrence. No one hears him, not even himself, but he is damned nevertheless. Similarly, Sister alienates herself from the family in the very act of trying to alienate Stella-Rondo.

However, the literary character that Sister resembles even more is Dostoevsky's Underground Man. As it is for Dostoevsky's nameless antihero, Sister's logic is not so much insane as it is the rational pushed to such an extreme that it becomes irrational and perverse. Sister's story, an apologia, but not an apology, is an argument that becomes nonsense. The whole story that Sister tells (not the story Welty creates) is nonsense, not because of the triviality of objects and concerns that the argument seems to be about, but rather because the subjective is completely cut off from objective reality. If the story is about schizophrenia, this is the nature of the pathology. Although, as is typical of her, Sister accuses the members of her family of "cutting off your nose to spite your face," this is exactly what she does to herself. By pulling herself into her underground P.O., by casting off everything except her own subjectivity, Sister, like Dostoevsky's underground man, becomes involved in a constant verbal defense of the autonomy of the self that only serves to further destroy the self, to eat it up with its own subjectivity.

At the end of the story when Sister's "revolution" against the family on the Fourth of July has divided up the whole town into two camps that correspond to her own divided self, she believes she has established a separate peace. "Peace, that's what I like. ... I want the world to know I'm happy." But as long as everything in Sister's life is "cater-cornered," which is indeed the way she likes things, she will never have peace. Like the Ancient Mariner, she will grab every Wedding Guest who enters the P.O. and once again tell her oblique and slanted story, therefore never uniting her ghost-like subjective self with the objective world of others. The real drama of the story is the reader's discovery of the logical and phenomenological circle in which Sister is trapped.

ROBERT PENN WARREN[1]

The Love and the Separateness in Miss Welty

He could understand God's giving Separateness first and then giving
Love to follow and heal in its wonder, but God had reversed this, and
given Love first and then Separateness, as though it did not matter to
Him which came first.

—"A Still Moment."

If we put *The Wide Net*, Eudora Welty's present collection of stories, up
against her first collection, *A Curtain of Green*, we can immediately observe a
difference: the stories of *The Wide Net* represent a specializing, an
intensifying, of one of the many strains which were present in *A Curtain of
Green*. All of the stories in *A Curtain of Green* bear the impress of Miss
Welty's individual talent, but there is a great variety among them in subject
matter and method and, more particularly, mood. It is almost as if the author
had gone at each story as a fresh start in the business of writing fiction, as if
she had had to take a new angle each time out of a joy in the pure novelty of
the perspective. There is the vindictive farce of "The Petrified Man," the
nightmarish "Clytie," the fantastic and witty "Old Mr. Marblehall," the
ironic self-revelation of "Why I Live at the P. O.," the nearly straight realism
of "The Hitch-Hikers," the macabre comedy and pathos of "Keela, the
Outcast Indian Maid." The material of many of the stories was sad, or
violent, or warped, and even the comedy and wit were not straight, but if

From *Critical Essays on Eudora Welty*. W. Craig Turner and Lee Emling Harding, eds. © 1989 by
W. Craig Turner and Lee Emling Harding. Originally from *Kenyon Review* 6 (Spring 1944):
246–59. © 1958 by Robert Penn Warren.

read from one point of view, if read as a performance, the book was exhilarating, even gay, as though the author were innocently delighted not only with the variety of the world but with the variety of ways in which one could look at the world and the variety of things which stories could be and still be stories. Behind the innocent delight of the craftsman, and of the admirer of the world, there was also a seriousness, a philosophical cast of mind, which gave coherence to the book, but on the surface there was the variety, the succession of surprises. In *The Wide Net* we do not find the surprises. The stories are more nearly cut to one pattern.

We do not find the surprises. Instead, on the first page, with the first sentence, we enter a special world: "Whatever happened, it happened in extraordinary times, in a season of dreams ..." And that is the world in which we are going to live until we reach the last sentence of the last story. "Whatever happened," the first sentence begins, as though the author cannot be quite sure what did happen, cannot quite undertake to resolve the meaning of the recorded event, cannot, in fact, be too sure of recording all of the event. This is coyness, of course; or a way of warning the reader that he cannot expect quite the ordinary direct lighting of the actual event. For it is "a season of dreams"—and the faces and gestures and events often have something of the grave retardation, the gnomic intensity, the portentous suggestiveness of dreams. The logic of things here is not quite the logic by which we live, or think we live, our ordinary daylight lives. In "The Wide Net," for example, the young husband, who thinks his wife has jumped into the river, goes out with a party of friends to dredge for the body, but the sad occasion turns into a saturnalian fish-fry which is interrupted when the great King of the Snakes raises his hoary head from the surface of the river. But usually, in the present stories, the wrenching of logic is not in terms of events themselves, though "The Purple Hat" is a fantasy, and "Asphodel" moves in the direction of fantasy. Usually the events as events might be given a perfectly realistic treatment (Dreiser could take the events of "The Landing" for a story). But in these cases where the events and their ordering are "natural" and not supernatural or fantastic, the stories themselves finally belong to the "season of dreams" because of the special tone and mood, the special perspective, the special sensibility with which they are rendered.

Some readers, in fact, who are quite aware of Miss Welty's gifts, have recently reported that they are disturbed by the recent development of her work. Diana Trilling, in her valuable and sobering comments on current fiction, which appear regularly in the *Nation*, says that the author "has developed her technical virtuosity to the point where it outweighs the uses to which it is put, and her vision of horror to the point of nightmare." There are two ideas in this indictment, and let us take the first one first and come to the second much later. The indictment of the technique is developed along these lines: Miss Welty has made her style too fancy—decorative, "falsely poetic" and "untrue," "insincere." ("When an author says 'look at me' instead of 'Look at it,' there is insincerity ...") This insincerity springs from "the extreme infusion of subjectivism and private sensibility." But the subjectivism leads not only to insincerity and fine writing but to a betrayal of the story's obligation to narrative and rationality. Miss Welty's stories take off from a situation, but "the stories themselves stay with their narrative no more than a dance, say, stays with its argument." That is the summary of the argument.

The argument is, no doubt, well worth the close attention of Miss Welty's admirers. There is, in fact, a good deal of the falsely poetic in Miss Welty's present style, metaphors that simply pretend to an underlying logic, and metaphors (and descriptions) that, though good themselves, are irrelevant to the business in hand. And sometimes Miss Welty's refusal to play up the objective action—her attempt to define and refine the response rather than to present the stimulus—does result in a blurred effect. But the indictment does not treat primarily of such failures to fulfill the object the artist has set herself but of the nature of that object. The critic denies, in effect, that Miss Welty's present kind of fiction is fiction at all: "It is a book of ballets, not of stories."

Now is it possible that the critic is arguing from some abstract definition of "story," some formalistic conception which does not accommodate the present exhibit, and is not concerning herself with the question of whether or not the present exhibit is doing the special job which it proposes for itself, and, finally, the job which we demand of all literature? Perhaps we should look at a new work first in terms of its effect and not in terms of a definition of type, because every new work is in some degree, however modest, wrenching our definition, straining its seams, driving us back from the formalistic definition to the principles on which the definition was based. Can we say this, therefore, of our expectation concerning a piece of literature, new or old: that it should intensify our awareness of the world (and of ourselves in relation to the world) in terms of an idea, a "view." This leads us to what is perhaps the key statement by Diana Trilling concerning *The Wide Net*: she grants that the volume "has tremendous emotional impact, despite its obscurity." In other words, she says, unless I misinterpret her, that the book does intensify the reader's awareness—but *not* in terms of a presiding idea.

This has led me to reread Miss Welty's two volumes of stories in the attempt to discover the issues which are involved in the "season of dreams."[2] To begin with, almost all of the stories deal with people who, in one way or another, are cut off, alienated, isolated from the world. There is the girl in "Why I Live at the P. O."—isolated from her family by her arrogance, meanness, and sense of persecution; the half-witted Lily Daw, who, despite the efforts of "good" ladies, wants to live like other people; the deaf-mutes of "The Key," and the deaf-mute of "First Love"; the people of "The Whistle" and "A Piece of News," who are physically isolated from the world and who make their pathetic efforts to reestablish something lost; the travelling-salesman and the hitch-hikers of "The Hitch-Hikers" who, for their different reasons, are alone, and the travelling-salesman of "Death of a Travelling Salesman" who, in the physically and socially isolated backwoods cabin, discovers that he is the one who is truly isolated; Clytie, isolated in family pride and madness and sexual frustration, and Jennie of "At the Landing," and Mrs. Larkin of "A Curtain of Green," the old women of "A Visit of Charity" and the old Negro woman of "A Worn Path"; the murderer of "Flowers for Marjorie" who is cut off by an economic situation and the pressure of that great city; Mr. Marblehall in his secret life; Livvie, who, married to an old man and trapped in his respectable house, is cut off from the life appropriate to her years; Lorenzo, Murrell, and Audubon in "A Still Moment," each alone in his dream, his obsession; the old maids of "Asphodel," who tell the story of Miss Sabina and then are confronted by the naked man and pursued by the flock of goats. In some of the cases, the matter is more indirectly presented. For instance, in "Keela, the Outcast Indian Maid," we find, as in "The Ancient Mariner," the story of a man who, having committed a crime, must try to reestablish his connection with humanity; or in the title-story of *The Wide Net*, William Wallace, because he thinks his wife has drowned herself, is at the start of the story cut off from the world of natural joy in which he had lived. "The Petrified Man" and "A Memory" present even more indirect cases, cases which we shall come to a little farther in the discussion.

We can observe that the nature of the isolation may be different from case to case, but the fact of isolation, whatever its nature, provides the basic situation of Miss Welty's fiction. The drama which develops from this basic situation is of either of two kinds: first, the attempt of the isolated person to escape into the world; or second, the discovery by the isolated person, or by the reader, of the nature of the predicament. As an example of the first type, we can remember Clytie's obsessed inspection of faces ("Was it possible to comprehend the eyes and the mouth of other people, which concealed she knew not what, and secretly asked for still another unknown thing?") and her attempt to escape, and to solve the mystery, when she lays her finger on the face of the terrified barber who has come to the ruinous old house to shave her father. Or there is Jennie, of "At the Landing," or Livvie, or the man of

"Keela." As an example of the second type, there is the new awareness on the part of the salesman in "The Hitch-Hikers," or the new awareness on the part of the other salesman in the back-country cabin. Even in "A Still Moment" we have this pattern, though in triplicate. The evangelist Lorenzo, the outlaw Murrell, and the naturalist and artist Audubon stand for a still moment and watch a white heron feeding. Lorenzo having seen a beauty greater than he could account for (he had earlier "accounted for" the beauty by thinking, "Praise God, His love has come visible"), and with the sweat of rapture pouring down from his forehead, shouts into the marshes, "Tempter!" He has not been able to escape from his own obsession, or in other words, to make his definition of the world accommodate the white heron and the "natural" rapture which takes him. Murrell, looking at the bird, sees "only whiteness ensconced in darkness," and thinks that "if it would look at him a dream penetration would fill and gratify his heart"—the heart which Audubon has already defined as belonging to the flinty darkness of a cave. Neither Lorenzo nor Murrell can "love" the bird, and so escape from their own curse as did, again, the Ancient Mariner. But there remains the case of Audubon himself, who does "love" the bird, who can innocently accept nature. There is, however, an irony here. To paint the bird he must "know" the bird as well as "love" it, he must know it feather by feather, he must have it in his hand. And so he must kill it. But having killed the bird, he knows that the best he can make of it now in a painting would be a dead thing, "never the essence, only a sum of parts," and that "it would always meet with a stranger's sight, and never be one with the beauty in any other man's head in the world." Here, too, the fact of the isolation is realized: as artist and lover of nature he had aspired to a communication, a communion, with other men in terms of the bird, but now "he saw his long labor most revealingly at the point where it met its limit" and he is forced back upon himself.

"A Still Moment," however, may lead us beyond the discussion of the characteristic situation, drama, and realization in Miss Welty's stories. It may lead us to a theme which seems to underlie the stories. For convenience, though at the risk of incompleteness, or even distortion, we may call it "Innocence and Experience." Let us take the case of Audubon in relation to the heron. He loves the bird, and innocently, in its fullness of being. But he must subject this love to knowledge; he must kill the bird if he is to commemorate its beauty, if he is to establish his communion with other men in terms of the bird's beauty. There is in the situation an irony of limit and contamination.

Let us look at this theme in relation to other stories. "A Memory," in *A Curtain of Green*, gives a simple example. Here we have a young girl lying on a beach and looking out at the scene through a frame made by her fingers, for the girl can say of herself, "To watch everything about me I regarded grimly and possessively as a need." (As does Audubon, in "A Still Moment.") And further: "It did not matter to me what I looked at; from any observation I would conclude that a secret of life had been nearly revealed to me...." Now the girl is cherishing a secret love, a love for a boy at school about whom she knows nothing, to whom she has never even spoken, but whose wrist her hand had once accidentally brushed. The secret love had made her watching of the world more austere, had sharpened her demand that the world conform to her own ideas and had created a sense of fear. This fear had seemed to be realized one day when, in the middle of a class, the boy had a fit of nose-bleed. But that is in the past. This morning she suddenly sees between the frame of her fingers a group of coarse, fat, stupid, and brutal people disporting themselves on the sand with a maniacal, aimless vigor which comes to climax when the fat woman, into the front of whose bathing suit the man had poured sand, bends over and pulls down the cloth so that the lumps of mashed and folded sand empty out. "I felt a peak of horror, as though her breasts themselves had turned to sand, as though they were of no importance at all and she did not care." Over against this defilement (a defilement which implies that the body, the breasts which turn to sand, had no meaning), there is the refuge of the dream, "the undefined austerity of my love."

"A Memory" presents the moment of the discovery of the two poles— the dream and the world, the idea and nature, innocence and experience, individuality and the anonymous, devouring life-flux, meaning and force, love and knowledge. It presents the contrast in terms of horror (as do "The Petrified Man" and "Why I Live at the P. O." when taken in the context of Miss Welty's work), and with the issue left in suspension, but other stories present it with different emphases and tonalities. For instance, when William Wallace, in "The Wide Net," goes out to dredge the river, he is acting in terms of the meaning of the loss of his wife, but he is gradually drawn into the world of the river, the saturnalian revel, and prances about with a great cat-fish hung on his belt, like a river-god laughing and leaping. But he had also dived deep down into the water: "Had he suspected down there, like some secret, the real true trouble that Hazel had fallen into, about which word in a letter could not speak ... how (who knew?) she had been filled to the brim with that elation that they all remembered, like their own secret, the elation that comes of great hopes and changes, sometimes simply of the harvest time, that comes with a little course of its own like a tune to run in the head, and there was nothing she could do about it, they knew—and so it had turned into this? It could be nothing but the old trouble that William Wallace was finding out, reaching and turning in the gloom of such depths."

This passage comes clear when we recall that Hazel, the wife who is supposed to have committed suicide by drowning, is pregnant: she had sunk herself in the devouring life-flux, has lost her individuality there, just as the men hunting for the body have lost the meaning of their mission. For the river is simply force, which does not have its own definition; in it are the lost string of beads to wind around the little negro boy's head, the cat fish for the feast, the baby alligator that looks "like the oldest and worst lizard," and the great King of the Snakes. As Doc, the wise old man who owns the net, says: "The outside world is full of endurance." And he also says: "The excursion is the same when you go looking for your sorrow as when you go looking for your joy." Man has the definition, the dream, but when he plunges into the river he runs the risk of having it washed away. But it is important to notice that in this story, there is not horror at the basic contrast, but a kind of gay acceptance of the issue: when William Wallace gets home he finds that his wife had fooled him, and spanks her, and then she lies smiling in the crook of his arm. "It was the same as any other chase in the end."

As "The Wide Net," unlike "A Memory," does more than merely present the terms of contrast, so do such stories as "Livvie" and "At the Landing." Livvie, who lives in the house of wisdom (her infirm husband's name is Solomon) and respectability (the dream, the idea, which has withered) and Time (there is the gift of the silver watch), finally crosses into the other world, the world of the black buck, the field-hand, in his Easter clothes—another god, not a river god but a field god. Just after Solomon's death, the field-hand in his gorgeous Easter clothes takes Livvie in arms, and she drops the watch which Solomon had given her, while "outside the redbirds were flying and crisscrossing, the sun was in all the bottles on the prisoned trees, and the young peach was shining in the middle of them with the bursting light of spring."

If Livvie's crossing into the world of the field god is joyous, the escape of Jennie, in "At the Landing," is rendered in a different tonality. This story assimilates into a new pattern many of the elements found in "A Memory," "The Wide Net," "Livvie," and "Clytie." As in the case of Clytie, Jennie is caught in the house of pride, tradition, history, and as in the case of Livvie, in a house of death. The horror which appears in "A Memory," in "Clytie," re-appears here. The basic symbolisms of "Livvie" and especially of "The Wide Net" are again called into play. The river, as in "The Wide Net," is the symbol of that world from which Jennie is cut off. The grandfather's dream at the very beginning sets up the symbolism which is developed in the action:

> The river has come back. That Floyd came to tell me. The sun
> was shining full on the face of the church, and that Floyd came

around it with his wrist hung with a great long catfish.... That Floyd's catfish has gone loose and free.... All of a sudden, my dears—my dears, it took its river life back, and shining so brightly swam through the belfry of the church, and downstream.

Floyd, the untamed creature of uncertain origin, is William Wallace dancing with the great catfish at his belt, the river god. But he is also, like the buck in "Livvie," a field god, riding the red horse in a pasture full of butterflies. He is free and beautiful, and Jennie is drawn after him, for "she knew that he lived apart in delight." But she also sees him scuffling playfully with the hideous old Mag: the god does not make nice distinctions. When the flood comes over the Landing (upsetting the ordered lives, leaving slime in the houses), Floyd takes her in his boat to a hill (significantly the cemetery hill where her people are buried), violates her, feeds her wild meat and fish (field and river), and when the flood is down, leaves her. She has not been able to talk to him, and when she does say, "I wish you and I could be far away. I wish for a little house," he only stares into the fire as though he hadn't heard a word. But after he has gone she cannot live longer in the Landing; she must set out to find him. Her quest leads her into the woods (which are like an underwater depth) and to the camp of the wild river people, where the men are throwing knives at a tree. She asks for Floyd, but he is not there. The men put her in a grounded houseboat and come in to her. "A rude laugh covered her cry, and somehow both the harsh human sounds could easily have been heard as rejoicing, going out over the river in the dark night." Jennie has crossed into the other world to find violence and contamination, but there is not merely the horror as in "Clytie" and "A Memory." Jennie has acted out a necessary role, she has moved from the house of death, like Livvie, and there is "gain" as well as "loss." We must not forget the old woman who looked into the dark houseboat, at the very end of the story, and understands when she is told that the strange girl is "waiting for Billy Floyd." The old woman nods, "and nodded out to the flowing river, with the firelight following her face and showing its dignity."

If this general line of interpretation is correct, we find that the stories represent variations on the same basic theme, on the contrasts already enumerated. It is not that there is a standard resolution for the contrasts which is repeated from story to story; rather, the contrasts, being basic, are not susceptible to a single standard resolution, and there is an implicit irony in Miss Welty's work. But if we once realize this, we can recognize that the contrasts are understood not in mechanical but in vital terms: the contrasts provide the terms of human effort, for the dream must be carried to, submitted to, the world, innocence to experience, love to knowledge, knowledge to the fact, individuality to communion. What resolution is possible is, if I read the stories with understanding, in terms of the vital effort. The effort is a "mystery," because it is in terms of the effort, doomed to failure but essential, that the human manifests itself as human. Again and again, in different forms, we find what we find in Joel of "First Love": "Joel would never know now the true course, or the true outcome of any dream: this was all he felt. But he walked on, in the frozen path into the wilderness, on and on. He did not see how he could ever go back and still be the boot-boy at the Inn."

It is possible that, in my effort to define the basic issue and theme of Miss Welty's stories, I have made them appear too systematic, too mechanical. I do not mean to imply that her stories should be read as allegories, with a neat point-to-point equating of image and idea. It is true that a few of the stories, especially some of those in the present volume, such as "The Wide Net," do approach the limit of allegory, but even in such cases we find rather than the system of allegory a tissue of symbols which emerge from, and disappear into, a world of scene and action which, once we discount the author's special perspective, is recognizable in realistic terms. The method is similar to the method of much modern poetry, and to that of much modern fiction and drama (Proust, James, Kafka, Mann, Isak Dinesen, Katherine Anne Porter, Pirandello, Kaiser, Andreyev, O'Neill, for example); but at the same time it is a method as old as fable, myth, and parable. It is a method by which the items of fiction (scene, action, character, etc.) are presented not as document but as comment, not as a report but as a thing made, not as history but as idea. Even in the most realistic and reportorial fiction, the social picture, the psychological analysis, and the pattern of action do not rest at the level of mere report; they finally operate as expressive symbols as well.

Fiction may be said to have two poles, history and idea, and the emphasis may be shifted very far in either direction. In the present collection the emphasis has been shifted very far in the direction of idea, but at the same time there remains a sense of the vividness of the actual world: the picnic of "The Wide Net" is a real picnic as well as a "journey," Cash of "Livvie" is a real field-hand in his Easter clothes as well as a field god. In fact, it may be said that when the vividness of the actual world is best maintained, when we get the sense of one picture superimposed upon another, different and yet somehow the same, the stories are most successful.

The stories which fail are stories like "The Purple Hat" and "Asphodel" in which the material seems to be manipulated in terms of an idea, in which the relation between the image and the vision has become mechanical, in which there is a strain for atmosphere, in which we do find the kind of hocus-pocus deplored by Diana Trilling.

And this brings us back to the criticism that the volume "has tremendous emotional impact, despite its obscurity," that the "fear" it engenders is "in inverse ratio to its rational content." Now it seems to me that this description does violence to my own experience of literature, that we do not get any considerable emotional impact unless we sense, at the same time, some principle of organization, some view, some meaning. This does not go to say that we have to give an abstract formulation to that principle or view or meaning before we can experience the impact of the work, but it does go to say that it is implicit in the work and is having its effect upon us in immediate aesthetic terms. Furthermore, in regard to the particular work in question, I do not feel that it is obscure. If anything, the dream-like effect in many of the stories seems to result from the author's undertaking to squeeze meaning from the item which, in ordinary realistic fiction, would be passed over with a casual glance. Hence the portentousness, the retardation, the otherworldliness. For Miss Welty is like the girl in "A Memory":

> ... from any observation I would conclude that a secret of life had been nearly revealed to me, and from the smallest gesture of a stranger I would wrest what was to me a communication or a presentiment.

In many cases, as a matter of fact, Miss Welty has heavily editorialized her fiction. She wants us to get that smallest gesture, to participate in her vision of things as intensely meaningful. And so there is almost always a gloss to the fable.

One more word: It is quite possible that Miss Welty has pushed her method to its most extreme limit. It is also possible that the method, if pursued much farther, would lead to monotony and self imitation and merely decorative elaboration. Certainly, the tendency to decorate elaboration is sometimes present. Perhaps we shall get a fuller drama when her vision is submitted more daringly to the fact, when the definition is plunged into the devouring river. But meanwhile *The Wide Net* gives us several stories of brilliance and intensity; and as for the future, Miss Welty is a writer of great resourcefulness, sensitivity, and intelligence, and can probably fend for herself.

NOTES

1. Originally published in the *Kenyon Review* 6 (Spring 1944): 246–59; reprinted in *Selected Essays* (Random House, 1958), 156–69. Copyright 1958 by Robert Penn Warren. Reprinted with permission of the author.

2. Limitation of space has prohibited any discussion of the novelette, *The Robber Bridegroom*, but I do not feel that it breaks the basic pattern of Miss Welty's work.

WARREN FRENCH

"All Things Are Double":
Eudora Welty as a Civilized Writer

Nothing else in American literature is quite like *The Robber Bridegroom*—even among Eudora Welty's other writings; and, as with many unique gifts, we recipients haven't known quite what to make of it. Because of its fairy-tale qualities, a tendency has been to display it on the bric-a-brac shelf with the Hummel figures; whereas, it ought to find its place with such rare attempts to find archetypal patterns an American home as "Rip Van Winkle" and Thomas Cole's magnificent canvases of "The Voyage of Life."

The relatively little attention that the tale has attracted has been dominated since the original reviews by observations about its relationship to European fairy tales, especially the Grimm Brothers' story of the same title. Most commentators have, if not echoed, at least paralleled John Peale Bishop's remarks in the *New Republic* (16 November 1942), "If Miss Welty meant to establish that our tall tale is the equivalent of the European folk tale she fails to do so." Bishop was the most subtly perceptive of the early judges of the tale, however, for he recognized the transformation that gave the narrative its direction and observed, "All bridegrooms, she seems to be saying, are robbers," who steal a woman's love; "but in time, the hurt is healed and at last the robber bridegroom is seen as a prosperous gentleman of the world .... nothing is easier than the transfer of a bandit into a merchant."

From *Thirteen Essays: Selected from Eudora Welty: Critical Essays*. Peggy Whitman Prenshaw, ed. © 1983 by the University Press of Mississippi.

Although Bishop was too exclusively preoccupied with the sexual aspects of the tale, many subsequent critics have not followed the plot as far as he did (for plot there is, despite some reviewers' doubts). Generally the tale has been treated as a delightful, but dubiously successful tour de force. Even one of its most impressed readers, Alfred Appel, Jr., after describing *The Robber Bridegroom* as "a joyful wedding of the European fairy tale and the lore of the American frontier," concludes that it is an example of "the comic spirit," in which "Miss Welty succeeds in capturing the lost fabulous innocence of the American frontier, its poetry and comedy."[1]

Innocence, however, is far from the principal concern of the tale, in which innocence is, if anything, doomed or at least relegated to the subservient role of a force of vanishing authority. John Peale Bishop did not quite get the point, either, when he speculated that Welty's "deepest interest would seem to be in the question of identity" and that "nothing is what it seems," for her point cannot be so tidily resolved in terms of Aristotelian categories. Eudora Welty is concerned rather with the quite non-Aristotelian notion that people are two things at once and that their "identity" at any given moment is determined by the context in which they are discovered. Although Bishop comments early in his review on the ominous setting in the "violent country" of the old Natchez Trace, he fails to read this fable of identities against the background of the specific time and place in which it is set. He was working without the benefit of some of the author's strictures on the significance of setting, but today we need to consider her observation in "Place in Fiction" that "every story would be another story and unrecognizable as art, if it took up its characters and plot and happened somewhere else" (*ES*, p. 122). Fantasy must be grounded in the concrete facts of place, she advises. Although "all bridegrooms" may be robbers, a particular robber/bridegroom's behavior may be modified by (circumstances of time and place that Bishop does not take into account.

J. A. Bryant, Jr. comes closer than other commentators to getting at the grounding of the story. He first establishes the worlds of difference in time and place that separate Eudora Welty's *The Robber Bridegroom* from the Grimm Brothers' story with the same title, in which a girl has "two suitors, a bad one to outwit and a good one to live with happily ever after." If the European tale had put the two together as Miss Welty does, Bryant argues, it "would have spoiled all the 'fabulous innocence' and made, a solution impossible."[2] Bryant perceives, further, the importance of wanderer/planter Clement Musgrove's speech to his daughter Rosamond about "doubles" as the pivotal point in this tale of transformations: "... all things are double, and this should keep us from taking liberties with the outside world, and acting too quickly to finish things off. All things are divided in half—night and day, the soul and body, and sorrow and joy and youth and age ..." (p. 126). The principal embodiment of this doubling comes in *The Robber Bridegroom* in the recognition scene in which Rosamond wipes berry stain from her robber/bridegroom's face and learns that he is also the Jamie Lockhart who has been her father's respected dinner guest (p. 134). Even before this revelation, however, Musgrove has worked out through the case of the mysterious bridegroom the practical application of his principle about a person's double nature: "If being a bandit were his breadth and scope, I should find him and kill him for sure.... But since in addition he loves my daughter, he must be not the one man, but two, and I should be afraid of killing the second" (p. 126).

As a result of Musgrove's caution, he ultimately sees Jamie and Rosamond rewarded "with a fine mansion, a hundred slaves, and rich merchants to go boating with" and himself rewarded "with the knowledge that his children have such things."[3] Curiously, however, having perceived the importance of the embodiment of robber and bridegroom in the same person, Bryant misses the very sentence that John Peale Bishop had spied as the key to the denouement of the tale, "the outward transfer from bandit to merchant had been almost too easy to count it a change at all, and [Jamie] was enjoying all the same success he had ever had" (pp. 184–85). By bringing these two readings together—in a fashion peculiarly appropriate to a tale of doubling—we can perhaps perceive the significance of Eudora Welty's choice of the "concrete facts of place" for *The Robber Bridegroom*.

Although Clement Musgrove meditates on several manifestations of doubleness (all of which play a role in the tale), Welty is most concretely concerned with a particular set of doubles in both character and situation. Rosamond is not the first to discover Jamie Lockhart's secret. Earlier in the novel, Jamie has on one occasion "just started to stain his face with the berry juice" (p. 107) that transforms him into the bandit of the violent Trace when he is interrupted by "sounds of screaming out of a cave in the hillside." He comes upon the bandit Little Harp and a kidnapped girl and, as a result of becoming involved in this episode, compromises himself; for Little Harp recognizes him: "Your name is Jamie Lockhart and you are the bandit in the woods, for you have your two faces on together and I see you both."

"At that," the narrator explains, "Jamie staggered back indeed, for he allowed no one who had seen him as a gentleman to see him as a robber, and no one who knew him as a robber to see him without the dark-stained face, even his bride." He pulls out his dirk to kill Little Harp, but is restrained when something seems to speak to him and say, "This is to be your burden, and so you might as well take it" (p. 112). This moment when the two Jamies are recognized by the actual physical division of his face into differing halves is also the psychological dividing point of the tale. From here forward the behavior of the two Jamies, hitherto entirely at odds with one another, merges more and more into a single pattern until Jamie discovers at last that he need not conceal his doubleness since it proves really no burden at all to his success within the law. He can abandon the refuge of masks; the berry juice can be left in the forest.

Nathaniel Hawthorne knew well the doubleness that Eudora Welty explores through Jamie. At a late point in *The Scarlet Letter*, after Hester, Dimmesdale and Pearl have met in the woods, they meet again in the city on a great holiday and Pearl asks her mother, "Was that the same minister that kissed me by the brook?" "Hold thy peace, dear little Pearl!" whispers Hester. "We must not always talk in the market-place of what happened to us in the forest."

Much of the history of what has happened to the New World Columbus discovered can be brought into focus through examining events in relation to this dichotomy of "the market-place" and "the forest." When this continent was discovered by (and for) the Europeans, it was entirely "forest" and much of its subsequent history has been of its transformation into "market-place." Jamie Lockhart is only one of the many implicated in the consequences of this transformation.

Our mythmakers have been of at least two minds about this phenomenon. Some would preserve the forest, while others would further the market-place. As Hester's caution suggests, the forest is the place of greater freedom, spontaneity, naturalness, but also of greater dangers from the robbers who operate under cover of its darkness; behavior in the marketplace must be conventional, controlled, artificial—one must respect established codes—but one receives in exchange for a loss in one's freedom the seeming security and safety of the community.

William Faulkner stands as the outstanding spokesman for the vanishing forest. In "The Bear," Ike McCaslin traces the corruption of our culture back to the division of the unbounded woods to serve the needs of self-aggrandizing men of the market-place. Ike tells his cousin that he cannot "repudiate" his inheritance because: "It was never mine to repudiate.... Because it was never Ikkemotubbe's fathers' fathers' to bequeath Ikkemotubbe to sell to Grandfather or any man because on the instant when Ikkemotubbe discovered, realized, that he could sell it for money, on that instant it ceased ever to have been his forever...." In a companion story, "Delta Autumn," some final words of this last man of the forest render a verdict on the triumph of the market-place: "No wonder the ruined woods I used to know don't cry for retribution! ... The people who have destroyed it will accomplish its revenge." By breaking his mystical tie to nature to exploit the forest, man at last destroys himself.

Scott Fitzgerald's Nick Carraway stands poised precariously as middleman in this generally wistful debate, as spokesman for those who lament the destruction of the forest but see it—as Hawthorne himself did in "Earth's Holocaust"—as the inevitable consequence of man's inadequacy to match the potential of the unspoiled natural world. At the end of *The Great Gatsby*, Carraway describes the early visitors: "for a transitory enchanted moment man must have held his breath in the presence of this continent, compelled into an aesthetic contemplation he neither understood nor desired, face to face for the last time in history with something commensurate to his capacity for wonder." But at the very beginning of Nick's account, we have discovered that he wants "no more riotous excursions with privileged glimpses into the human heart," but rather "the world to be in uniform and at a sort of moral attention forever." Men must congregate in the market-place because of their incapacity to cope with the aesthetic challenge of the forest. Faulkner's stories present—along with Mark Twain's *The Adventures of Huckleberry Finn*, for example—the anti-civilized position, while Fitzgerald's novel presents—as Melville had even more forbiddingly—the reluctantly civilized.

Faulkner's fellow Mississippian Eudora Welty stands, however, at the farthest end of the spectrum from him; and recognition of *The Robber Bridegroom*'s place in our fiction can restore a balance that often seems missing. While I dislike digressing into personalities in literary criticism, I do think it appropriate to mention here Victor H. Thompson's pointing out that "the newspapers present Miss Welty as perhaps the most amiable and inoffensive writer that America has ever produced."[4] What this statement suggests is that she is a thoroughly "civilized" person, something that, for whatever reasons, few of our writers have been. Many of her contemporaries have proved as wild and flighty as the talking raven in *The Robber Bridegroom*.

We have been slow to perceive Eudora Welty for the civilized writer she is, because we haven't especially been seeking fictionists of this temperament. Lately literate Americans—reacting against their genteel forebears—tend toward nostalgia and fancy themselves sons of the pioneers, so that they equate being civilized—much as Huck Finn did—with being effete, prissy and overly inhibited. Most of the proponents of civilization in our fiction—like William Dean Howells and Willa Cather—have come from frontiers and have had serious misgivings about civilized society that have increased as they have aged and withdrawn into their private forests. Hardly anyone among our writers before Welty had been able to find more enjoyment than displeasure in the products of civilization, and most of the few that did—like Henry James and Gertrude Stein—felt compelled to spend most of their lives abroad. I think that the reason why critics have scarcely known what to make of Eudora Welty's work is that most of them, like the writers with whom they identify, can flourish only on denunciations of the very civilization that makes their trade possible. (In the forest, they see themselves, of course, "called" as shamans.)

This is not to say that Welty is naively unaware of the discontents and displeasures of urban society (for we are here in a necessarily limiting way equating "civilization" with "the market-place"). Scarcely a wide-eyed innocent in an adolescent success story, she is able to maintain her stance because she has an adequate sense of irony to perceive that our choices are not usually between the better or best of alternatives but between the lesser of evils—a stance that manifests itself as early in her work as *The Robber Bridegroom*.

The forest is really never given much of a chance in this tale. The "innocence" that Welty ascribes at the beginning of the narrative to the only thoughtful character, Clement Musgrove—with a first name wonderfully symbolic of merciful judgment—has been misconstrued. He is hardly, as John Peale Bishop would have it, "guileless," for he is often wary in his dealings; nor is he *innocent* in the sense that crops up so often in discussions of Faulkner's egomaniacs, that of being unaware of the conventions of society and thus uninhibited in one's actions. Rather, Musgrove is innocent in the simple sense of "guiltless." He wishes no one ill, nor does he scheme or connive against anyone; he strives only to make the land productive and to please his loved ones with presents. "My time is over," he observes after a long meditation on the cycle of the seasons, "for cunning is of a world I will have no part in" (p. 142).

The Indians in this tale are even more clearly doomed, for they do not, like the white characters, have two faces; and this lack of doubleness works to their disadvantage. Early in the novel Musgrove muses that despite the redmen's success in one raid that killed most of his loved ones, "The Indians know their time has come.... They are sure of the future growing smaller always, and that lets them be infinitely gay and cruel" (p. 21). Near the end of the book, after another Indian uprising that claims Musgrove's duplicitous second wife, he muses again, "The savages have only come the sooner to their end; we will come to ours too. Why have I built my house, and added to it? The planter will go after the hunter, and the merchant after the planter, all having their day" (p. 161).

This meditation carries us beyond the point that we have reached in this argument and hints of its end; but, as in the sequential process described here, we must dispose of the forest before moving to town, because if the day of the merchant will at last end, it has now arrived—"the time of cunning has come," as Musgrove recognizes (p. 142). He himself has led a double life and has been torn between the forest and the cultivated field: "he was an innocent of the wilderness, and a planter of Rodney's Landing, and this was his good" (p. 182). With what time is left to him, after having seen his child settled and refusing to stay with her, he returns to the plantation, feeling that it grows smaller as he grows older. Finally even for Jamie Lockhart, who has been divided by his two faces between the forest and the market-place, it is the forest visage that has been the affectation. He has had to stain his face with berry juice to maintain his standing as a robber of the Trace and to keep his genteel identity entirely separate; but, when he realizes that "the bandit's life is done with" (p. 166), he has only to remove his mask to claim his place in the city—unlike the Harps who are not cunning enough to survive the transition.

By setting her story thus on the already vanishing Natchez Trace just at that time early in the nineteenth century when the American economy was shifting from one dominated by the trailblazers of the forest and tillers of the fields to one dominated by city merchants, Welty has grounded her fantasy in "the concrete facts of place." *The Robber Bridegroom* is, paradoxically, a legend of civilization, a fantastic representation of a very real movement as the nineteenth century began of the United States from a primarily wild country to the international market-place it had become by the time the century ended.

Eudora Welty does not, however, like the ebullient boosters of our "go-getter" tradition, equate change with progress. In *The Robber Bridegroom*, a shift in the controlling elements of society brings into power not a new class of persons but the most resourceful figures from the older order of things, wearing new guises. The observation that binds together the wandering threads of the tale is, as already pointed out, that for Jamie "the outward transfer from bandit to merchant had been almost too easy to count it a change at all." The implications of this wry summary is that no *inner* change has been required by the transformation—merchants are quite like bandits operating within legal sanctions in a civilized community. The further comment that Jamie "was enjoying all the same success he had ever had" indicates that the same talents are required for the two callings.

This putdown of mercantile probity reveals also that the tale itself partakes of an as yet unmentioned double identity as part of two literary traditions, although its origins in primitive folktale only have usually been observed. Although I have maintained earlier that there is nothing else like *The Robber Bridegroom* in American literature, it finds a kindred spirit elsewhere in one of the wellsprings of "civilized" urban literature, John Gay's

The Beggar's Opera (1728), which created much of its enduring impact with such ironic statements as merchant Peachum's: "A rich rogue now-a-days is fit company for any gentleman; and the world, my dear, hath not such a contempt for roguery as you imagine," and again, "In one respect, indeed, our employment may be reckon'd dishonest, because, like great Statesmen, we encourage those who betray their friends." The most marked similarity occurs at the end of the pieces: the ostensible beggar-author of Gay's play observes, in a statement that matches Welty's about Jamie Lockhart, that "it is difficult to determine whether (in the fashionable vices) the fine gentlemen imitate the gentlemen of the road or the gentlemen of the road the fine gentlemen." (For Eudora Welty, of course, no dilemma exists, for the two are one, imitating none, but turning only toward differing situations the appropriate face. Macheath's final revelation after his fantastic reprieve that he is married to Polly Peachum may hint as well that this robber/bridegroom, too, may find the transition to inheritor of Peachum's mercantile empire scarcely a change at all.)

The Robber Bridegroom thus weds two traditions of fantasy—the primitive fairy tale of ancient rural cultures with the "Newgate pastoral" of the bourgeois ascendancy in England.

A further evidence of cultural transition is afforded by Welty's handling of the loose frame story of the legendary American riverboatman Mike Fink. He appears at the beginning of the tale as the third lodger with whom Clement Musgrove and Jamie Lockhart must share a bed for the night. Despite his physical prowess, Fink is outwitted by the cunning Jamie and, as we learn later, loses his standing in his own community because of the way he has been gulled by apparent spooks. Rosamond encounters him near the end of the story come "down in the world" from his former splendor to be a mail rider, though still a gifted teller of tall tales. Fink flourished during the days of the conquest of the forest through his physical strength; but in the new era of mercantile princes, physical force is no match for cunning, and he becomes a servant rather than a master of a culture that depends upon communication rather than confrontation. He thus shares the fate of a similar character in a story that Eudora Welty herself has commented upon in a much different context, Stephen Crane's "The Bride Comes to Yellow Sky" (*ES*, pp. 86–87). In Crane's story, Scratchy Wilson, "the last one of the old gang that used to hang out along the river here," continues to terrorize a Western community as in frontier days until the coming of Marshal Potter's bride emblemizes the triumph of civilization. Scratchy even turns up later in a too much neglected counterpart story, "Moonlight on the Snow," as Marshal Potter's deputy. Although we are assured in *The Robber Bridegroom* that Mike Fink's name was "restored to its original glory" (p. 180), he must return to a life already fading into legend; whereas Jamie Lockhart can abandon his stealthy life on the Trace to take an honored place in the rising city.

Jamie can make the transition, among other reasons, because he is unburdened by guilt. He is not, like Musgrove, guiltless; but he finds guilt "a burdensome thing to carry about in the heart.... I would never bother with it." After this announcement, Musgrove salutes Jamie as "a man of the times" (p. 27). Jamie has found also a useful wife in Rosamond, a talented liar. Yet despite the gain in luxury and security that the pair enjoy, something is lost— even this tale acknowledges—in the transition from forest to market-place. The talking raven that once rode on Mike Fink's finger as emblem of man's affinity with wild and wise things is caged and neglected after Jamie acquires it; and, at last, after the Indians during a final outbreak burn the robbers' hideout, it "flew out over the treetops and was never seen again" (p. 148). The mystical tie with the forest is gone.

In the course of these speculations I have not just idly linked *The Robber Bridegroom* with such acclaimed works as "The Bear" and *The Great Gatsby* and "The Bride Comes to Yellow Sky," for it seems to me that this usually too lightly dismissed tale (let us not quarrel about "novels" and "novellas" when the important antecedents are evident) deserves to take its place beside these others as the unflaggingly beguiling embodiment of one of several points of view toward the experience central to American culture of the transformation of "the forest" into a patchwork of "trading districts" centered around "the market-place." Perhaps because like Faulkner's Ike McCaslin our heart is in the forest or like Fitzgerald's Nick Carraway we feel defeated by our possession of capacities we cannot manage, we are more impressed by these works than by Eudora Welty's delicate polishing of the cutting cynicism of the tradition of *The Beggar's Opera*; but it is no small achievement to have fashioned from scraps of tradition the fitting vehicle for any position toward an inescapable aspect of man's experience.

What Welty meant to "establish," if John Peale Bishop's rather pompous term fits her storytelling at all, is not our tall tale "as the equivalent of the European folk tale," but the contribution that both this ancient vehicle and the later fantasies of city wits can make to the fictional embodiment of a stage in the development of a culture that moved with unprecedented suddenness from forest to market-place. She subsumes both fairy tale and "Newgate pastoral" within her own peculiarly original form to suggest the continuation of the past in a present beyond which most people's consciousnesses do not extend. "Yet no one can laugh or cry so savagely in this wilderness as to be heard by the nearest traveler or remembered the next year. A fiddle played in a finished hut in a clearing is as vagrant as the swamp breeze. What will the seasons be, when we are lost and dead?" muses Clement Musgrove, losing himself so deeply in his reverie that the Indians are able to seize him once more (p. 144). What indeed would be remembered next year but for the intervention of the artist whose words fix the fleeting seasons?

It may be useful to view what—as Eudora Welty suggests—may be the passing triumph of the market-place through the detached consciousness of a civilized writer rather than the claims of its celebrators and detractors, who, whether they are impetuously guileless or deliberately duplicitous, produce more outrageous fantasies than *The Robber Bridegroom*.

NOTES

1. *A Season of Dreams* (Baton Rouge: Louisiana St. Univ. Press, 1965), pp. 69, 72.
2. *Eudora Welty* (Minneapolis: Univ. of Minnesota Press, 1968), p. 19.
3. Bryant, p. 20.
4. *Eudora Welty: A Reference Guide* (Boston: G. K. Hall, 1976), p. ix.

SUZANNE MARRS

"The Treasure Most Dearly Regarded": Memory and Imagination in Delta Wedding

By the fall of 1942, Eudora Welty had written all of the stories to be published in *The Wide Net* (1943), but afterward, for more than a year, she did not write fiction. Worry about the nature of war, the course of the war, the dangers into which friends and family had been or would be placed—all these things distracted Welty from creative pursuits. As a result, she busied herself instead with work for the war effort, with gardening, with the writing of "Some Notes on River Country" for *Harper's Bazaar*, and with reviewing for the *New York Times*. When she finally was able to return to fiction, she returned haltingly at first but ultimately found that "The Delta Cousins," begun as a short story, was the impetus toward the novel *Delta Wedding*, a novel that would encompass more and more details from Mississippi's past, from stories John Robinson had brought to her attention, and from her own memories of childhood. Welty once again relied on the past as she had in *The Robber Bridegroom* and *The Wide Net*, and again her look backward drew criticism. Critics felt her first novel was essentially escapist in nature. Its nostalgic portrait of the 1923 Mississippi Delta, they claimed, ignored the ugly realities that plagued the contemporary South. A review in *Time* magazine even labeled *Delta Wedding* a "Cloud-Cuckoo Symphony."[1]

Since the novel's publication in 1946, Welty readers have typically recognized that the charges of nostalgia are wrong-headed, but few have

---

From *One Writer's Imagination: The Fiction of Eudora Welty*. © 2002 by Louisiana State University Press.

realized how closely, if obliquely, tied to contemporary issues *Delta Wedding* actually is. Albert Devlin is a notable exception. He writes that because the novel "was written in wartime and published in 1946," it involves a "probing for a humane order." Indeed, writing in the midst of war profoundly governed the sort of novel Welty would produce and the sort of order she would implicitly seek. By late 1943 when Welty began work on "The Delta Cousins," the threat of an Axis victory had diminished, but the threat of spiritual devastation in the wake of war remained full blown. This threat was still of preeminent concern when Welty completed the novel in September 1945. Not able to address directly this worry, Welty was able to "translate" her concern into what she later called "domestic or other dimensions of my writing"[2]; therefore, though the events of *Delta Wedding* are set in the past, the issues it investigates were of great importance in Welty's present. In the novel Welty explores the importance of courageously confronting the imminence of death and loss, of recognizing the urgency that life's transience brings to our lives, of discovering the continuity of love and the humanity of others, and of perceiving life's beauty despite its many horrors. Surely these traits are ones she must have felt to be endangered by totalitarian regimes during the war, and surely these traits are the ones she desperately hoped would survive the war years.

The story of *Delta Wedding*'s composition has been perceptively recounted by both Michael Kreyling and Albert Devlin, but Kreyling and Devlin are primarily concerned with aesthetic issues, not with the novel's connection to the political and social context from which it emerged.[3] That connection is deep and strong, as a comprehensive look at Welty's life and work between 1943 and 1946 helps to reveal.

Of course, two reviews Welty wrote in 1942–43 in lieu of writing fiction might be taken as a sign that she embraced a respite from the war-torn present. It is true that in reviewing novels about the pre–World War II South, Welty declined to level the charges of escapism that later would be directed at *Delta Wedding*. She accepted these books on their own terms, but she did not retreat from criticizing or commending the values they conveyed. Welty firmly believed that values particularly relevant in the 1940s could and should be integral to books about the past. In a review of *But You'll Be Back* by Marguerite Steedman, for instance, Welty praises Steedman's ability to re-create the surface of southern life, but objects to the novel's lack of passion: "Her thesis that no little town need die is laudable and full of interest, but the mind and heart and spirit of the town that would prove this thesis and rise above it are not examined. A glimpse of the town's real core of feeling and a timid hint of imagination are in the last chapter or so, but much more could have been made of the town's story and its overtones of medieval pride and joy in its work." Steedman, Welty argues, does not embody the values of small-town life in her story's plot, and it is those values Welty expects the author to be passionately committed to: "The author herself has not been emotionally affected by her ethical ideas, one feels. She is sure of them, often enthusiastic, sometimes sentimental, but not possessed."

In her review of *Sweet Beulah Land* by Bernice Kelly Harris, Welty praises Harris for providing a wide-ranging portrait of "a section of river plantation country in North Carolina," a section whose "inhabitants include river gentry, sharecroppers and Negroes, and their in-betweens." And Welty particularly praises Harris for her openness to diversity, for her lack of judgmental class consciousness. Welty believes that Harris is "completely at ease in every mansion, cottage, or shack" and that Harris "never preaches in any social-study manner."[4] In reviewing these novels of the South, Welty may have been looking ahead to the story and later novel she would write about a plantation region in Mississippi and its wide range of characters, but she may also have been anticipating the sort of passionate ethical statement she would embed in her plot and the sort of acceptance of diversity for which her novel would call—a statement and an acceptance that might provide a vision for a meaningful postwar existence.

Certainly by summer 1943, Welty was feeling impatient with her inability to write fiction and was perhaps contemplating a fictional world like Steedman's and Harris's. But as fall arrived, she had been unable to create such a world. She wrote to Katherine Anne Porter, "For myself, I haven't written anything—in a year at least—except for a little article that was commissioned (Harper's B.) and I had to. I hope some day to be able to start again. It's not lack of concentration, but concentration on other things, and things I can't help—a form of indulgence in the long run maybe—if you can call dwelling on the warfront an indulgence." To the war Welty attributed her year-long fictional silence, but her anxieties about the war would ease, though not disappear, in the last few months of 1943. As she told Porter, "My friend John [Robinson] who was in the invasion and battle of Sicily came out of it all right, with nothing worse than a little fever they all got from bites got sleeping in haystacks etc., and a week in hospital—and is now doing something confidential for the British in Africa.... My little brothers are both still in this country at this writing." The comfort Welty drew from the current safety of those she loved and the catharsis she experienced in the aftermath of Robinson's first danger seem ultimately to have freed her to write again. She must also have taken heart from Robinson's posting to North Africa and from the humorous anecdotes he felt able to tell. The very fact that Robinson chose to report on his comically annoying French landlady in Africa—the woman who had requested that he "please swallow up nothing in the bedroom and bathroom and also to not sit on the bed"— marked his well-being and helped to move Welty herself toward new fiction with a comic vision.[5] Not surprisingly, when Welty did write fiction again, she wrote about a world John Robinson had shown her.

During the thirties, Robinson had taken Welty to visit his family homes, homes upon which *Delta Wedding*'s Shellmound and The Grove would be based, and had introduced her to the distinctive ambiance of the Mississippi Delta. Sometime in October 1943, Welty began writing "The Delta Cousins," a story drawing upon what Robinson had taught her of the Delta and a story that would eventually become the novel *Delta Wedding*. On November 5, 1943, immediately upon completing this story, Welty mailed it to Robinson, in Africa.[6] Perhaps she sought to send a piece of home to Robinson who could not come home himself.

The story must have delighted Robinson with its descriptions of typical Mississippi Delta settings and characters. It opens with nine-year-old Laura Kimball making a train journey like ones Robinson had often made, a journey from Jackson to see her Shelton cousins who live in the Delta, cousins much like Robinson's own. The story then goes on to detail Laura's love for Uncle Raymond, the visit she and cousins Cindy and India make to Parthenia's house and to the store, the adventure India and Laura share when they go the house that would be called Marmion in *Delta Wedding*, the hostile behavior of Maurine toward Laura, the experience Laura has making mayonnaise with Aunt Mim, and the Sheltons' picnic on the banks of the Sunflower River.

Yet however much "The Delta Cousins" owes to John Robinson, the story also draws heavily upon Welty's memories of her own childhood and college years. The games Laura and her cousins play, the party favors they receive, the movies they have seen, the books Laura reads, Laura's love of bottles and boxes—all these aspects of her 1943 story Welty drew from memories of childhood. And memories of her college years in Columbus, Mississippi, at the Mississippi State College for Women (1925–27), also played a role for Welty. The train on which Laura rides is like the one Welty took from Artesia to Columbus as a college student, and one significant location in the story is based upon a Columbus landmark Welty had often visited, a deserted antebellum home called Waverley. This house served as a model for the bee man's house in "The Delta Cousins" and eventually for Marmion in *Delta Wedding*.

Recalling details from such a distance seems to have helped Welty view actual events in the metaphoric and transforming light of the imagination. Welty has written that "without the act of human understanding ...

experience is the worst kind of emptiness; it is obliteration, black or prismatic.... Before there is meaning, there has to occur some personal act of vision. And it is this that is continuously projected as the novelist writes, and again as we, each to ourselves, read" (*ES*, 136–7). Recalling the long ago seems to have made a "personal act of vision" possible for Eudora Welty as it has for many writers, including her friend Elizabeth Bowen. Indeed, Bowen has noted that "remote memories, already distorted by the imagination, are the most useful" ones for a writer of fiction to use in constructing a scene.[7] Not surprisingly, then, Welty calls her memory "the treasure most dearly regarded by me, in my life and in my work as a writer" (*OWB*, 104). The present world may be too intractable, too much itself, to be manipulated by the writer, but the past is not. In turning to the past for material, therefore, Welty was not denying the significance of present events, but was discovering strategies to convey the import of those events. Indeed, she has written that "the events in our lives happen in a sequence in time, but in their significance to ourselves they find their own order, a timetable not necessarily—perhaps not possibly—chronological" (*OWB*, 68–69).

If the passing of time encourages a metaphoric use of memory, a metaphoric sensibility seems to summon a long-held memory from its place in the unconscious. The mathematician Jules Poincaré, for instance, believed that his theories had their origins in an aesthetic impulse. And according to Rollo May, an aesthetic impulse "is why the mathematicians and physicists talk about the 'elegance' of a theory. The utility is subsumed as part of the character of being beautiful. The harmony of an internal form, the inner consistency of a theory, the character of beauty that touches one's sensibilities these are significant factors determining why a given idea emerges."[8] With Welty, then, we can speculate that the harmony between her past experiences and her worries of the 1940s, the ways in which a particular place or event from her own past could define the characters she was just now creating in "The Delta Cousins," enabled Welty's thematic investigation of time and change, of love and death, to emerge. Moreover, discovering connections between her past and her work in the present, as she had not been able to do for more than a year, must have been reassuring to Welty as she continued to anticipate the traumatic changes World War II would inevitably bring about—some things at least promised to endure.

Reassuring or not, it was months before Welty would begin to revise "The Delta Cousins." Shortly after Welty finished the story in late 1943, Diarmuid Russell and *Harper's Bazaar* fiction editor Mary Lou Aswell suggested strategies for revision. Welty adopted none. Instead, for four months she wrote no fiction. Then in the spring of 1944 Welty began work on "A Sketching Trip" and mailed it to Russell by early May. In "A Sketching

Trip," Welty once again turned to her distant past to find her story's subject. As a child of five or six, Welty had joined her mother and brother Edward in a retreat from the summer heat of Jackson. They spent two or three weeks in residence at a small establishment twenty or so miles southwest of Jackson; this establishment, called Hubbard's Wells, offered room and board, a number of wells with mineral waters thought to cure a variety of ailments, and weekend dances with music provided by Eddie Stiles. This very real place becomes Fergusson's Wells in Welty's story, and Delia Farrar, the story's adult protagonist, returns on a sketching trip to this spot she had visited as a young girl in the company of her mother. She also returns to visit the nearby haunted house, the ruins of an early-nineteenth-century house based upon an actual house that had belonged to someone in John Robinson's family. This is all the story has in common with actuality; the subsequent plot is Welty's invention. That plot deals with betrayal and loss and desolation, and it deals with the nature of memory. Delia recalls a childhood tour of the haunted house led by an "old maid" who fancies herself an artist, and she recalls the lurid story the old woman has told about the house, the story of a husband discovering his wife and her lover, murdering his wife, and then dying himself even as he kills the lover in a duel. Delia further recalls that a similar, though somewhat ludicrous, incident was part of her childhood stay at Fergusson's Wells. Mr. Fergusson had discovered his wife's infidelity and, in the midst of festivities for all guests, had shot at Mr. Torrance, her unlikely looking lover, with a rabbit gun. The young Delia and all the other guests had then abandoned Fergusson's Wells, but on her return years later Delia discovers that Mr. Fergusson, now a drunk, still lives at the wells and that he had not killed Mr. Torrance after all. Instead, Mr. Torrance and Mrs. Fergusson have set up housekeeping a mere forty miles down the road. The story's first words are "Violence! Violence!" and this is a story about the destructive violence called forth by betrayal. It is also a story about hope for renewal. When Delia returns to the haunted house, she sees that "it rose taller than any happenings or any times that forever beset the beauty itself of life. It was no part of shelter now, it was the survivor of shelter, an entity, glowing, erect, and a fiery color, the ancient color of a phoenix."[9] On a domestic scale, this story concerns the very issues and the very values that concerned Welty about the international scene of 1944—violence, betrayal, and the survival of "the beauty itself of life"—and these issues would prove central, if less melodramatic, in Delta Wedding.

A week after sending Russell this story, Welty went to New York and on June 1 began working at the New York Times Book Review. At the Times, she later recalled, were the rather hostile Lester Markel and an even more hostile colleague who refused to work in the same room with a woman. But such negative experiences were few, and Welty relished her May-to-October stay in the city. Robert Van Gelder proved to be a wonderful boss, Welty's copyediting and writing for the *Review* were sources of fulfillment, and the theaters and galleries of New York delighted her as they always had. Welty was particularly amused by a Mae West production of *Catherine Was Great*. Before this play opened at a theater within sight of her office, Welty occasionally managed to watch rehearsals. There she saw West, as Catherine the Great, inspect her identically clad troops, singling out one young man for special notice: "You're new here, aren't you," West inquired as she looked him over, up and down. More than fifty years after these events, Welty continued to repeat Mae West's line with great relish and enjoyment. Welty's fabled sense of humor was thoroughly engaged during her New York stint, and it seems especially appropriate that Welty reviewed S. J. Perelman's *Crazy Like a Fox* while she was on the staff of the book review. Humor had not been killed by war, and Welty's revitalized sense of humor signaled that she once again possessed the aesthetic distance required for a major achievement in fiction.

Good times notwithstanding, Welty remained concerned with the war. Operation Overlord had been launched in June, and by September 1 victory in Europe seemed to be in the offing. In the summer and fall of 1944, Welty's reviews of books about war displayed both confidence in victory and distress at the continuing casualties. Writing under the name Michael Ravenna, Welty reviewed George Biddle's book *Artist at War* for the 16 July *Book Review*. Biddle had gone to Africa and then Italy with U.S. troops for the express purpose of providing "a pictorial record of the war." In her review, Welty deems Biddle's record both admirable and inadequate. She feels that his sketches "fail in immediate impact" because, unlike the drawings of Goya, they show the "aftermath of disaster" rather than "disaster in the act." Goya, Welty writes, "often showed human beings at the moment they met death, but at that moment they were supremely alive, aware—the very passion of his feeling for war's horror seemed to dictate this moment to him for its translation into art." Biddle, Welty suggests, seems not to recognize the intimate connection of life and death. However, Welty does praise the sense of humor in the text Biddle wrote to complement his drawings: "He has an eye out for the absurdities that make life even on the front bearable from one minute to the next." And Welty offers high praise for the nature of the project itself. The idea of trying to show people at home something real and concrete about the individual soldier at war, Welty contends, "is an interesting and hopeful example of a new, a human and subjective attitude of a country toward war, that may be a sign in itself that we can never tolerate another one."[10] Welty's comments about the Biddle book are, of course, very relevant to the sort of story she had written in "The Delta Cousins" and to the sort of changes she would make in transforming it into a novel. Her focus upon loss and upon the importance of facing "death on its way" would grow as her manuscript did. So too would her focus upon the urgency that death brings to our lives, her focus upon the importance of humor, and her focus upon "a human and subjective attitude" toward her subject.

By mid-October 1944, Welty had returned to Jackson, her internship at the *New York Times Book Review* at an end. Russell viewed Welty's departure from New York with ambivalence. He wrote to say that she would be missed, but added, "Its [sic] probably not a bad thing that you went for you'd never do any work up here and you write too well for us to accept that very happily." Back in Jackson, Welty had decided that a visit to John Robinson's cousins in Webb, Mississippi, might spur her revisions to "The Delta Cousins." Russell wrote to encourage this visit, saying "I hope you can manage to visit the people in the Delta because I am looking forward so eagerly to see what the story becomes." That visit didn't occur for several months. But in February 1945, Russell wrote to Welty about her imminent trip to the Delta:

> I'll be curious to know how your visit to the Delta turns out. I think it will produce something inside your head, perhaps not anything that you ever thought of. But the place is ancient in its way and historied and somthing [sic] of that is bound to affect you and if you can see old journals with accounts of the day to day life you will be moved. I don't really care if it results or not in rework of the story, though that is the ostensible reason. But I am sure that a dip into the past of the South will have some effect—even if it only means that you start dressing in crinolines.[11]

The trip did indeed have a profound effect; Welty read the nineteenth-century diaries of Nancy McDougall Robinson and found the impetus for turning "The Delta Cousins" into *Delta Wedding*. Those diaries told of a young bride coming to the 1832 Mississippi Delta and eventually facing isolation, yellow fever, war, and loss. Nancy Robinson's struggles and her ability to cope with the ravages of time and change struck Eudora Welty, who was herself confronting the devastation wrought by the war, who was only now learning the full horror of Hitler's Final Solution, and who knew that a changed world lay ahead. Welty would remove her characters in *Delta Wedding* from the mind-boggling difficulties of 1945, but by setting her story in 1923 and by granting her Fairchild characters an ancestor like Nancy Robinson, Welty placed the Fairchilds in line for the changes of the Great

Depression and World War II and made Nancy Robinson a model for the way they might eventually be able to cope with change. If Welty could not turn the horrors of Hitler's Germany into fiction, her novel would stress the importance of facing life's terrors directly, of understanding the meaning of one's own experience. The diaries show that sort of ability, an ability Welty finds lacking in most of her novel's characters.

Even as Welty was revising and expanding "The Delta Cousins" in the light of her visit to the Delta and her discovery of Nancy Robinson's diaries, she continued to write reviews. Of particular interest is her May 1945 review of William Sansom's *Fireman Flower*. In this review, Welty centers her commentary upon the volume's title story about a fireman attempting to save London buildings from the fires caused by bombings. At the end of this story, she tells us, "Fireman Flower is consumed inwardly by a vision of love—a quiet love for all he sees and knows through the greater vision of the world."[12] Writing this review even as she was writing *Delta Wedding*, Welty recognized in Sansom the very values that she would place at the heart of her novel. As *Delta Wedding*, though not "The Delta Cousins," closes, a love of the beautiful and the continuity of love promise to sustain young Laura McRaven.

On May 8, 1945, V-E Day was celebrated, and by mid-June Welty was roughly halfway through the writing of *Delta Wedding*. When victory over Japan was achieved in August, Welty was well into the second half of her novel, and by September 11 the entire manuscript was in Diarmuid Russell's hands. Fostered by the growing assurance of victory in war and by the survival of ones near and dear, Welty had completed the novel. She had found her inspiration in the need to communicate with a beloved friend, the emergence of personal memories from the unconscious, the careful reading of books she had been hired to review, and the need to define sustaining values in the face of devastation and social upheaval.

The transformation of "The Delta Cousins" into *Delta Wedding* is the record of Welty's growing emphasis upon the very values that she hoped would survive and triumph over the world Hitler envisioned. That transformation sharpens and deepens Welty's stress upon the significance of love in the face of time's inexorable movement, upon the need to face life's dangers courageously, upon the reality of beauty despite the horrors of experience, and upon the importance of granting each individual his humanity—all themes that had been central to Welty's reviews of the Biddle and Sansom wartime books. In particular, Welty's revisions and additions to actual settings, to historical contexts, and to the development of peripheral characters serve to develop ideas only touched upon in her short story.

A key setting in "The Delta Cousins," for instance, takes its source in Eudora Welty's own experience, but becomes increasingly emblematic in the process of revision. During her two years at the Mississippi State College for Women, Welty and her classmates would occasionally hike out into the country, take the ferry across the Tombigbee River, and visit Waverley, a once grand plantation home that had become derelict. Almost twenty years after first entering this house, first seeing its double stairway ascending to a cupola with sixteen windows, and first standing beneath the massive chandelier that hung suspended from the top of the cupola, Welty chose to use Waverley as a model for the bee man's house in "The Delta Cousins" and eventually for Marmion in *Delta Wedding*.

In 1943, when in her mind's eye she journeyed back to days as a student at MSCW, Welty remembered Waverley in great detail. She recalled that the ferry man who had brought her across the river to the derelict house was also a bee man, that the gardens approaching the house were filled with boxwood, that the large octagon-shaped foyer of the house was topped by a cupola, that a double stairway in the foyer led to three tiers of galleries, and that a chandelier hanging from the cupola had once been lighted by gas manufactured from the plantation's own pine knots. The house still contained some furnishings, most notably a piano with mother-of-pearl keys, but its only inhabitants were dirt daubers and wasps, wrens and sparrows, chimney swifts, bats, and woodpeckers. Waverley's desolation, Welty remembered, seemed symbolized by the dead goldfinch she saw on the house steps during one of her visits. As she recalled these details, moreover, Welty knew that they, lit by the light of imagination, defined her deepest concerns. In "The Delta Cousins," when Laura and her cousin India come to the bee man's house, a dead finch on the house steps and the chandelier "like a pendulum that wants to swing in a clock but no one starts it" seem ominous and suggest the finality of death. But the truly sinister threat to the young girls' innocence lies not in such images of time's power, but in the bee man. As the girls return to his boat, he touches "his trousers and a little old fish seemed to come out."[13] The two cousins never realize what they have seen, but the visit to the house has been a potential sexual initiation as well as a potential initiation into the power of time itself.

These suggestions persist, are more subtly developed, and are closely tied to episode after episode in *Delta Wedding*. In the novel, the threat is not one of violation, as it had been in the story and in earlier stories like "At the Landing." In the novel, Laura and her cousin Roy Fairchild (not India, as in the story) must confront the intensity that the looming presence of death brings to life and love, the very intensity Welty had discussed in her review of George Biddle's *Artist at War*. The short story is only peripherally concerned with the power of time. Not so with the novel. In the novel, it is life's transience that most members of the Fairchild family refuse to face, and it is this aspect of reality that young Laura McRaven encounters when she and Roy come alone to Marmion. But suggestions of danger and death do not wholly define the experience Laura and Roy have at Marmion. The very chandelier that is like a stopped pendulum to Laura has seemed "like the stamen in the lily down-hanging" (*DW*, 122) to her older cousin Dabney. Dabney thinks of the house, or the chandelier at least, in sexual terms. And Roy and Laura's experience at Marmion reiterates those terms. The house's tower around which the adventurous Roy runs and the delicate piano that Laura plays seem to embody the union of masculine and feminine that the forthcoming marriage of Troy and Dabney, an event that plays no role in the story, will bring to the house. From the tower Roy can see "the whole creation," while inside the house Laura focuses her attention on the beautiful piano, "looking small as a fairy instrument" (*DW*, 176). Thus, when the old black woman Aunt Studney, a character based upon an actual woman Welty had heard of during visits to the Delta, a character who appears in the novel though not the story, and one who has entered Marmion with Roy and Laura, sounds "a cry high and threatening like the first note of a song at a ceremony, a wedding or a funeral" (*DW*, 176), she captures the double spirit of the house and the nature of the initiation that Laura undergoes there. Chandelier, tower, and piano—Welty has recognized a harmony between these elements of an actual place and the evolving concerns of her novel, and she has transformed the house and its furnishings into metaphor. Death, she suggests, is the source of life's urgency, of the need to cherish love and marriage and procreation. Writing as World War II moved toward its close, Welty reasserted the value of love that war's destruction had made so evident in other contexts.

The use of an actual place to define or confine the novel's concerns, of course, may involve a tension within a writer, a tension between the free flights of imagination and the restraining forces of memory, or between the demands of thematic development and the demands of verisimilitude, or between the desire to use invented details that will seem credible in a story and the desire to describe a very real locale in an accurate fashion. And tension itself seems to characterize all sorts of creative endeavors. According to John Briggs, psychiatrist Albert Rothenberg believes that "polarities and oppositional elements are pervasive in creative thinking," and Briggs adds that for creative individuals, "contradictory feelings are experienced not as mere conflict or ambivalence, but as possibilities, potentials, mystery, openness." Briggs's assertion well describes not only the way that seemingly contradictory images converge in *Delta Wedding* but also the way that possibility and potential arise for Welty from a polarity between the real world and her story's needs. Her metaphoric concept of place, in fact, embodies a possibility or potential for harmony. As Rothenberg has written, "a metaphor is a unity referring simultaneously to disparate aspects of experience." That sort of unity was missing in "The Delta Cousins," for as her agent Diarmuid Russell noted, "every individual section seems good and yet as a whole it doesn't quite have the effect it ought to have." And as Mary Lou Aswell later added, the bee man episode was not "integral" to the story.[14] Marmion, however, is an integral part of *Delta Wedding*. In this setting, past and present, memory and vision, are harmoniously united, as are images of love and death, and all converge to develop Welty's most central concerns and values.

But a particular memory cannot always provide the writer with appropriate imagery, and when it cannot, the polarity between reality and fiction must be resolved in another way. Robert Penn Warren discusses the writer's reliance on memories that emerge from the unconscious mind, and he argues that the ability to break free from such memories is crucial to creativity. A "creative reverie," Warren asserts, does not deny "the needs of the unconscious," but "it gives new contexts to the images arising from the unconscious and criticizes projections of it, and in that process 'liberates.'"[15] Welty makes much the same assertion when she states that "the writer must accurately choose, combine, superimpose upon, blot out, shake up, alter the outside world for one absolute purpose, the good of his story. To do this, he is always seeing double, two pictures at once in his frame, his and the world's" (*ES*, 124–5). In "The Delta Cousins," Welty has chosen aspects from Waverley for inclusion and exclusion, but in *Delta Wedding* she has more thoroughly altered that setting and combined it with other settings for the good of her story. And whether Welty selects elements from the outside world or invents details in order to establish her own world, she is working "in a state of constant and subtle and unfooled reference between the two." Indeed, Welty believes this state of conscious and "unfooled reference" is at the heart of any writer's achievement. And she knows that "at the moment of the writer's highest awareness of, and responsiveness to, the 'real' world, his imagination's choice (and miles away it may be from actuality) comes closest to being infallible for his purpose" (*ES*, 125).

In *Delta Wedding*, as in "The Delta Cousins," Welty locates Marmion, alias Waverley, literally "miles away" from actuality. (A story or novel about so distinctive a region as the Delta can hardly have one of its major locales one hundred miles to the east, in Columbus.) Yet in developing her novel's most crucial themes, Welty needed a landscape described in more detail than her story had permitted. Thus, the novel's first view of Marmion occurs when Dabney, who is scarcely mentioned in "The Delta Cousins," who is not a bride-to-be in that story, and who does not visit the bee man's house, comes alone on horseback to look across the Yazoo River, not the Tombigbee, at the "magnificent temple-like, castle-like house" (*DW*, 122). The location of the house on the Yazoo River and near a Delta swamp is integral to the thematic development of the novel. When Dabney rides away from Marmion, for example, she seizes "a last chance to look" at the river's backwater "before her wedding," and she sees the swamp in a rather suggestive light. She dismounts from her horse, parts "thronged vines of wild grapes, thick as legs," and looks at snakes in the bayou and at "vines and the cypress roots" growing in the water "more thickly than any roots should grow, gray and red" some of which "moved and floated like hair." Dabney then ponders a whirlpool: "And the whirlpool itself—could you doubt it? doubt all the stories since childhood of people white and black who had been drowned there, people that were dared to swim in this place, and of boats that would venture to the center of the pool and begin to go around and everybody fall out and go to the bottom, the boat to disappear? A beginning of vertigo seized her, until she felt herself leaning, leaning toward the whirlpool" (*DW*, 123). Dabney never describes this experience to anyone, not even to her future husband, though she, as Louise Westling has noted, dearly associates the tangled vines and the dangerous whirlpool with the mysteries of sex and marriage. And just as clearly, Dabney associates the whirlpool with the dissolution of self and the inescapable mortality which she must face to enter adulthood. Life and death are linked in her perceptions of the Delta landscape just as Welty had thought they should be linked in illustrations demonstrating the reality of a soldier's existence.

When Laura and her cousin Roy visit Marmion, the landscape surrounding the house becomes even more complexly emblematic. As we have already seen, Welty uses elements drawn from *Waverley* to associate the house with death as well as love, and when Roy throws Laura into the Yazoo River, not the Sunflower River of "The Delta Cousins," these concepts reappear: "As though Aunt Studney's sack had opened after all, like a whale's mouth, Laura opening her eyes head down saw its insides all around her— dark water and fearful fishes" (*DW*, 178). Laura, whose only previous swim has been in Jackson's Pythian Castle with the protection of water wings, is immersed in the Yazoo, literally the River of Death, which is now linked to Studney's sack. Roy believes her mysterious sack is the place his mother "gets all her babies," while Studney's home beyond the Deadening makes her seem an emblem of mortality.[16] In "The Delta Cousins" Laura undergoes no such immersion, and the metaphorical Studney is nowhere in evidence. In the novel, however, both Studney's sack and the Delta's Yazoo River bring Laura an awareness of life's most fundamental mysteries, of its transience, and of the consequent urgency to love.

In expanding her story into a novel, Welty, even as she transformed the environs of Waverley, thus added descriptions of the swamps and rivers that had survived the Delta's metamorphosis from wilderness to plantation country. Dabney gazing into the whirlpool and Laura immersed in the River of Death encounter the frontiers of their own experience, the wilderness of their own emotional lives. The untamed physical world Welty describes is a psychological landscape as well. These descriptions, however, spring not from Welty's intuitive reliance upon archetypal concepts, but upon her very conscious decision to read and use the at times mundane, at times exciting, and always concrete diaries of Nancy McDougall Robinson, John Robinson's great-grandmother. Welty read the diaries over a year after she had completed her short story. Indeed, Welty's agent Diarmuid Russell wrote to her on Valentine's Day in 1945, predicting that the as yet unread diaries would have a powerful effect upon her.[17] Russell's remarks were prophetic, for Welty's venture into the journals led to her transformation of "The Delta Cousins" in both overt and oblique ways.

The diarist, Nancy Robinson, came to the Delta as a young bride in 1832, and her journals reveal just how much a frontier region nineteenth-century Mississippi was. Her first Delta home, Robinson writes, was a house made of "sticks and mud like a dove's nest" where she lived "more than 150 miles from any near relative in the wild woods of an indian nation, a stranger and unknown sitting in a low roofed cabbin [sic] by a little fire, nothing to be heard (that is cheerful) save the shrill note of the skylark the loud shriek of the night owl or the tinkling of a distant bell."[18] Robinson goes on to describe the bears her husband and later sons killed in the wilderness, the visits from plantation to plantation that family members made or received, the yellow fever epidemics that threatened the Delta population, her efforts to nurse both blacks and whites afflicted by fever, the devastating effects of the Civil War, the arrival of a federal steamboat on the bayou, and the 1869 conflict between her son and a business associate, a conflict that resulted in the associate shooting at her son Douglas, and in Douglas returning fire and killing his assailant.

In "The Delta Cousins," Welty makes no attempt to re-create a sense of the Delta past and makes little attempt to re-create the untamed Delta landscape. But in *Delta Wedding* the diaries have clearly inspired the Fairchild family history that Welty presents, the dark waters into which Laura has plunged, and the bayou landscape that Dabney encounters before her marriage. The frontier in *Delta Wedding* embodies that world that the Fairchilds typically attempt to repress, the world of mystery and the unknown, and the frontier persists in the land that planters have yet to bring under their control and into cultivation. The Fairchilds, of course, pay homage to their frontier past, hanging portraits of their ancestors, consulting the old cookbooks and diaries, but in doing so they fail to discover anything that is profoundly relevant to their lives. When Tempe sees the firearms displayed in the Fairchild living room, she sighs with distress and along with India looks for a moral: "There was Somebody's gun—he had killed twelve bears every Saturday with it. And Somebody's pistol in the lady's work-box; he had killed a man with it in self-defense at Cotton Gin Port, and of the deed itself he had never brought himself to say a word; he had sent the pistol ahead of him by two Indian bearers to his wife, who had put in it this box and held her peace, a lesson to girls" (*DW*, 98).[19] Both Tempe and India ignore the powerful and complex questions the firearms might evoke and arrive at a motto that neither can live by—that women should quietly accept the actions of their men.

Dabney and George, however, are not guilty of simplistic and comic distortions. They seem to feel what their ancestors felt and to revere the mysterious heroism of those who confronted the Delta wilderness. Dabney gazes at the portrait in which Mary Shannon has circles under her eyes, "for that was the year the yellow fever was worst and she had nursed so many of her people, besides her family and neighbors; and two hunters, strangers, had died in her arms" (*DW*, 41). Here, as Welty enlarges upon Nancy Robinson's experiences with yellow fever and superimposes the appearance of Eudora Carden Andrews, Welty's own grandmother, upon the fictional Mary Shannon, the relevance of the past is clear (*OWB*, 49). Dabney, anticipating her own marriage and the challenges it may involve, recognizes the heroism of her great-grandmother, who married, left her parents and friends, and came to the unsettled Delta: "How sure and how alone she looked, the eyes so tired. What if you lived in a house all alone and away from everybody with no one but your husband" (*DW*, 41). Like Dabney, George reveres those who can face the unknown with courage and serenity. Robbie believes that for George, "old stories, family stories, Mississippi stories, were the same as very holy or very passionate, if stories could be those things. He looked out at the world, at her, sometimes, with that essence of the remote, proud, over-innocent Fairchild look that she suspected, as if an old story had taken hold of him—entered his flesh. And she did not know the story" (*DW*, 191). George, like Dabney, grants family stories their meaning, a meaning that embraces rather than denies mystery; as a result, the past is not prismatic to uncle or niece. These two individuals recognize the courage with which their ancestors confronted isolation, death, the unknown, the courage with which they faced those realities rather than retreating from them. Writing in 1945 to readers of the forties, Welty clearly relied upon dramatic irony: She and her readers knew that neither George, Dabney, nor any of the Fairchilds would be able to remain in the relatively secure world of 1923. They would have to face a severe economic depression and a world war; the courage of their ancestors would have to become their own if they were to lead meaningful lives.

Although Welty relied upon Nancy McDougall Robinson in creating these Fairchild ancestors, she felt free to create her own history for the house she re-names Marmion. The actual house, Waverley, was constructed by Colonel George Hampton Young, probably in 1852. During the Civil War, Confederate officers, including General Nathan Bedford Forrest on at least one occasion, met there. The mansion was abandoned in 1913 when Young's last surviving son died. A Delta house near Greenwood would be unlikely to have such a history, and Welty uses none of this information in "The Delta Cousins" or in *Delta Wedding*. In "The Delta Cousins," Welty provides no history for the house; its origins are wholly mysterious and no Shelton seems ever to have owned it. But in *Delta Wedding*, she tells us that Marmion— Welty, like the owners of Waverley, found a name for her house in the works of Sir Walter Scott—was built in 1890 by James Fairchild, father of Denis, Battle, George, Tempe, Jim Allen, Primrose, and Annie Laurie, and abandoned in the same year after James Fairchild was killed in a duel. As the novel begins, we learn that it is to be the home of Dabney and Troy once they are married. And one day Laura may live at Marmion, for it is her rightful inheritance from her mother. Laura's inheritance from her dead mother, however, consists not only of this property, but also of the ability to accept the complex terms of human existence. Appropriately, then, Welty establishes one as the symbol of the other. In the novel, though not the story, Annie Laurie, who left the Delta in order to marry Laura's father, has inherited Marmion, and Marmion therefore should one day be Laura's. As Carol Moore and Peggy Prenshaw have noted, when Annie Laurie makes her young daughter a doll and names the doll Marmion, she looks forward to the legacy that will be Laura's.[20] The doll is aptly linked to the house, for Annie Laurie will bequeath a knowledge of love and death to Laura—the love she has given her daughter, the love implicit in her making of the doll, but also death, her own death. Ellen believes that Uncle George is the only Fairchild who sees "death on its way" (*DW*, 188), but she is wrong. Nine-year-old Laura shares this perception. Laura will be able to live in Marmion because she can appreciate its history of loss and its return to life during the tenure of Troy and Dabney.

The fictional history of Marmion is perfectly appropriate for a novel located in the slow-to-be-developed lands of the Delta interior.[21] More importantly, it focuses attention on the empowering nature of Laura's dual inheritance, not on the sterile memories of a lost cause; it suggests the possibility of renewal, not merely the reality of desolation. And as Welty wisely invents a family history for the house, she also fortuitously discovers in her own experience the metaphor of the doll. Welty's memory of her own mother making a stocking doll one rainy day, gratifying her daughter's wish almost as soon as it was expressed, becomes in *Delta Wedding* an emblem of a mother's love and the promise of love's continuity. And that promise enables Laura to embrace her Fairchild aunts and uncles and cousins and to see the beauty in the world around her. At the novel's close, "One great golden star [goes] through the night falling," to be followed by another. And Laura joyously responds to this beauty, holding out both arms "to the radiant night" (*DW*, 247). Here again Welty must "choose, combine, superimpose upon, blot out, shakeup, alter the outside world" to serve the purposes of her story. Here again the success of her story has emerged from the tension between the demands of memory and the demands of the story and from the writer's ability to know when those demands coincide and when they do not. And here again Welty asserts the power of love's continuity and of life's beauty despite the pain of loss, a domestic version of the power she describes in her review of William Sansom's World War II stories, the only power capable of redeeming a war-torn world.

Redemption of that world, Welty further suggests in her novel, lies in granting each individual his humanity, and Welty revised "The Delta Cousins" in order to focus on this very issue. In "The Delta Cousins," Parthenia is an amusing figure. Suspected by Ellen of taking her garnet pin, Parthenia effectively fends off Dip's tentative inquiries about the pin and relishes the attention her drawer leg hat commands. The scene is an amusing but somewhat stereotypical one. Not so in the novel. In *Delta Wedding*, Welty grants Partheny her humanity as most of her white characters do not. The plantation-owning Fairchilds deal with their servants in a congenial fashion, white and black children play together, and Ellen Fairchild sees to the health and well-being of black servants. But these surface relationships mask a very deep separation. When the black matriarch Partheny is subject to spells of mindlessness, for instance, the Fairchilds are sympathetic, but they never see the tragic import of the spells. Partheny, whose seizures resemble those experienced by Jackson midwife Ida M'Toy, describes her latest spell to Ellen Fairchild: "I were mindless, Miss Ellen. I were out of my house. I were looking in de river. I were standing on Yazoo bridge wid dis foot lifted. I were mindless, didn't know my name or name of my sons. Hand stop me. Mr. Troy Flavin he were by my side, gallopin' on de bridge. He laugh at me good—old Partheny! Don't you jump in dat river, make good

white folks fish you out! No, sir, I ain't goin' to do dat! Guides me home"
(*DW*, 78). Partheny's "mindlessness" takes a particularly appalling form—she
loses all sense of her identity. Mindlessness for Aunt Shannon Fairchild takes
the form of senility, not of blackouts; she is able to "talk conversationally
with Uncle Denis and Aunt Rowena and Great-Uncle George, who had all
died no telling how long ago, that she thought were at the table with her"
(*DW*, 13). The white woman retreats into the past. Partheny doesn't know
her own name or the names of her sons. She recalls no past. In fact, Partheny
scarcely has a past of her own. Her life has been focused upon the Fairchilds.
Her contact with the family has been close and affectionate; she attended
Ellen Fairchild at the birth of her daughter Shelley, was the nurse to several
of Ellen's children, and assists in the final preparations for Dabney's wedding
to Troy Flavin; Ellen Fairchild, similarly, has ministered to the ailing
Partheny, provided her with Shellmound Plantation's old wicker furniture,
and refused to criticize Partheny's appropriation of insignificant Fairchild
possessions. But no other family members even think about Partheny except
as she plays a role in family activities. They take her for granted; never
questioning that her life should be devoted to them, never realizing that she
had been denied a separate past of her own. Though they are more sensitive
than Troy, the overseer who laughs as he stops Partheny from jumping into
the Yazoo River, the Fairchilds' empathy for their servants is limited. There
is no indication that Welty intended this implicit indictment of racism to
serve as a commentary upon wartime issues. Nevertheless, writing in 1945 as
Nazi anti-Semitic and racist atrocities were becoming widely known, Welty
portrays the attitudes that along with greater economic opportunity had led
many black Mississippians to emigrate northward during the war years and
that ironically failed to match the nobility of the American crusade again
Nazism. At the same time, her characterization of Partheny conveys the hope
that those attitudes may yet change.

We can thus learn much about one writer's imagination by studying the
origins of "The Delta Cousins" and *Delta Wedding*. The reliance upon distant
memories, the impetus to metaphoric thought that distance in time can
provide, the intuitive recognition that a remembered place can define issues
and values crucial to the present moment, a tension between the power of
memory and the demands of fiction—these elements all characterize Eudora
Welty's creative process and are crucial to the achievement of *Delta Wedding*.
More crucial perhaps are the values that emerge from this process, values
that Welty believed must answer the challenges posed by World War II.
Implicit in Eudora Welty's *Delta Wedding* is an affirmation of faith that
William Faulkner would later explicitly make: It is the writer's privilege,

Faulkner wrote, "to help man endure by lifting his heart, by reminding him of the courage and honor and hope and pride and compassion and pity and sacrifice which have been the glory of his past."[22] In *Delta Wedding* Eudora Welty surely prefigured Faulkner's Nobel Prize address and proved herself deserving of that very honor.

NOTES

1. "Cloud-Cuckoo Symphony," *Time* 47 (22 April 1946): 104, 106, 108.

2. Albert Devlin, "The Making of *Delta Wedding*," in *Biographies of Books*, ed. James Barbour and Tom Quick (Columbia: University of Missouri Press, 1996), 227; Ruas, 66.

3. Kreyling, *Eudora Welty's Achievement of Order*, 55–76; Devlin, "The Making of *Delta Wedding*," 226–61.

4. Eudora Welty, *A Writer's Eye: Collected Book Reviews*, ed. Pearl Amelia McHaney (Jackson: University Press of Mississippi, 1994), 5, 6, 7.

5. Welty to Porter, [October 1943], Katherine Anne Porter Papers, Special Collections, University of Maryland Libraries. John Robinson turned the incident mentioned here into a story titled "Room in Algiers" (*New Yorker* 22 [19 October 1946]: 89–95).

6. "The Delta Cousins," Welty Collection, MDAH.

7. Elizabeth Bowen, "Notes on Writing a Novel," in *The Mulberry Tree*, ed. Hermione Lee (San Diego, New York, London: Harcourt Brace Jovanovich, 1986), 40.

8. Rollo May, *The Courage to Create* (New York: Norton, 1975), 68.

9. Eudora Welty, "A Sketching Trip," *Atlantic Monthly* 175 (June 1945): 62, 70.

10. Welty, *A Writer's Eye*, 33, 34, 35, 36.

11. Russell to Welty, 19 October 1944, 31 October 1944, 14 February 1945, restricted papers, Welty Collection, MDAH.

12. Welty, *A Writer's Eye*, 67.

13. Welty, "The Delta Cousins," 24, 26.

14. Briggs, 93, 110; Albert Rothenberg, "The Process of Janusian Thinking in Creativity," in *The Creativity Question*, ed. Albert Rothenberg and Carl Hausman (Durham: Duke University Press, 1976), 317; Russell to Welty, 10 November 1943, restricted papers, Welty Collection, MDAH, and as cited by Kreyling, *Author and Agent*, 103; Aswell to Welty, 16 December 1943, enclosed in Russell letter to Welty 21 December 1943, restricted papers, Welty Collection, MDAH.

15. Robert Penn Warren, "A Poem of Pure Imagination: An Experiment in Reading," in *Selected Essays* (New York: Random House, 1958), 288.

16. The argument I advance in this paragraph appears in a different context in my 1986 article "The Metaphor of Race in Eudora Welty's Fiction" and in my 1988 book *The Welty Collection*. In 1980, Carol Moore discussed the significance of Aunt Studney's sack at some length and in similar terms ("Aunt Studney's Sack," *Southern Review*, n.s. 16 [1980]:591–6). Her discussion of the bees that emerge from the sack and of their symbolic import is of particular interest, though Louise Westling persuasively takes exception to Moore's conclusions (*Sacred Groves and Ravaged Gardens* [Athens: University of Georgia Press, 1985], 89–90).

17. Russell to Welty, 14 February 1945, restricted papers, Welty Collection, MDAH.

18. Nancy McDougall Robinson, Diary 1832, Mississippi Department of Archives and History, Jackson, n.pag.

19. There is actually a town named Cotton Gin Port in the Columbus, Mississippi, vicinity.

20. Waverley, Subject File, Mississippi Department of Archives and History, Jackson; Moore, 591–6; Peggy W. Prenshaw, "Woman's World, Man's Place," in *Eudora Welty: A Form of Thanks*, ed. Louis Dollarhide and Ann J. Abadie (Jackson: University Press of Mississippi, 1979), 51.

21. The Mississippi Department of Archives and History reports that "The 4,000,000 rich acres in the interior of the Mississippi Delta were sparsely settled before 1880 because of flooding from the Mississippi River and its many tributaries" ("The New Cotton Kingdom," Exhibition text, Old Capitol Museum, Jackson, Mississippi). In the novel, the nineteenth-century Fairchilds live at the Grove, "a cypress house on brick pillars" (*DW*, 37), until Marmion is built in 1890, and they return to the Grove when tragedy seems to taint that house. The early house on pillars would have been, before 1880, far better suited to the landscape of the Delta interior and far more feasible to construct there.

22. William Faulkner, "William Faulkner's Speech of Acceptance upon the Award of the Nobel Prize for Literature," in *The Faulkner Reader* (New York: Random House, 1954), 4.

ELIZABETH BOWEN

The Golden Apples[1]

W hen one speaks of "imaginative writing," one may use the term too vaguely and widely. Fiction is often no more than *inventive* writing—the plot is found, the characters are made lifelike, the scene of the story assumes a short-term reality. All this requires, on the part of the writer, hard concentration and patient ingenuity: the result is entertainment which gives pleasure, and for which thanks should be due. But the fact that much fiction is written to formula cannot be ignored. The formula is created by the wish of the public to be told, yet once again, what it knows already, or to have the same tune played, with slight variation, on a range of feelings of which it is already aware. The inventive writer has to his or her credit a new *story*, but the ideas conveyed by (or feelings contained in) the story have been taken from stock. No new world has been created, no unique vision sheds light, nothing of significance has been laid bare. The reader, having been held for a sum of hours, agreeably, by the inventive novel or book of stories, closes the volume and puts it down again. That is that. He is, as far as he knows, satisfied—nothing disturbs him, nothing haunts him. He has been left, in fact, where he was before. Like a child automatically stretching out its hand for another bun, he heaves himself out of his chair and goes to his book-table, or puts on his hat and goes to his library, in search of another work of fiction which shall resemble the one before.

From *Seven Winters*. © 1962 by Elizabeth Bowen.

If imaginative writers were more numerous, the inventive less so, there would be a less rapid turnover of fiction. The work of imagination causes a long, reflective halt in the reader's faculties. It demands to be reread, to be brooded over, to be ingested, to be lived with and *in*.

Eudora Welty is an imaginative writer. With her, nothing comes out of stock, and it has been impossible for her to stand still. Her art is a matter of contemplation, susceptibility, and discovery: it has been necessary for her to evolve for herself a language, and to arrive, each time she writes, at a new form. She has given us two collections of stories—*A Curtain of Green* and *The Wide Net*—a fairyless fairy tale called *The Robber Bridegroom*, and a novel, *Delta Wedding*. Now comes *The Golden Apples*.

The Golden Apples consists of seven stories similar in scene, playing upon the same cast of characters, dramatically different in time, and so placed in relation to one another as to develop a theme and bring out a pattern. The scene is the little town of Morgana, in the southern American state of Mississippi. The characters—whom we see in childhood, in adolescence, in maturity, in love, in death—are dwellers in and around Morgana. We more than see these people; we become identified with them, as though their nerves, senses, and thoughts had been, by some operation, spliced into our own. The MacLains, the Starks, the Spights, the Morrisons, the Raineys, and their neighbours, each serve to illuminate for us intense moments of experience, which are at once their own and universal.

From whence has Miss Welty drawn her title? She had in mind those golden apples which, rolled across Atalanta's course as she ran, sent her chasing sideways, and made her lose the race. Outwardly, existences in Morgana—remote, sleepy, and past-bound—are conventional: one goes to school, goes to work, marries, raises one's family, dies. Inwardly, each of these human beings gropes his or her way along—perplexed, solitary (in spite of the neighbourliness), and from time to time blinded by flashing illuminations. We have the gentle albino, Snowdie MacLain, and her almost magic relationship with her great, handsome, errant husband. We have hoydenish Virgie Rainey, with her abused music and her miscarried life. And young Loch Morrison, spying on love and insanity in the deserted next-door house. There are the MacLain twins (born of "the shower of gold") and there is Jinny Love Stark, with her endless girlhood enclosed in a gaunt marriage. Maideen, wearer of dainty gloves, takes her own life after a hallucinated episode of love. Cassie keeps her mother's name written in growing flowers. Old King MacLain, all passion not quite spent, makes terrifying grimaces at a funeral.

This is great, tender, austere stuff, shot through from beginning to end with beauty. Miss Welty does not merely decorate her style with similes and images, she uses them to enlarge it—such as here: "*Behind the bed the window was full of cloudy, pressing flowers and leaves in heavy light, like a jar of figs in syrup held up.*" The seven episodes, or stories, in *The Golden Apples* are not to be separated from one another; they relate at once meaningly and closely: their dramatic total is only to be grasped at the very end—when time, with its action, and change, with its crushing force, seem, with Katie Rainey's burial, to reach full circle. So far as the stories *can* be made to stand apart, "The Shower of Gold," "June Recital," "Moon Lake," and "The Wanderers" are likely to be judged the most nearly perfect.

In *The Golden Apples*, Miss Welty would seem to have found, for her art, the ideal form. But, for a writer of her stature, nothing is conclusive—what comes next? American, deliberately regional in her settings, she "belongs," in the narrow sense, to no particular nation or continent, having found a communication which spans oceans.

NOTE

1. *The Golden Apples*, by Eudora Welty. New York: Harcourt, Brace; 1949.

MARILYN ARNOLD

The Strategy of Edna Earle Ponder

V arious commentators have remarked on the narrative role of Edna Earle
Ponder in Eudora Welty's *The Ponder Heart*. Having cornered a stranger at
the Beulah Hotel in Clay, Mississippi, someone stranded there because of car
trouble, Edna Earle proceeds to tell her captive audience of Daniel Ponder's
trial marriage with Bonnie Dee Peacock and his courtroom trial for her
murder. Ruth Vande Kieft, who calls *The Ponder Heart* "a light-hearted
'murder-mystery'" (*Eudora Welty* [1962] 70), later suggests that ideally the
reader enters the dramatization as Edna Earle's audience, her guest at the
hotel ("The Question of Meaning" 30). Brenda G. Cornell, like reviewer
Coleman Rosenberger, also assumes the reader's identification with the
stranger, indicating that an important "narrator-reader intimacy" is
established as the reader becomes a confidant of Edna Earle (210). Kurt
Opitz is less than impressed with what he calls the novel's "artificial narrator"
(88). In his view, Edna Earle displays a "loquaciousness [that] strikes us as
hollow." Instead of developing scene or defining plot, her talk serves merely
to "introduce the author's *ego*" by being calculatedly witty (87).

Critical assessments of Edna Earle Ponder, in acknowledging her
function as an apologist for Daniel Ponder, her childlike uncle, say nothing
of her role as a cunning strategist. Edna Earle and Daniel, who is a few years
her chronological senior but many years her mental junior, constitute the last

From *Eudora Welty: Eye of the Storyteller*. Dawn Trouard, ed. © 1989 by The Kent State
University Press.

spunky remnants of a family in decline. In some sense, yes, the reader is
drawn into unusually active participation in the story in response to Edna
Earle's intimately chatty revelations to "you," her listener. In my view,
however, the narrative ear is a character in her own right; her identity and
Edna Earle's moderately subversive purposes in telling her about Daniel are
important to our understanding of the novel. Furthermore, Edna Earle *is*
intelligent, at least by Clay standards. We should not dismiss her matter-of-
fact boast that she has always been hopelessly bright, having passed Daniel in
the seventh grade though she hated to do it. She shamelessly confesses, "It's
always taken a lot out of me, being smart" (10). Although her view of herself
is not universally shared—*Harper's* reviewer Gilbert Higher, for example,
regards the book as a satire on women of the Edna Earle type, "a tale told by
an idiot"—it can be argued that Edna Earle is clever enough to entertain a
hidden agenda as well as a shy young guest.

Surprisingly, at least two reviewers assume the guest to be a traveling
salesman (Pritchett and the anonymous author of "The Human Comedy").
Their views notwithstanding, she is most certainly young and female, and
probably shy and naive as well. In a manner appropriate only for addressing
a younger woman, Edna Earle warns her guest in the novel's first paragraph
that when Daniel "sees you sitting in the lobby of the Beulah, he'll take the
other end of the sofa and then move closer up to see what you've got to say
for yourself; and then he's liable to give you a little hug and start trying to
give you something. Don't do you any good to be bashful" (7). Later, she
says, "He's smart in a way that you aren't, child." Every indicator in the novel
points to a listener whose gender, youth, innocence, and social status could
make her a likely candidate—in Edna Earle's mind—to be Daniel's next
bride.

Throughout the novel the adroit Edna Earle travels the course of her
story selecting details meant to charm and impress a young woman, and at
the same time she sets forth the expectations that would govern a liaison
between her guest and Daniel. Edna Earle can be both strategically cryptic
and frankly blunt: "I size people up," she warns. "I'm sizing you up right
now" (11). And she is. Apparently, Edna Earle is at least preliminarily
satisfied with what she sees—a young woman of an acceptable social class
who is independent enough to be journeying on her own, yet reticent
enough to allow Daniel full rein. Edna Earle indicates that she and her
grandfather selected his first wife, Miss Teacake Magee, but "it was bad luck.
The marriage didn't hold out" (27). Daniel himself picked his second wife,
with uncanny appropriateness but without premeditation or consultation, in
the ten cent store; and that marriage ended in comic disaster. The marriage
also killed Grandpa Ponder, who could not handle the shock of his son's

marrying a low-class Peacock. Even if he had survived the marriage, he would probably have died at the upshot of it. First, Bonnie Dee up and left Daniel, then returned and threw him out, then died of heart failure from being tickled during a thunderstorm. She was clearly inferior stock. If Edna Earle has her way, any future brides will be first sized up, then courted, then forewarned and foreordained by Daniel's niece and protector.

It is obvious throughout the novel that Edna Earle's first concern is Daniel's happiness, for Daniel "loved happiness like I love tea" (14). He can give away the family fortune or marry white trash for all she cares, so long as he is happy. When Bonnie Dee leaves him forlorn and heartbroken, it is Edna Earle who places an ad—in verse, mind you—in the Memphis paper to tempt her back. Edna Earle will even endure the Peacocks if she can count on Daniel's happiness. And now, in an effort to secure that happiness, she informs her guest through an ingenious circumlocution that it is time for Daniel to fall in love again, at least it is if he holds true to his established pattern: "He went from giving away to falling in love, and from falling in love to talking, and from talking to losing what he had, and from losing what he had to being run off, and from being run off straight back to giving away again" (148–49). Logically, his next step is to fall in love again.

In Edna Earle's view, the current status quo is unacceptable. The trial is over, Daniel has moved back to the Beulah, and not a soul has entered the hotel for three days. Daniel, whose greatest pleasures are talking and giving away anything that can be owned, has no one to talk to and nothing left to give away. Small wonder he is not himself just now. When he turned his trial into a circus by waltzing through the courtroom pitching money in every direction, he won his acquittal but lost his audience. As Edna Earle explains, "You see, that money has come between the Ponders and everybody else in town. There it is, still on their hands.... Here Clay sits and don't know what to do with it" (155). The whole disappointing town is avoiding Daniel, and that is the one condition intolerable to him. "He comes down a little later every night" (155), Edna Earle sighs. She can put him up at the hotel and she can prepare his supper, "But he don't enjoy it any more. Empty house, empty hotel, might as well be an empty town. He don't know what's become of everybody" (154). At the very least, Edna Earle sees the newcomer as an audience for Daniel, and that alone should lift him out of the doldrums. On the other hand, with the right kind of encouragement this particular hotel guest might turn into a permanent audience for Daniel—a wife.

Daniel can always rely on Edna Earle and her unflagging loyalty; but she knows her devotion is not enough, and his dejection worries her. Slim as the pickings are in the way of brides in this town, a young, unattached stranger is practically heaven-sent. Edna Earle must be careful, however. Not only must she market Uncle Daniel's charms, but she must also prepare the young woman for a demanding new role and test her capacity to fill the expectations of that role. There is more at stake here than Edna Earle's penchant for talk, more than her finding someone with whom to pass the time of day. There is, in fact, a sense of urgency in her chatter. Uncle Daniel is losing ground and may soon require "a good course of calomel-and-quinine" (155). When the young guest attempts to escape with a book, Edna Earle intercepts and insists on telling her story. "And listen; if you read, you'll put your eyes out. Let's just talk" (11), meaning, don't read; listen to me. Daniel will be coming down to supper soon; and Edna Earle, his self-appointed guardian and general family caretaker, must lay the groundwork for a possibly auspicious meeting. Everything in her story is a preparation for Daniel's entrance, and it is no accident that the subject of her discourse is brides and marriage. In a dozen subtle and not so subtle ways, Edna Earle flatteringly gathers her young visitor into her confidence. Her opening sentence, for example, is broadly familiar and assuring: "My Uncle Daniel's just like your uncle." His only weakness, she confesses, is that "he loves society and he gets carried away" (7).

After extending a prefatory caution that Daniel might proffer a hug and a gift or two, Edna Earle launches into her campaign. Borrowing method from John Alden, she exclaims over Daniel's sweet disposition, his large-size hat (implying that he is blessed with a goodly share of the legendary Ponder brains in spite of his childlike nature), his generosity, his popularity, and his father's money. Then she shifts to a physical description of Daniel, painting a romantic portrait for one she deems to be an impressionable and not overly discriminating young woman. Edna Earle is especially careful to stress Daniel's youthfulness in spite of his fifty-plus years ("Don't believe it if you don't want to" [11]), and she takes every opportunity to mention that Bonnie Dee was only seventeen when Daniel married her and still looked only seventeen in her coffin. Age difference, Edna Earle implies, is inconsequential with Uncle Daniel. What's more, he has stature in a crowd, and style: "He's unmistakable. He's big and well known." His "short white hair" is "thick and curly, growing down his forehead round like a little bib." As a bonus, "He has Grandma's complexion. And big, forget-me-not blue eyes like mine, and puts on a sweet red bow tie every morning," and a "large-size Stetson" that he has always "just swept ... off to somebody." Daniel "dresses fit to kill ... in a snow-white suit"; but more important, he is "the sweetest, most unspoiled thing in the world. He has the nicest, politest manners—he's good as gold." No one can "hold a candle to Uncle Daniel for looks or manners" (11).

Edna Earle strengthens her case by emphasizing the prominence, wealth, and superior social standing of the Ponders and by suggesting that Daniel's marital failures can be traced to his marrying beneath him, even though the practice is common. The young bridal candidate apparently passes muster on this point because Edna Earle addresses her as one of "us" and refers frequently to the inferior Baptists and Peacocks. The ingenuous Daniel is too naive to be discriminating and therefore must be protected from himself. He "didn't mind old dirty people the way you and I do" (91), she confides. Moreover, he finds nearly all young women fascinating, from Intrepid Elsie Fleming and her motorcycle to the burlesque dancers at the fair. In spite of his sweetness, "he's a man, same as they all are" (16), she admits.

Impressing her guest with the Ponders in general and Daniel in particular is only one part of Edna Earle's design, however. Assuming that the young woman is interested, and knowing how quickly Daniel acts if the inclination strikes him, it is possible Edna Earle sees this as her sole opportunity to influence the course of Daniel's next marriage. She must accomplish a great deal in this conversation. Since Edna Earle is the only person living or dead who understands Daniel and knows how to handle him, it is her example any future bride must follow. Even Daniel's father, Edna Earle's grandpa, though he "worshiped Uncle Daniel" (12), did not know that an attempt to teach Daniel a lesson by sending him to an asylum would end in calamity. Daniel quite innocently turned the tables on Grandpa and came home, leaving Grandpa in custody instead of himself. Furthermore, Edna Earle assures her listener, "they couldn't find anything the matter with [Daniel]" (15).

From the time he was very small, Daniel had lived virtually without restraint. "They had him late—mighty late," she says. "They used to let him skate on the dining room table" (9). And this is no time, as Grandpa discovered, to try a different mode of operation. "He's as good as gold," Edna Earle cautions, "but you have to know the way to treat him" (16). Her narrative becomes in part a lesson on how to treat Daniel: that is, how to protect him and let him do whatever makes him happy, even if it means perjuring oneself in court for his sake and letting him indiscriminately dispense the family fortune to the Peacocks and half the town of Clay. "It *was*," after all, "cheering him up" (148), she says. Edna Earle virtuously reminds her listener that if anyone had a stake in shutting off Daniel's spontaneous philanthropy, she did: "Now I'll tell you something: anything Daniel has left after some future day is supposed to be mine. I'm the inheritor. I'm the last one, isn't that a scream? The last Ponder. But with one fling of the hand I showed the mayor *my* stand: I'd never stop Uncle Daniel for the world." Sensing some disapprobation in her guest, Edna Earle exclaims parenthetically, "(And I don't give a whoop for your approval!)" (146). She instantly remembers herself, however, and seeks the young woman's sympathy for her benevolent perjury and her efforts to keep Daniel from revealing how Bonnie Dee really died. "(You don't think I betrayed him by not letting him betray himself, do you?)" (148), she asks. Whatever Edna Earle does, she convinces herself that her motive is Uncle Daniel's happiness. Her last instruction to her guest before calling Daniel to supper is in fact a plea to humor him should he try to give her something: "Make out like you accept it. Tell him thank you" (156).

Essentially, Edna Earle's advice to her guest, to anyone who might marry Daniel, is to please him at all costs, to allow him to do whatever he likes, to accept his loving nature, and to forget about changing him. A very large order. She even drops hints about things he likes, such as divinity candy. Again, Edna Earle suggests that her own example is the one to follow: "I don't even try, myself, to make people happy the way they should be: they're so stubborn. I just try to give them what they think they want" (57). She does, that is, if "they" happen to be Daniel.

Perhaps the most important skill to be acquired by Edna Earle's apprentice is the art of listening. It is probably Welty's little joke that the one who preaches listening does nothing but talk, but anyone who marries Daniel has to know that he loves an audience. Moreover, Edna Earle's lengthy monologue makes it quite clear that love of an audience is a Ponder trait that afflicts niece as well as uncle. The irony is that Edna Earle sees the trait in Daniel but not in herself. Welty, however, knows that Ponder heaven is a new face with ready ears. Edna Earle may be summing up the measure of her own happiness as well as Daniel's when she says, "if he wasn't in the thick of things, and couldn't tell you about them when they did happen, I think he'd just pine and languish" (67). It would be humanly impossible for Daniel to remain silent at his own trial with an eager audience already assembled. And with him, talking and giving are two manifestations of the same impulse; they function alternately, not simultaneously. As chance would have it, just as he is about to tell the court how Bonnie Dee died from his tickling her (to distract her from her fright at the storm), he remembers the greenbacks stuffed in his pockets, money he had earlier withdrawn from the bank. He abruptly stops talking and begins to hand it out. In the bedlam that follows, the court never learns the precipitative cause of Bonnie Dee's death, though Edna Earle wants the prospective bride to know that Bonnie Dee was killed by love, not hate.

Edna Earle's lesson is this: if you want to keep Daniel from giving, let him talk. And listen without interrupting him. Grandpa, who did not handle

Daniel wisely, was "the poorest listener in the world" (17). The "perfect listener" is someone like Mr. Ovid Springer, the traveling salesman whose chief entertainments when he comes to town are treating Edna Earle to the movies and listening to Daniel's stories. He came in "seldom enough to forget between times" and knew the Ponders "well enough not to try to interrupt." Moreover, he was "too tired to object to hearing something over" (17–18). In fact, he would beg Daniel to tell his favorite tales. But when Edna Earle realizes that Mr. Springer's ill-conceived efforts to help at the trial would have provided Uncle Daniel with a motive for murder, she questions his judgment and his loyalty. This episode predicts Mr. Springer's scarcity in Clay and creates additional pressure on Edna Earle to cultivate a new listener.

It appears that Edna Earle is indeed cultivating a new listener, and testing one at the same time. If the young woman can listen attentively to Edna Earle, then she can listen attentively to Uncle Daniel. The guest apparently does set her book aside, interrupting Edna Earle at perhaps only the one point mentioned above, near the end of the narrative. Even a single interruption, it appears, draws a rather curt response. At times, too, Edna Earle pushes beyond impressing, instructing, and testing her young visitor. Her tone is never threatening, but occasionally it warns. A prospective bride must know what is required, must accept the ground rules in the Ponder league. Daniel could make another Peacock marriage, but Edna Earle will do all in her power to lead him into a different kind. Since he is likely to be as happy with one sweet young thing as another, he might as well have one that has been tutored by Edna Earle. The next bride, if there is one, must learn that the lovable but totally irresponsible Daniel requires someone to "mind out for him" (36).

For years, now, that someone has been Edna Earle; and a prospective bride should be apprised that Edna Earle is not likely to disappear regardless of Daniel's marital status. Edna Earle is proprietor of more than the Beulah Hotel, and she does not let her listener forget it. There is a double purpose to her strategy, to find Daniel a bride and to carve out a permanent place for herself in Daniel's life. She reasons, for instance, that "I don't really think Uncle Daniel missed Bonnie Dee as much as he thought he did. He had me" (54). And when "all the other children and grandchildren went away to the ends of the earth or died and left only me and Uncle Daniel—the two favorites," naturally "we couldn't leave each other" (55). Furthermore, the first time Edna Earle reports that Daniel was going to be accused of murder, she says, "they *charged* us" (80). Her emphasis is on the word "charged"; mine would be on the word *us*. Regretting Daniel's isolation from the town since the trial, she says that nevertheless, "*I'm* here, and just the same as I always was and will be, but then he never was afraid of losing me" (154). Lest there be misunderstanding about the matter, Edna Earle indoctrinates her listener to the view that a marriage with one of the two remaining Ponders is a threesome rather than a twosome. Her subject is purportedly her own contemplated marriage with Mr. Springer, but her point is clear: "I'm intended to look after Uncle Daniel and everybody knows it, but in plenty of marriages there's three—three all your life. Because nearly everybody's got somebody" (26). And in the end her intent is confirmed; Daniel and the young woman will not eat dinner alone. "Narciss!" she calls, "Put three on the table!" (155).

The visitor is served notice not only that a Ponder marriage is a package deal but also that a Ponder bride must take up residence in the groom's home a few miles from Clay. It is empty and waiting for Daniel's return, and Daniel is not the sort who can live among strangers unschooled in the ways of the Ponders. To the young woman's credit, she is at least "somebody from nearer home." Indirectly, Edna Earle also warns her guest against venturing too far from friendly faces (such as those she would find in Clay) herself. Walking the thin line between threat and persuasion, Edna Earle clarifies her position:

> The stranger don't have to open his mouth. Uncle Daniel is ready to do all the talking. That's understood. I used to dread he might get hold of one of these occasional travelers that wouldn't come in unless they had to—the kind that would break in on a story with a set of questions, and wind it up with a list of what Uncle Daniel's faults were: some Yankee. (17)

The listener has to see herself in the captious reference to "occasional travelers that wouldn't come in unless they had to," but Edna Earle diverts the insinuation by making a Yankee the suppositional culprit and by concluding with the reassurance that "he'd [Daniel] be crazy about you" (17).

There is just one more point Edna Earle wishes to make, one more strategic purpose for her narrative. She wishes to warn any future Mrs. Daniel Ponder that most of the Ponder money disappeared in the courtroom fiasco and that it would be unwise in any case to marry for whatever may be left. Her narrative suggests that the selfish prospect of social position and financial ease were what persuaded Bonnie Dee to accept Daniel's proposal. Moreover, she left Daniel and was brought back by the promise of "retroactive allowance." It was, in fact, the termination of that allowance that prompted her to summon him on the fateful day of the storm. As was mentioned earlier, too, the townspeople turned from Daniel because he showered money on them, converting their greed into shame. In the end, Edna Earle's warning is explicit: "The worst thing you can give away is money—I learned that if Uncle Daniel didn't. You and them are both done for then, somehow; you can't go on after it, and still be you and them. Don't ever give me a million dollars! It'll come between us" (149).

No doubt Edna Earle, like Eudora Welty, tells her story largely for the pure love of telling. She has experienced a few slow days at the Beulah and welcomes new blood herself. At the same time, there are enough indicators of a more strategic purpose in the back of Edna Earle's mind to suggest that she is already sizing up a possible candidate to be the next bride of Daniel Ponder, a candidate whom she both instructs and tests, both woos and warns.

Welty herself may also have minor strategic purposes she only hints at. Though her tone is light and her wit ready, an edge of ache encircles her tale. Less obvious than Sister's ache in "Why I Live at the P.O.," Edna Earle's is defined by her loneliness, especially in her new relation to the town since the trial. Moreover, her relationship with Ovid Springer has been permanently altered, if not terminated, by his thoughtless betrayal. Edna Earle's narrative, like that of her counterpart in "Why I Live at the P.O.," reveals more about herself than about Daniel or anyone else. It may be, too, that Welty has purposefully obscured the identity of Edna Earle's guest—so much so that more than a few readers have assumed the guest to be male—because some part of Edna Earle wants the guest to be male, yearns for a new love interest to replace Mr. Springer. In a manner reminiscent of John Alden, she wishes she were doing the courting for herself. Nevertheless, she will seize whatever opportunity presents itself and make the best of it, in this instance, a potential bride for Daniel. Edna Earle, like Carson McCullers's Frankie, may not be the bride, but she is determined to be a member of the wedding.

RUTH M. VANDE KIEFT

The Bride of the Innisfallen:
A Collection of Lyrics

T he first impression given by the stories collected in *The Bride of the Innisfallen* (1955) is that a number of departures have been made from the patterns of Eudora Welty's earlier fiction. A major change is the predominant shift from her usual regional settings and Southern characters. Four of the seven stories have their settings outside Mississippi. "Circe," set on a legendary island and based on the Circe episode in the *Odyssey*, is Eudora Welty's only explicit use of a Greek myth. The title story depicts a group of chiefly Irish people en route from London to Cork; "Going to Naples," a group of Italian-Americans on a ship headed for Italy; the viewpoint, in both cases, is largely that of an outsider. "No Place for You, My Love" has a Southern setting (the delta country south of New Orleans), but one unfamiliar to Eudora Welty; furthermore, the two principal characters of this story are an open-faced, self-conscious young woman from the Middle West and a sophisticated Eastern businessman.

"Kin" is one of the three stories with a Mississippi setting, but its point of view is that of a girl who at the age of eight moved away from the state to the urban North and is making a return visit. "The Burning" is Eudora Welty's first and only Civil War story. Only in "Ladies in Spring" do we return to something familiar: rural Mississippians in their own setting, in and near a tiny town named Royals.

From *Eudora Welty*. © 1987 by G.K. Hall & Co.

Experiment, range, and variety are apparent in the stories. Only the initiated may, at first, be able to perceive the continuity with Eudora Welty's earlier stories—the focus on place and on the themes of love and separateness, the human mysteries, vulnerability, the sense of exposure and need for protection, the rarity of genuine communication, the glory of one precious moment of personal insight and fulfillment. Though much happens in the stories, little can be summarized. The climaxes are internal and difficult to locate: they are likely to occur in a series of moments, or realizations, which do not usually effect a turning point in external action or behavior. Brilliant descriptions, pictures, moods, snatches of conversation, epigrammatic summations contribute to the whole, which tends to be a dominant impression rather than a clear rational design.

The differences between the earlier stories and those of *The Bride* emerge more clearly through comparison. "A Worn Path" and the "The Wide Net" are both stories of journey or quest. In each case a journey is taken for a specific purpose: Old Phoenix goes to fetch the "soothing medicine" for her grandson; William Wallace and his entourage drag the river to recover the body of Hazel. In each case episodes, stages, and diversions engage the attention of characters and readers; the journey becomes a progression in which the final purpose is temporarily lost sight of (as when William Wallace dances with the fish in his belt, or Old Phoenix forgets why she made her trip). In each case the trip also takes on a ceremonial significance and becomes a symbol for a whole life, in which processes and rituals carry us, unwitting, to our goals and destinies.

"The Bride of the Innisfallen," "No Place for You, My Love," and "Going to Naples" are also stories of quest or journey. But whose is each journey, why is it taken, what is its significance? In the title story the central character is not, as might be expected, the bride, but the American girl for whom the bride, never identified, seems to represent love at its pristine moment of joy, hope, expectancy. Contrasted with the motivations of Phoenix or William Wallace, her motivation for taking the journey is as obscure as her central "problem." Perhaps recently married herself, she seems to have run from her husband in London in order to rediscover and affirm an inner self, a "primal joy" threatened both by her marriage and by the grayness of London. An excess of hope and joy, an openness to life, expectation and outgoing love of it, have become a burden on her heart because these feelings cannot be shared or acted upon. This motivation is not incomprehensible: it seems to me both credible and moving. But it is somewhat ratified and difficult for the reader to discover, especially outside the context of Eudora Welty's work as a whole; and part of this difficulty is the lack of the immediate, tangible human relationships found in "A Worn Path" or "The Wide Net."

A similar vagueness surrounds the flight of the young woman in "No Place for You, My Love." We know only from the Easterner's point of view, that back home she must be involved in some hopeless love relationship (possibly with a married man), that there may recently have been a "scene," since she has on her temple a bruise which affects her "like an evil star," that her frantic need is for escape and the protection of distance and anonymity, and that her painful obsession is with exposure. But if the heroine's situation is vague, we know from Eudora Welty's account in "Writing and Analyzing a Story,"[1] that it is intended to be; we also know that the point of view was neither the woman's nor her companion's but that of a mysterious third presence:

> It was ... fished alive from the surrounding scene. As I wrote further into the story, something more real, more essential, than the characters were on their own was revealing itself. In effect, ... there had come to be a sort of third character along on the ride— the presence of a relationship between the two. It was what grew up between them meeting as strangers, went on the excursion with them.... I wanted to suggest that its being took shape as the strange, compulsive journey itself, was palpable as its climate and mood, the heat of the day....
>
> I wanted to make seen and believed what was to me, in my story's grip, literally apparent—that secret and shadow are taken away in this country by the merciless light that prevails there, by the river that is like an exposed vein of ore, the road that descends as one with the heat—its nerve (these are all terms in the story), and that the heat is also a visual illusion, shimmering and dancing over the waste that stretches ahead.... I was writing of exposure, and the shock of the world; in the end I tried to make the story's inside outside and then leave the shell behind.[2]

Eudora Welty accomplished what she set out to do, but it was a perilous undertaking. She took a human feeling—a panicky, raw-nerved sense of exposure—and invested an entire landscape and journey with that feeling; she rendered a strong emotional effect without supplying much information about its cause. The vivid impressionism of this method is strangely exciting, but the story is not as fully and solidly alive as is a story like "A Worn Path," in which there seems never to have been a shell to leave behind because every part—plot, character, setting, theme—seems essential to every other part.

Experimentation in narrative technique is also evident in "The Burning." The characters in this story are clearly conceived, but monolithic: a pair of genteel maiden sisters, and an obedient young slave, Delilah. The narrator is usually hovering in and around the consciousness of Delilah, recording what is said and done in a language subtly adjusted to the minds, mode of life, relationships, and idiom of the three women. The description is sharply detailed, textural, impressionistic. Frequent gaps in the action have the effect of averted eyes; confusions and ambiguities are abundant.

The action that can be pieced together is sufficiently horrible. Two of Sherman's soldiers, with a white horse, invade the home of the two ladies; though it is not clear how the soldiers attack the women, it is implied that Miss Myra and Delilah are raped, and all three women are put out; the house is looted by soldiers and slaves, then burned with a child named Phinney in it. The three women, who witness the burning, wander toward and through a devastated Jackson; Miss Theo murders her sister by hanging; then, with Delilah's help, she tries to hang herself but apparently succeeds only in breaking her neck and dies by inches in the grass. After a day or two Delilah returns to the blackened ruins of the house, finds and takes Phinney's bones, and is seen, finally, with a "Jubilee cup" set on her head, advancing across the Big Black River.

The effect of all these grim happenings is not what the facts would suggest. It is weirdly diffused, muted, diverted by the variety of irrelevant detail that swamps Delilah's consciousness and by the quaint, ladylike speech, behavior, and "props" of the two old maids. Only the slightest hint notifies the reader of some new horror: "the soldier ... dropped on top of her" tells us Miss Myra is being raped; "when it came—but it was a bellowing like a bull, that came from inside—Delilah drew close" tells us that Phinney is being burned alive. Then the profuse details come flooding: pictures of the elegant interior of the house, "glimmering with precious, breakable things white ladies are never tired of"; or outdoors, of butterflies and insects and "black-eyed susans, wild to the pricking skin, with many heads nodding." Or there are bits of dainty, playful argument or assertion, which are madly inappropriate to the grim occasion, such as this one of Miss Theo, who is tying the noose for Miss Myra: "I learned as a child how to tie, from a picture book in Papa's library—not that I ever was called on.... I guess I was always something of a tomboy." Because the felt reactions often have no correlation with the events, the effect on the reader is ironic almost to the point of perversity.

There are two main reasons for this apparent perversity. The first is that the old style of Southern gentlewoman behaves with faultless consistency, which means, in extreme circumstances (as in Faulkner's "A

Rose for Emily"), that she may behave insanely. The proud Miss Theo has the godlike strength that befits her name. Sufficiently warned of the coming destruction, she can't "understand" the message, pulls down the shutters, and goes on living as if nothing is going to happen; attacked, turned out, she retains her dignity and consummates her protest with suicide.

Miss Myra is even more insane. A delicate, childish woman with purple eyes and bright gold hair, she seems a parody of the Lady of Shalott living in a fantasy world of chivalry. When she first sees the mirror image of the intruding soldier on his white horse, she asks, "Will you take me on the horse? Please take me first" as though he were a knight on a rescue mission. She imagines Phinney to be her child by "an officer, no, one of our beaux that used to come out with Benton." But the child is black, and appears, from Miss Theo's comments, to have been their brother Benton's child by a slave—probably Delilah, who thinks of him as "her Jonah, her Phinney."

If Miss Myra's delusions and Miss Theo's strong-willed resistance to outrage and cruelty are a source of confusion, the use of Delilah as a main center of consciousness is another reason for the strange narrative technique. Delilah is innocent and does not understand the meaning of the horror and catastrophe that she witnesses. Her world is shattered into fragments, but she cannot make a tragic shape out of the fragments. Like Little Lee Roy in "Keela, the Outcast Indian Maiden," she is incapable of the moral comprehension of her experience.

The major symbol in "The Burning" is an important container of the story's meaning. In the parlor is a large Venetian mirror, the ornate "roof" of which is supported by two black men (Moors), who stand on either side of it and appear almost to be looking into the glass themselves. When the soldiers and horse invade the house at the beginning of the story, the two ladies raise their eyes to the mirror and regard the intruders reflected there instead of turning to face them directly. While Miss Myra is attacked, Delilah's vision is turned away from the violence and fixed on the mirror; it reflects her, obediently holding the white horse, and the tranquil parlor interior with the "bare yawn" of the hall reaching behind. The elegant mirror is the symbol of a way of life: placid, decorative, sheltered, lived at a remove, out of touch with reality, and supported by slaves.

Returning to the ruins after the burning, Delilah finds the mirror. The black men are now "half-split away, flattened with fire, bearded, noseless as the moss that hung from swamp trees"; the glass is clouded "like the horse-trampled spring." Peering into it, Delilah has a hallucinatory vision in which the mirror's decoration (images of aristocratic Venetian life) are blended with images of "Jackson before Sherman came"; then, "under the flicker of the sun's licks, then under its whole blow and blare, like an unheard scream, like an act of mercy gone, as the wall-less light and July blaze struck through from the opened sky, the mirror felled her flat." And finally, in a phantasmagoria of destructive images, Delilah sees and feels her world violently shattered.

Elaborateness, subtlety, and sophistication are distinguishing marks of the stories in *The Bride of the Innisfallen*. These qualities are visible not only in choice and motivation of character, structure, and narrative technique, but also in style. The changes, though in no way absolute and already visible in some of the stories of *The Wide Net*, may be illustrated by a comparison of the opening sentences of a few stories from A *Curtain of Green* and *The Bride of the Innisfallen*. Following are three from the first-mentioned:

> R. J. Bowman, who for fourteen years had traveled for a shoe company through Mississippi, drove his Ford along a rutted dirt path. It was a long day! ["Death of a Traveling Salesman"]

> I was getting along fine with Mama, Papa-Daddy and Uncle Rondo until my sister Stella-Rondo just separated from her husband and came back home again. ["Why I Live at the P.O."]

> It was December—a bright frozen day in the early morning. Far out in the country there was an old Negro woman with her head tied in a red rag, coming along a path through the pinewoods. Her name was Phoenix Jackson. ["A Worn Path"]

And following are two opening sentences from *The Bride of the Innisfallen*:

> They were strangers to each other, both fairly well strangers to the place, now seated side by side at the luncheon—a party combined in a free-and-easy way when the friends he and she were with recognized each other across Galatoire's. ["No Place for You, My Love"]

> There was something of the pavilion about one raincoat, the way—for some little time out there in the crowd—it stood flowing in its salmony-pink and yellow stripes down toward the wet floor of the platform, expanding as it went. ["The Bride of the Innisfallen"]

Striking in the first set of opening sentences is directness of style. Characters, setting, time of day or season, the beginnings of situation or action are at once set before the reader purely and plainly in short, simple statements. By comparison, the style of the second pair of opening sentences is oblique and sophisticated. Characters are introduced without their names (in these two stories they never get them). Questions are raised, and the reader knows instinctively that answers may not be immediately forthcoming. The pertinence of each opening to the central action is subtle rather than explicit. The style is that of a storyteller who knows there are a thousand different ways of getting into a story rather than the one of simply beginning with persons, places, and things.

The changes in style in *The Bride of the Innisfallen* must be considered in their relation to character, situation, and point of view. The sophistication of style in "No Place for You, My Love," for example, is fitted to the sophistication of the two main characters and their situation: two self-conscious modern people, briefly whirled together and then apart, whose relationship is determined by the environment they encounter together and by the heat and speed of their journey, as much as by their own natures. The self-consciousness of the relationship pervades the style. Even the metaphors are difficult to interpret, as, for instance, the following, which appears toward the end of the story, just after the couple have returned to New Orleans and are about to leave each other: "Something that must have been with them all along suddenly, then, was not. In a moment, tall as panic, it rose, cried like a human, and dropped back." Without the help of the author's explanation, one might puzzle over that metaphor long and fruitlessly. She says the cry was that of "that doomed relationship—personal, mortal, psychic—admitted in order to be denied, a cry that the characters were first able (and prone) to listen to, and then able in part to ignore. The cry was authentic to my story: the end of a journey *can* set up a cry, the shallowest provocation to sympathy and love does hate to give up the ghost."[3] The metaphor is odd, but it was born legitimately out of an odd story with an odd point of view.

It is, finally, the storyteller who reveals sophistication in the stories of *The Bride of the Innisfallen*: a writer who is far more aware of multiple choices, the varieties of form and technique possible to the creative imagination, than was the writer of *A Curtain of Green*. As an artist, Eudora Welty seems to have gone through the kind of change she has so often described in her fiction: the passage from innocence to experience. What is lost in this process is simplicity, purity, lucidity, immediacy in relation to the materials of fiction, a natural and instinctive grace, an intuitive perception and realization of form, and relative ease and spontaneity of creation. The sophistication that is gained at the expense of the loss of innocence has a compensating value: the stories provide the delight that comes from the experience of an art beautifully and skillfully executed, varied, mature, experimental. And throughout, the power of feeling has never been lost. Indeed, an undercurrent of certain kinds of feeling provides a sort of unity among these seemingly disparate stories.

Michael Kreyling has shown convincingly that the stories of *The Bride of the Innisfallen* are related in several ways. He finds a new, "metaphysical" interest in place—"the lively medium that makes things possible and confers identity." He finds rhythmic motion, patterns recurring in time but leading to an inner form through which is achieved, in T. S. Eliot's phrase, "the stillness, as a Chinese jar still / Moves perpetually in its stillness." He finds "the motifs of pilgrimage" (frequently involving water, images of crossing, meetings and partings, rivers, bridges and separating seas), "passages toward fulfillment of dream, lonely souls in need of response, calls sent out in hope of connecting with other lonely hearts."[4] Except in "Kin," where the pleading call is that of an old man remembering, the call is a woman's, as in "Ladies in Spring"—secret, plaintive, unanswered. A small boy named Dewey, "playing hooky" and gone fishing with his father Blackie, hears him called and feels intuitively the desolation of that lonely girl's cry. Each of the heroines is abandoned by her potential or actual lover: even the powerful Circe, semideity that she is, must endure the departure of the mortal Ulysses. Yet each of the love-burdened heroines retains the virtues of openness to life, the capacity to love, to renew hope and joy, to achieve an inner poise, steadiness, or stillness, even when alone. These resources are costly, for each is troubled not only by the finality of partings, but by the inhibitions of propriety, everything that gnaws and nibbles away at joy and fulfillment.

In "Going to Naples," among the literal and figurative pilgrims on board the *Pomona*, is plump young Gabriella Serto, on her own quest for love and fulfillment. She is given to screams that often seem "endeavors of pure anguish or joy that youth and strength seemed able to put out faster than the steady pounding quiet of the voyage could ever overtake and heal." Anxiously hovering over Gabriella is a mama too impressed with her own and everyone's "terrible responsibility," running "her loving little finger over the brooches settled here and there on her bosom like St. Sebastian over his arrows." Precious few candidates are available even for a "shipboard romance," but there is one budding musician, a cellist named Aldo, whose courtship begins with Ping-Pong, and flowers the moment when he buries his face in Gabriella's blouse. He produces a lifting of the soul in onlookers as they "contemplate among companions the weakness and the mystery of the flesh" and feel "something of an old, pure loneliness come back to them—like a bird sent over the waters long ago, when they were young...."

Gabriella is abandoned by Aldo on "Gala Night." The sea turns heavy; and like many others, finally including Mama Serto, Aldo succumbs to seasickness. But Gabriella enjoys a physical triumph that turns metaphysical when she dances solo on the heaving ocean against pitching floors; a few intrepid survivors, "*indisposti* or not," witness and applaud her triumph:

> That great, unrewarding, indestructible daughter of Mrs. Serto, round as an onion, and tonight deserted, unadvised, unprompted, and unrestrained in her blue dress, went dancing around this unlikely floor as lightly as an angel.... Some radiant pin through her body had set her spinning like that tonight, and given her the power—not the same thing as permission, but what was like a memory of how to do it—to be happy all by herself.

This speaks not so much of a *discovery* of her own "primal joy" as her *performance* of it, for "how can we know the dancer from the dance?" In that innermost steadying of her turbulent adolescent passion, the eye of her storm, the axis of that "radiant pin" through her whirling body, we have the equivalent of a Chinese jar or Grecian urn—a kinesthetic one: the point at which time freezes into no-time and life into art.

Approached with the set of expectations we bring to the reading of lyric poetry, the stories of this collection will often yield to the reader of "willing imagination" experiences of surpassing beauty reminiscent, in their texture and meaning, of great Romantic poetry, most often that of Keats, but also that of Wordsworth. Surely the "primal joy," "the kind you were born and began with," related as it so often is to the act of seeing and the need for telling, "being able to prophesy, all of a sudden" ("Kin"), singing, even screaming from sheer intensity ("Going to Naples"), resembles the phenomenon Wordsworth sang of so memorably in his "Ode on Intimations of Immortality": the experience of splendor in the objects of sense, "the glory and the freshness of a dream." Threatened, lost, recoverable by the characters in the stories of *The Bride*, it is recovered by their creator through the lyric feeling captured in those stories.

Even more impressive in the stories are echoes of and parallels with the poetry of Keats: in their nostalgia and ineffable yearning, their questing and questioning, their sensuous texture and richness of imagery, their use of synesthesia, their bitter sweetness through juxtaposition of joy and sorrow, their themes of time and eternity, truth and beauty, life and art. The poet who, "in embalmed darkness," bathed in the myriad springtime odors and pictured images of flowering trees and fragrant blossoms, listens to a bird "pouring forth [his] soul abroad," is not far from Dewey ("Ladies in Spring") roaming in "drenched and sweet" places, and standing quietly, half-buried in fragrant flowers and vines, listening to "the lonesomest sound in creation, an unknown bird singing through the very moment when he was the one that listened to it." Something of Keats's ineffable yearning is what Dicey sees in the portrait of her great-grandmother ("Kin"), her romantically tragic history known from family stories, now viewed in all her openness, vulnerability, and courage, through eloquent eyes. Dicey feels "kin" to this ancestor who had felt "the wildness of the world," and knows the two of them, Dicey and her "divided sister," were "homesick for somewhere that was the same place"—perhaps a place where love is fresh, sweet, and forever, existing now in her old dying Uncle Felix's (happy) fevered nostalgia as he yearns to recover a girl named Daisy, by some nameless river, in a midnight tryst. The whole romantic story is squeezed into the three words scribbled on the note he presses into Dicey's hand—"River—Daisy—Midnight"; the pathos to Dicey, and to us, lies in the fourth word, "Please."

The parallels with Keats's odes are most remarkable in the title story, through the experience of the American girl who comes to Cork with her questing heart and her burden. As the *Innisfallen* sails toward the harbor, church bells ring along the river; time past and present blend as "an older, harsher, more distant bell rang from an inland time: *now*." Walking the streets of Cork, she feels the spring with the intensity of sense impressions merged, of the metamorphosis of branch and blossom to bird to song, of tree to golden goddess. "The trees had almost rushed with light and blossom; they nearly had sound, as the bells did. Boughs that rocked on the hill were tipped and weighted as if with birds, which were really their own bursting and almost-bursting leaves. In all Cork today every willow stood with gold-red hair springing and falling about it, like Venus alive. Rhododendrons swam in light, leaves and flowers alike; only a shadow could separate them into colors."

She wants to *tell* this joy, but cannot; she can only see, feel, and finally know:

> I see Cork's streets take off from the waterside and rise lifting their houses and towers like note above note on a page of music, with arpeggios running over it of green and galleries and belvederes, and the bright sun raining at the top. Out of the joy I hide for fear it is promiscuous, I may walk for ever at the fall of evening by the river, and find this river street by the red rock, this first, last house, that's perhaps a boarding house now, standing full-face to the tide, and look up to that window—that upper window, from which the mystery will never go. The curtains dyed

so many times over are still pulled back and the window looks out open to the evening, the river, the hills, and the sea.

This remarkable sequence of images, in which the horizon of a town becomes the rising and falling of musical notation, and architectural decoration with nature's green becomes arpeggios and light becomes rain, in which what is passing and temporal seems to become eternal, ends with an ordinary window looking out over the sea. But it is filled with mystery. The unheard music of the lifting houses and towers is magical, reminiscent of the eternal bird whose song "Charmed magic casements, opening on the foam / Of perilous seas, in faery lands forlorn." In the story Ireland is made to seem such a faery land opening out on perilous seas.

Briefly, the window has a tenant: the mood of the passage turns realistic, then shifts back to a tempered echo of another of Keats's odes:

> For a moment someone—she thought it was a woman—came and stood at the window, then hurled a cigarette with its live coal down into the extinguishing garden. But it was not the impatient tenant, it was the window itself that could tell her all she had come here to know—or all she could bear this evening to know, and that was light and rain, light and rain, dark, light, and rain.

As a mere window, however wonderfully perceived, is to a beautiful Grecian urn, so is the summation of "All ye know on earth, and all ye need to know" of window and urn. Yet the alternations of light and rain, surely suggestive of the weather of the mind, of joy and sorrow, is a simple truth made beautiful by a lyricist in prose.

But comedy defeats high romance, and few scenes in Eudora Welty's fiction are without comic relief. These intrusions are like the sudden "Tweeeet!" of outrageous old Papa's ten-cent whistle into "life's most precious moments" ("Going to Naples"). The title story ends, as it began, with the comedy of colorful Irish characters when the American girl throws away the message to her husband and plunges into a pub. At her entrance "a glad cry [goes] up" and they all call out "something fresh ... like the signal for a song."

Yet the whole collection, with the closing lines of "Going to Naples," brings together transformations of the "Ode on Melancholy," "Ode to a Nightingale," and "To Autumn." When the *Pomona* reaches Naples it is golden autumn; there are tender reunions and partings, tears are shed. Gabriella knows that Papa, the raucous old whistle-blower, has come home to die; her own Nonna turns out to be a fabulously ancient, tiny lady, bright-eyed with a brown face "creased like a fig-skin." Gabriella feels her long journey, every tumultuous event, every new thing seen and old thing remembered, "caught up and held in something: the golden moment of touch, just given, just taken, in saying good-by. The moment—bright and effortless of making, in the end, as a bubble—seemed to go ahead of them as they walked, to tap without sound across the dust of the emptying courtyard, and alight in grandmother's homely buggy, filling it." Then as the black horse pulling Nonna's buggy tosses its mane and they are about to leave, "the first of the bells in the still-hidden heart of Naples began to strike the hour."

A strangely haunting question ends the book. "'And the nightingale,' Mama's voice just ahead was beseeching, 'is the nightingale with us yet?'"

The question is rhetorical: the "immortal bird" is, of course, with Mama Serto as it was with the homesick Ruth in Keats's ode. The nightingale's song rises and falls like Gabriella's bright bubble of memory: both end buried, first in valley-glades or buggy, at last in the reader's memory. He may even come to think of the bride of the *Innisfallen*, forever surrounded by the pilgrims' delight in her sweet, shy loveliness as she stands alone by the rail in her white spring hat and dazzling little white fur muff, as Keats's "still unravished bride of quietness, ... foster child of silence and slow time."

Eudora Welty has said that "the source of the short story is usually lyrical." In the stories of this collection the completed artifact is as close to pure lyricism as she has ever come.

NOTES

1. *The Eye of the Story*, 107–15.
2. Ibid., 111–13.
3. Ibid., 114.
4. Michael Kreyling, *Eudora Welty's Achievement of Order* (Baton Rouge: Louisiana State University Press, 1980), 128–29.

SALLY WOLFF

"Foes well matched or sweethearts come together": *The Love Story in* Losing Battles

Returning on foot through a hot, dusty field to her estranged husband, Robbie Fairchild muses in *Delta Wedding* about the upcoming reunion with her spouse and wonders to herself, "What do you ask for when you love?" (*DW*, 146). The omniscient narration then adds: "So much did Robbie love George, that much the less did she know the right answer." Such a statement about the ambiguous, complex, and mysterious nature of love is the revelation at the heart of Eudora Welty's best fiction. From the lonely salesman in her earliest story to the infidels of *The Golden Apples* and the heartrending widow of *The Optimist's Daughter*, characters throughout Welty's works reach for love and answers to their "hearts' pull." The Natchez Trace, a boat landing, or a post office—and always the woods—provide settings for Welty's love stories.

From her first story of human relationships, "Death of a Traveling Salesman," Welty has written of the "pervading and changing mystery" people discover in responding to others. The mysterious quality of a relationship has been Welty's subject from her earliest days as a writer. The secret may simply lie in deserving to know the indecipherable identity of the lover; the search for a lover may prove elusive and mysterious; or the attempt—as in "Circe"—merely to fathom the indefinable idea of love may be futile. Love in Welty's stories is as mysterious and incomprehensible to

From *The Late Novels of Eudora Welty*. Jan Nordby Gretlund and Karl-Heinz Westarp, eds. © 1998 by the University of South Carolina.

those who experience it as for those who do not. "What do you ask for when you love?" becomes a keynote for Welty's long-held exploration of the ambiguous and infinitely complex fabric of relationships. Her characters who are willing to confront the mystery—and who are curious to know more of it—are those characters who often find the fulfillment they seek. William Wallace, in "The Wide Net," for instance, strains tirelessly for the entire story to understand secrets of human nature that seem withheld from him, especially regarding his wife's personality. In the last scenes of the story, he looks out from the porch, in the same direction of his wife's gaze, and at last he can see where she sees and know more of her perspective. Such characters usually grow in love and knowledge.

Welty's description of *Losing Battles* applies to much of her love literature: "I wanted to show that relationships run the whole gamut of love and oppression. Just like any human relationship has the possibilities of so many gradations of affection, feeling, passion, resistance, and hatred" (*C*, 221–22). These infinite "gradations" form the bases for most of her stories. From her early stories of searching through her first comic novels, later more meditative stories, and last novels of domesticity, Welty considers the many "alternatives and eventualities" in the world of relationships. Some couples know the "ancient communication" between two people, or the deep and time-tested commitment of Ellen and Battle Fairchild or Becky and Judge McKelva. She also depicts the harsh consequences that loss and death force people to confront. Paul Binding has observed that in fact "*Losing Battles* is dedicated to Welty's brothers—as *The Optimist's Daughter* was to be to Chestina Andrews Welty. These losses—in complex ways—stand behind both novels, giving them not just their darkness but their overall depth, their immensity of understanding. There are qualities of the heart in *Losing Battles* that were not even present in *The Golden Apples*."[1] Those who know and then lose or relinquish love are among Welty's most heartrending depictions. Laurel Hand is one such compelling figure, who has known and lost a marriage that was near-perfect in its wholeness, enriching and educating for both partners, as it was simultaneously one of challenge and security in providing mature life and love.

Welty's late novel *Losing Battles* returns to tested themes and narrative techniques from earlier works. She writes of a love that resembles those in *The Robber Bridegroom*, the early stories, and *Delta Wedding* in the focus on romance, domesticity, familial orientation, and happiness. She returns in *Losing Battles* to the "by ear" storytelling strategy, in which dialogue and dialect become almost as important to the story as the tale which it tells. Binding has seen this novel as "her largest scale tribute to the richness of Southern vernacular...."[2] Dialogue and dialect weave the tale in *Losing*

Battles, as Welty considers here, and in *The Optimist's Daughter*, serious questions about love. She reaches deeper, emotionally and philosophically, in these late novels than in some of her earlier works, such as *Delta Wedding*.

On the whole, *Losing Battles* is about love of different kinds. Joyce Carol Oates has termed it "a book about domestic love" in which "we hear about the young hero, Jack; we hear about his exploits, his courage, his foolishness, his falling in love with the young girl who is his teacher; we hear about the bride herself and about her infant girl; gradually ... understanding how the hero and his bride came to be separated and how they will be joined again." In a larger sense, she adds, the book concerns the importance of family life: "What is important is love—the bonds of blood and memory that hold people together, eccentric and argumentative and ignorant though these people are. The basic unit of humanity is the *family*, the expanded family and not the selfish little family of modern day."[3]

A great degree of loyalty, allegiance, and commitment to the family, even at the expense of community involvement, is not a new topic for Welty. In *Delta Wedding* Robbie Fairchild's feelings of rivalry with the Fairchild clan for her husband's love is the most extensive treatment of the topic, although the issue of community intervention in familial relations occurs in "Lily Daw and the Three Ladies," "Petrified Man," "Asphodel," and other early stories. In *Losing Battles* the dispute between loyalty to the family and the need for privacy reaches the most clamorous levels ever in Welty's fiction, and she answers her own question with characteristic ambiguity.[4] The tension between private relations and societal obligations and needs remains a central concern for Welty.

Perhaps more than any other pair in Welty's canon, Jack and Gloria Renfro grapple with the difficult questions of marital allegiance, insularity and privacy, and the proper balance of familial obligations with communal and social roles. Besides their financial worries, this dichotomy between private affairs and community is the crucial problem in the marriage between Jack and Gloria. Symbolized by Judge Moody's car, balanced precariously on a tree limb, hanging from a cliff, this tension keeps both husband and wife shifting a balance toward equilibrium in their marriage—and not always achieving it.

More than many characters, Jack and Gloria adapt to the necessity for living "most privately when things are most crowded," for they must renew their love, passion, and commitment in the midst of a family reunion. They have their intimate moments, and some naturally are "in front of the whole family": "First kiss of their lives in public, I bet a hundred dollars" (73), Aunt Cleo announces upon Jack's initial embrace of his wife. Other moments find them quite blissfully alone. Nonetheless, their predominant dilemma is the need for privacy and intimacy—only heightened by Jack's long absence in jail—juxtaposed with the equally demanding necessity of developing a viable social context. Jack hopes for a lasting reconciliation between his family and Gloria, and she hopes for private time apart from the "clannishness" of his family.[5]

The value of privacy understandably becomes skewed in Gloria's mind, since her lot is cast amid a family of new in-laws, whom she does not seem to like, for the duration of Jack's jail term. Early in the novel in-laws criticize Gloria's characteristic insistence upon her privacy: "'Mind out, Sister Cleo, Gloria don't like to tell her business,' Miss Beulah called" (48). Later when Aunt Birdie assumes the entire family will tell Jack about his new baby, born since he went to prison, Gloria brings the whole family up short with a reassertion of her sense of marital and familial intimacy: "She's my surprise to bring" (69). Even later when the family begs her for the surprise, Gloria stays inside the house and calls out the window that she is "tending to some of my business." Trespassing further into Gloria's territory, "the crowd" of this family becomes increasingly intent upon telling the secret of the baby: "'Gloria! What have you got for Jack? Ain't it just about time to show him?' The crowd caught up with her in the kitchen, clamoring to her. 'I'll be the judge,' said Gloria from the stove" (74). What Gloria is judging is the width of her territorial boundary of the private sphere within the larger family.

The first intimate moment Gloria shares with Jack is a precious one, given the intrusive and insistent family: "Chewing softly, he kept his eyes on Gloria, and now in a wreath of steam she came toward him. She bent to his ear and whispered her first private word. 'Jack, there's precious little water in this house, but I saved you back some and I've got it boiling'" (75). When Gloria finally does show Jack their baby, the family realizes that by confidential, epistolary means, Gloria has already revealed to Jack, during his jail term, the secret of the baby. The surprise is now the family's—to find that Jack knows all: "'Gloria told him what she had. That baby's no more a surprise than I am,' cried Aunt Nanny. '*I'm* not afraid of pencil and paper,' said Gloria" (94). After this pronouncement on this subject, Gloria firmly establishes not only her literacy, but also her views about the private sphere of her relationship with Jack: "'Lady May all along was supposed to be his surprise. *Now* what is she?' cried Aunt Birdie." Disappointment may reign in the ranks, but Gloria differentiates and sharply monitors the distinction between the public and the private domain, especially regarding the intimate subject of the birth of this child: "she was my surprise to tell" (92).

Conversely, Jack Renfro feels strong familial and social obligations. Reminiscent of George's conflict with Robbie (in *Delta Wedding*) about his loyalty to his family in maintaining large social context, Jack's entreaty to Gloria is to share with him in embracing his family: "'Say now you'll love 'em a little bit. Say you'll love them too. You can. Try and you can.... Honey, won't you change your mind about my family?' 'Not for all the tea in China,' she declared" (360). Jack wants Gloria to become his family in the broadest sense; his vision, like George's, is flexible and all-inclusive: "'Be my cousin,' he begged. 'I want you for my cousin. My wife, and my children's mother, and my cousin and everything.... Don't give anybody up.... Or leave anybody out.... There's room for everything, and time for everybody ...'" (361–62).

Typically, however, Gloria takes the opposite view: she wants to devote herself to the marriage and her core family. She keeps her mind on "the future" (434) and romantically dreams of a day when she, Jack, and the baby can move to a "two-room house, where nobody in the world could find us" (412): "'Oh, this is the way it could always be. It's what I've dreamed of,' Gloria said, reaching both arms around Jack's neck. 'I've got you all by myself, Jack Renfro. Nobody talking, nobody listening, nobody coming—nobody about to call you or walk in on us—there's nobody left but you and me, and nothing to be in our way'" (431). Jack feels "sudden danger" at these ideas, which are, as Michael Kreyling suggests, "very real to a man of Jack Renfro's mind, in which family means safety, companionship, defense against chaos."[6] John Hardy has also pointed out that "Even more fiercely than Robbie Reid, Gloria believes that it is possible to marry a man without marrying his whole kin. She has not quite succeeded in convincing Jack.... In her own mind, she is still a long way from being taken captive by the tribe."[7] Louise Gossett adds that "Welty doesn't promise escape, for as Gloria looks away from the house to the future, beyond the bright porch she couldn't see anything."[8] So the battle lines are drawn and set.

At the end of the novel the argument remains unresolved—the battle is neither won nor lost. Gloria wants her privacy from family, and Jack still maintains, "You just can't have too many, is the way I look at it" (435). Welty commented in an interview that "every instinct" in Gloria wants them to "go and live by themselves," and "Jack, of course, is just oblivious to the fact that there could be anything wrong with staying there and having the best of both" (*C*, 305). Welty takes sides only to show the rationale for each character: "Jack is really a good person, even though he is all the other things.... he allows himself to be used by everybody.... [But that] comes out of his goodness.... Yes, I really like Jack. He's a much better person than Gloria" (*C*, 306). The struggle characterizes their relationship, and the tension remains high.

Jack and Gloria face a dilemma—not of goodness versus evil, or right versus wrong, but of the forces of togetherness and opposition in the marriage—and in other relationships—which draw together and push apart the individuals who wish to share their feelings of love. Both positions in the argument have merit, and Welty indicates that to balance privacy and community, passion and society does prevent Jack and Gloria from slipping into isolation or clannishness. To preserve the integrity of their most intimate relationships, Welty's lovers in these stories dodge intrusion to maintain their private relations. At the same time the familial and social influence on the couple seems essential in supporting a love relationship. Indeed, such a communal context may be the vital thread without which characters such as Livvie, Robbie, and especially Gloria risk unraveling the fabric of which their marital lives are woven.

Despite the concerns of social and familial roles, the relationship of Jack and Gloria Renfro flourishes as one of Welty's most romantic unions. Three full decades after *Delta Wedding*, Welty again writes of a happy love in a domestic setting. The marriage of Jack and Gloria depends for inspiration not upon exotic travels away from home, scandalous infidelity, or fairy-tale fantasy, but upon love generated between the two people in a realistic setting within traditional marital boundaries. Like so many other Welty love stories, this one resembles in structure the Shakespearian separation of lovers and their eventual, sweet reunion. The seventy-five-page prelude to Jack's arrival is a masterful narrative that anticipates the entrance of the newlywed husband, the recent bride, their quickly begotten child, and Gloria's reaction to her husband's homecoming. As in preparation for a wedding, the "girl cousins" march ceremoniously around Gloria like flower girls, chanting what might easily be a wedding song: "Down on the carpet you must kneel / Sure as the grass grows in this field" (29). Time seems suspended until the lovers reunite. The throng of people parts in Biblical splendor for the intensely dramatic moment when Jack greets his wife:

> They divided and there stood Gloria. Her hair came down in a big puff as far as her shoulders, where it broke into curls all of which would move when she did, smelling of Fairy soap. Across her forehead it hung in fine hooks, cinnamon-colored, like the stamens in a Dainty Bess rose. As though small bells had been hung, without her permission, on her shoulders, hips, breasts, even elbows, tinkling only just out of her ears' range, she stepped the length of the porch to meet him ... Jack cocked his hands in front of his narrow-set hips as she came. Their young necks stretched, their lips tilted up, like a pair of rabbits yearning

toward the same head of grass, and Jack snapped his vise around her waist with thumbs met. (73)

Like India in *Delta Wedding*, the onlookers can try to see "what there was about a kiss." Welty even describes the cactus as the color of "mistletoe" (24), providing Jack with ample excuses for kissing in public. Poised as they are amid the throngs of family, rejoined, the romantic couple now takes center stage and full dramatic sympathy as Welty continues exploring her theme of *Delta Wedding*: "What do you ask for when you love?" (*DW*, 146).

The omniscient narration Welty chooses begins the unveiling of this story of love, as she reveals the first private conversations between a man and wife. Gloria presents her husband with the gift of a new shirt that she has saved relentlessly to buy for him. In the first of many intimate moments between them, she helps Jack dress in a scene deeply suggestive of their sexual attraction and need.

> Without ever taking his eyes from her, and without moving to get the old shirt off till she peeled it from his back, he punched one arm down the stiffened sleeve. She helped him. He drove in the other fist. It seemed to require their double strength to crack the starch she'd ironed into it, to get his wet body inside. She began to button him down, as his arms cracked down to a resting place and cocked themselves there....
>
> By the time she stood with her back against the door to get the last button through the buttonhole, he was leaning like the side of a house against her. His cheek came down against her like a hoarse voice speaking too loud.... She straightened him up and led him back into the midst of them. (78)

Their deep need cannot go unmet, and much like Jamie and Rosamund (in *The Robber Bridegroom*) and George and Robbie Fairchild (in *Delta Wedding*), Jack and Gloria leave for an afternoon alone together in the woods. Miss Beulah Renfro, Jack's mother, articulates what is almost always true for Welty's lovers as they reunite: "this minute is all in the world she's been waiting on" (94). Welty adorns the edenic couch for them with detail of a Southern Paradise: bees crawl "like babies into the florets" (98); and the birds move like "one patch quilt." The setting for love is the woods, much as it is for Milton's Adam and Eve or for Shakespeare's midsummer night's lovers.

> They walked through waist-high spires of cypress weed, green as strong poison, where the smell of weed and the heat of sun made

equal forces, like foes well matched or sweethearts come together. Jack unbuttoned his new shirt. He wore it like a preacher's frock-tailed coat, flying loose.... Then side by side, with the baby rolled next to Jack's naked chest, they ran and slid down the claybank, which had washed away until it felt like all the elbows, knees and shoulder, cinder-hot.... Keeping time with each other they stepped fast without missing a tie.... Jack reached for her.... (98)

The couch to which these two retire is not garlanded with Miltonic petals, however. Like Jamie and Rosamund's, the pallet has the Southern color of pine needles: "The big old pine over them had shed years of needles into one deep bed." The squirrels playing and courting over the lovers' heads reenact the playful romance in the human world below: "a pack of courting squirrels electrified a pine tree in front of them, poured down it, ripped on through bushes, trees, anything, tossing the branches, sobbing and gulping like breasted doves." Jack approaches Gloria with equal earnestness: his face rushes "like an engine toward hers" (99).

In two other love scenes during the novel's span of one day, Jack and Gloria plumb their passion, romance, and love. After accidentally bumping her head on a log, "Without stopping to be sorry for her head," Jack "crammed kisses in her mouth, and she wound her arms around his own drenched head and returned him kiss for kiss" (113). Jack comforts her as she explains the trauma of confronting Julia Mortimer in her opposition to the marriage: "He drew her near, stroking her forehead, pushing her dampening hair behind her ears.... He went on stroking her.... Gloria's tears ran down the face he was kissing" (168). And they reaffirm their vows to each other: "I ain't ever going to laugh at you, and you ain't ever going to feel sorry for me. We're safe." They agree that "being married" means "we're a family" (171).

Emotions run high, but the "deep bed" of pine holds them gently. Jack "held her in his arms and rocked her, baby and all, while she spent her tears. When the baby began to roll out of her failing arm, he caught her and tucked her into the pillow of the school satchel. Then he picked up Gloria and carried her the remaining few steps to that waiting bed of pinestraw" (171). Gloria returns from this brief, second honeymoon looking "like all the brides that ever were," and Jack confirms that she is still looking "just like a bride" (361) (even after the watermelon fight). In the ensuing discussion of Miss Julia's accusations of incest, Gloria reveals that her worst fears are all symbolized in three words: "null and void" (321). What she wants most is the marriage to Jack.

The moon, always a powerful romantic force in Welty's stories, intervenes "now at full power" (333) as Jack assuages Gloria's fears with his caring ways. The night-blooming cereus—that magical flower which lifts its blossoms triumphantly and nocturnally—joins the moon, too, as the natural world celebrates the reunion of the human lovers in a midsummer night's dream. This scene, typically depicting the lovers in their most intimate moments in the privacy of their bedroom, is complex in its illustration of the sacredness of the love communion and of the truths about the importance of privacy and sharing. Under the magical "white trumpets" of the night-blooming cereus, the moonstruck Gloria and Jack entreat one another in their third love scene of the day to protect the boundaries of their love and let no one intrude:

> She put her mouth quickly on his, and then she slid her hand and seized hold of him right at the root. And so she convinced him that there is only one way of depriving the ones you love—taking your living presence away from theirs; that no one alive has ever deserved such punishment ... and that no one alive can ever in honor forgive that wrong, which outshines shame, and is not to be forgiven until it has been righted. (362)

Like Shelley, the love observer in *Delta Wedding*, the young boy Vaughn in *Losing Battles*, still lying awake nearby, ponders the mysteries of love as he watches Jack and Gloria. He found them earlier in the day "lying deep in the woods together, like one creature" (363). The image of the lovers thus conjoined is reminiscent of that in Loch Morrison's mind in *The Golden Apples* as he gazes in half-innocence at the lovers in the abandoned house next door. Loch thinks they look "like a big grasshopper lighting, all their legs and arms drew in to one small body, deadlike, with protective coloring" (*CS*, 282). Vaughn may see the physical manifestation of love—two people joined as one creature—but he cannot comprehend the fuller meaning of love or the sexual and emotional ways of people "getting tangled up with each other." To this "moonlit little boy," who seems a young version of Jamie Lockhart, this mysterious phenomenon is a "danger"—and something for later and farther away. But Jack and Gloria have found the end of waiting. Love is in the here and now—not to be postponed an instant longer. As they drift to sleep by the light of the silvery moon, Jack and Gloria take their place among Welty's most joyful lovers, yet they have many battles ahead of them to be lost and won.

NOTES

1. Paul Binding, *The Still Moment Eudora Welty: The Portrait of a Writer* (London: Virago Press, 1994), p. 233.

2. Binding, *The Still Moment*, p. 229.

3. Joyce Carol Oates, "Eudora's Web," *Atlantic* 225 (1970): 118–19.

4. See Gail L. Mortimer, *Daughter of the Swan: Love and Knowledge in Eudora Welty's Fiction* (Athens & London: University of Georgia Press, 1994) for discussion.

5. Michael Kreyling, *Eudora Welty's Achievement of Order* (Baton Rouge & London: Louisiana State University Press, 1980), p. 35.

6. Kreyling, *Eudora Welty's Achievement*, p. 149.

7. John Edward Hardy, "Marrying Down in Eudora Welty's Novels," in *Eudora Welty: Critical Essays*, ed. Peggy W. Prenshaw, (Jackson: University Press of Mississippi, 1979), p. 105.

8. Louise Gossett, "Eudora Welty's New Novel: The Comedy of Loss," *Southern Literary Journal* 3 (Fall 1970): 128.

REYNOLDS PRICE[1]

The Onlooker, Smiling:
An Early Reading of The Optimist's Daughter

On March 15, this year *The New Yorker* published an issue half filled with a story by Eudora Welty called *The Optimist's Daughter*. The story is some 30,000 words long, 100 pages of a book—much the longest work published by Miss Welty in fourteen years, since her fourth collection of stories, *The Bride of the Innisfallen* in 1955. In those years, in fact, fewer than twenty pages of new fiction by her have appeared (two extraordinary pieces rising from the early civil rights movement, "Where Is the Voice Coming From?" and "The Demonstrators"). Now there is this novella—and, close behind it, news of a long comic novel, more stories, a collection of essays.

A *return*, in our eyes at least (Miss Welty could well ask "From where?"); and some eyes (those that haven't raced off after the genius-of-the-week) have got a little jittery with time. Returns in the arts are notorious for danger—almost always stiff-jointed, throaty, short-winded, rattled by nerves and ghosts of the pressures which caused the absence. There have been rare and triumphant exceptions—among performers in recent memory, Flagstad and Horowitz, grander than ever. But who among creators? American arts are uniquely famous for silent but audibly breathing remains—novelists, poets, playwrights, composers. The game of naming them is easy and cruel, and the diagnoses multiply. Yet why must I think back seventy years to Verdi's return with *Otello* thirteen years after

From *Critical Essays on Eudora Welty*. W. Craig Turner and Lee Emling Harding, eds. © 1989 by W. Craig Turner and Lee Emling Harding. Originally from *Shenandoah* 20 (Spring 1969): 58–73 © by Washington and Lee University.

Aïda and the *Requiem* for an ample precedent to Miss Welty's present achievement?

I have known the new story for less than a month and am straining backward to avoid the sort of instant apotheosis which afflicts the national book-press; but I don't feel suspended over any fool's precipice in saying this much—*The Optimist's Daughter* is Eudora Welty's strongest, richest work. For me, that is tantamount to saying that no one alive in America now has yet shown stronger, richer, more useful fiction. All through my three readings, I've thought of Turgenev, Tolstoy, Chekhov—*First Love*, *The Cossacks*, *The Steppe*—and not as masters or originals but as peers for breadth and depth.

—And an effortless power of *summary*, unity (of vision and means). For that is what I have felt most strongly in the story—that Miss Welty has now forged into one instrument strands (themes, stances, voices, genres) all present and mastered in various pieces of earlier work (many of them, invented there) but previously separate and rather rigidly compartmented. I'm thinking especially of "comedy" and "tragedy." In her early work—till 1955—she tended to separate them as firmly as a Greek dramatist. There is some tentative mingling in the larger works, *Delta Wedding* and the linked stories of *The Golden Apples*, but by far the greater number of the early stories divide cleanly—into rural comedy or farce, pathos or tragic lament, romance or lyric celebration, lethal satire. This is not to say that those stories over-select to the point of falsification (fear and hate lurk in much of the laughter, laughter in the pain); but that the selection of components-for-the-story which her eye quickly or slowly made and the subsequent intensity of scrutiny of those components (place, character, gesture, speech) exhibited a temporary single-mindedness as classical as Horace's, Vermeer's.

But now in *The Optimist's Daughter* all changes. If the early work is classic, this might be medieval—in its fullness of vision, depth of field, range of ear. Jesus *and* goblins, Macbeth *and* the porter. There is no sense however of straining for wholeness, of a will to "ripeness," no visible girding for a major attempt. The richness and new unity of the story—its quality of summary—is the natural image produced by *this action* as it passes before Miss Welty's (literal) vision—look at a room from the perfect point, you can see it all. She has found the point, the place to stand to see this story—and we discover at the end that she's seen far more than that. Or perhaps the point drew her—helpless, willing—towards it, her natural pole?

For it is in this story that she sustains most intensely or has the fullest results extracted from her by the stance and line-of-sight which, since her first story, have been native to her—that of the onlooker (and the onlooker's avatars—the wanderer, the outsider, the traveling salesman, the solitary artist, the bachelor or spinster, the childless bride). Robert Penn Warren in his essay "Love and Separateness in Eudora Welty" defined the stance and theme as it formed her early stories—

> We can observe that the nature of the isolation may be different from case to case, but the fact of isolation, whatever its nature, provides the basic situation of Miss Welty's fiction. The drama which develops from this basic situation is of either of two kinds: first, the attempt of the isolated person to escape into the world; or second, the discovery by the isolated person, or by the reader, of the nature of the predicament.

And a catalogue of her strongest early work and its characters is a list of onlookers, from R. J. Bowman in "Death of a Traveling Salesman" (her first story) and Tom Harris in "The Hitch-Hikers" (both lonely bachelors yearning for the richness which they think they glimpse in the lives of others—mutual love, willful vulnerability), to the young girl (a would-be painter) in "A Memory" and Audubon in "A Still Moment" (the artist who must hole-up from life, even kill it, to begin his effort at description and comprehension), to the frightening and hilarious spinsters of "Why I Live at the P.O." and *The Ponder Heart* or the more silent but equally excluded Virgie Rainey of *The Golden Apples*, to the recently orphaned Laura who visits her Fairchild cousins in *Delta Wedding* as they plunge and surface gladly in their bath of proximity, dependence, love.

You might say—thousands have—that the onlooker (as outsider) is the central character of modern fiction, certainly of Southern fiction for all its obsession with family, and that Miss Welty's early stories then are hardly news, her theme and vision hardly unique, hardly "necessary," just lovely over-stock. Dead-wrong, you'd be.

In the first place, her early onlookers are almost never freaks as they have so famously been in much Southern (and now Jewish) fiction and drama. (Flannery O'Connor, when questioned on the prevalence of freaks in Southern fiction, is reported to have said, "It's because Southerners know a freak when they see one.") They have mostly been "mainstream" men and women—in appearance, speech and action at least. Their visions and experiences have been far more nearly diurnal—experiences comprehensible at least to most men—than those of the characters of her two strong contemporaries, Carson McCullers and Flannery O'Connor, whose outsiders (often physical and psychic freaks) seem wrung, wrenched, from life by a famished special vision.

In the second place, the conclusions of Miss Welty's early onlookers, their deductions from looking—however individual and shaped by character, however muted in summary and statement—are unique. Their cry (with few exceptions, her salesman the most eloquent) is not the all but universal "O, lost! Make me a *member*" but something like this—"I am here alone, they are there together; I see them clearly. I do not know why and I am not happy but I do see, and clearly. I may even understand—why I'm here, they there. Do I need or want to join them?" Such a response—and it is, in Miss Welty, always a response to vision, literal eyesight; she has the keenest eyesight in American letters—is as strange as it is unique. Are we—onlookers to the onlookers—moved to sympathy, acceptance, consolation? Are we chilled or appalled and, if so, do we retreat into the common position?—"These people and their views are maimed, self-serving, alone because they deserve to be. Why don't they have the grace to writhe?" For our peace of mind (the satisfied reader's), there is disturbingly little writhing, only an occasional moment of solemn panic—

> "She's goin' to have a baby," said Sonny, popping a bite into his mouth.
>
> Bowman could not speak. He was shocked with knowing what was really in this house. A marriage, a fruitful marriage. That simple thing. Anyone could have had that.
>
> Somehow he felt unable to be indignant or protest, although some sort of joke had certainly been played upon him. There was nothing remote or mysterious here—only something private. The only secret was the ancient communication between two people. But the memory of the woman's waiting silently by the cold hearth, of the man's stubborn journey a mile away to get fire, and how they finally brought out their food and drink and filled the room proudly with all they had to show, was suddenly too clear and too enormous within him for response....

Or a thrust through the screen, like Lorenzo Dow's in "A Still Moment"—

> He could understand God's giving Separateness first and then giving Love to follow and heal in its wonder; but God had reversed this, and given Love first and then Separateness, as though it did not matter to Him which came first. Perhaps it was that God never counted the moments of Time ... did He even know of it? How to explain Time and Separateness back to God,

Who had never thought of them, Who could let the whole world
come to grief in a scattering moment?

But such moments are always followed by calm—Bowman's muffled death or
Dow's ride onward, beneath the new moon.

Yet in those early stories the last note is almost invariably rising, a
question; the final look in the onlooker's eyes is of puzzlement—"Anyone
could have had that. Should I have tried?" Not in *The Optimist's Daughter*
however. The end clarifies. Mystery dissolves before patient watching—the
unbroken stare of Laurel McKelva Hand, the woman at its center. The story
is told in third person, but it is essentially seen and told by Laurel herself. At
the end, we have not watched a scene or heard a word more than Laurel;
there is not even a comment on Laurel which she, in her native modesty,
could not have made aloud. That kind of secret first-person technique is at
least as old as Julius Caesar and has had heavy work in modern fiction, where
it has so often pretended to serve Caesar's own apparent aim (judicial
modesty, "distancing") while in fact becoming chiefly a bulletproof shield for
tender egos, an excuse for not confronting personal failure (Joyce's *Portrait* is
the grand example), a technical act of mercy. But Laurel Hand is finally
merciless—to her dead parents, friends, enemies, herself; worst, to us.

This is what I understand to be the story—the action and Laurel's
vision of the action.

Laurel Hand has come on sudden notice (and intuition of crisis) from
Chicago, where she works as a fabric designer, to a New Orleans clinic where
her father Judge McKelva, age 71, is being examined for eye trouble. (The
central metaphor begins at once—vision, the forms of blindness; the story is
as troubled by eyes as *King Lear*, and our first exposure to Laurel's sensibility
suggests youth and quivering attentiveness.) In a clinic she has time to notice
this—

> ... Dr. Courtland folded his big country hands with the fingers
> that had always looked, to Laurel, as if their simple touch on the
> crystal of a watch would convey through their skin exactly what
> time it was.

Laurel's father is accompanied by his new wife Fay; and at the diagnosis of
detached retina, Fay's colors unfurl—hard, vulgar, self-absorbed, envious of
Laurel and, in Laurel's eyes, beneath the McKelvas and Laurel's dead
mother. The doctor advises immediate surgery, over Fay's protests that
nothing is wrong. The Judge declares himself "an optimist," agrees to eye-
repair; the surgery goes well, and Laurel and Fay take a room in New

Orleans to spell one another at the Judge's bedside—their important duty, to keep him still, absolutely motionless with both eyes bandaged through days of recovery. Friction grows between the two women but with no real discharge. Fay shows herself a kind of pet, baby-doll—her idea of nursing consisting of descriptions of her new shoes or earrings, her petulance at missing Mardi Gras whose time approaches loudly through the city. Laurel watches quietly, reading Dickens to her father, oppressed by his age and docility—

> He opened his mouth and swallowed what she offered him with
> the obedience of an old man—obedience! She felt ashamed to let
> him act out the part in front of her.

Three weeks pass, the doctor claims encouragement, but the Judge's deepening silence and submission begin to unnerve Fay and to baffle Laurel. (It is only now—nearly fifteen pages in—that we learn Laurel's age. She is older than Fay and perhaps Fay is forty. We are, I think, surprised. We had felt her to be younger—I'd have said twenty-four and only now do I notice that she bears a married name; yet no husband has been mentioned and will not be till just before the midpoint of the story. There is no air of caprice or trick about these crucial withholdings, only quiet announcement—"Now's the time for this.") Then on the last night of Carnival, Laurel in her rooming house senses trouble and returns to the hospital by cab through packed, raucous streets. (Inevitably, a great deal of heavy holy weather will be made over Miss Welty's choice of Carnival season for this opening section and the eve of Ash Wednesday for the first climax. So far as I can see, she herself makes almost nothing of it—the revelry is barely mentioned and then only as a ludicrously inappropriate backdrop to death. Even less is made of the city itself, almost no appeal to its famous atmosphere—it is simply the place where a man from the deep South finds the best doctors.) At the hospital, Laurel finds her foreknowledge confirmed. Fay's patience has collapsed. She shakes the silent Judge, shouts "Enough is enough"; and Laurel enters to watch her father die—

> He made what seemed to her a response at last, yet a mysterious
> response. His whole pillowless head went dusky, as if he laid it
> under the surface of dark pouring water and held it there.

While Laurel and Fay await the doctor's confirmation in the hospital lobby, they watch and listen to a Mississippi country family come to oversee their own father's death—the Dalzells, family of the Judge's deranged roommate.

(Their sizable appearance is not, as might first seem, a chance for Miss Welty to ease tension and pass necessary clock-time with one of her miraculously observed country groups. Funny and touching as they are—

> "If they don't give your dad no water by next time round, tell you what, we'll go in there all together and pour it down him," promised the old mother. "If he's going to die, I don't want him to die wanting water"—

the Dalzells make a serious contribution towards developing a major concern of the story. They are, for all their coarse jostling proximity, a *family* of finer feeling and natural grace than whatever is constituted here by Fay and Laurel; and they will soon return to mind, in sweet comparison with Fay's Texas kin who swarm for the funeral.) At final news of the Judge's death, Fay lunges again into hateful hysterics; but Laurel tightens—no tears, few words. Only in the ride through revellers toward the hotel does Laurel begin to see, with a new and steelier vision, meanings hung round people, which, she does not yet speak—

> Laurel heard a band playing, and another band moving in on top of it. She heard the crowd noise, the unmistakable sound of hundreds, of hundreds of thousands, of people *blundering*.

Part II opens with the train ride home to Mount Salus, Mississippi. (Laurel's view from the train of a single swamp beechtree still keeping dead leaves begins to prepare us for her coming strangeness, her as yet unexpected accessibility to ghosts.) Mount Salus is a small lowland town and is now home only to the dead Judge—Fay will inherit Laurel's childhood home but is Texan forever; Laurel will return to Chicago soon. But two groups of her friends survive in the town—her dead parents' contemporaries and her own schoolmates—and they rally to her, ambivalent hurtful allies, as Fay's kin—the Chisoms—arrive for the funeral. Led by Fay's mother, they cram the Judge's house like a troupe of dwarfs from a Goya etching, scraping rawly together in a dense loveless, shamingly vital, hilarious parody of blood-love and loyalty—"Nothing like kin. Yes, me and my brood believes in clustering just as close as we can get." It is they—Fay's mother—who at last extract from Laurel what we have not yet known, that Laurel is a widow—

> "Six weeks after she married him ... The war. Body never recovered."

"*You* was *cheated*," Mrs. Chisom pronounced ... "So you ain't got father, mother, brother, sister, husband, chick nor child." Mrs. Chisom dropped Laurel's finger to poke her in the side as if to shame her. "Not a soul to call on, that's you."

So the Chisoms stand at once—or pullulate—in Laurel's sight, as a vision of the family and of love itself as horror, hurtful, willfully vulnerable, parasitic. Yet one of them—Wendell, age seven, viewing the corpse—also provides her with a still point for temporary sanity, for "understanding" Fay and her father's love for Fay—

> He was like a young, undriven, unfalsifying, unvindictive Fay. His face was transparent—he was beautiful. So Fay might have appeared to her aging father, with his slipping eyesight.

That emergency perception and the cushioning care of friends prop Laurel through Fay's last hysterical kiss of the corpse and on through the burial.— Propped but stunned, and open on all sides—especially the eyes—for gathering menace to her saving distance. Above the graveyard, she sees a flight of starlings—

> ... black wings moved and thudded in perfect unison, and a flock of migrant starlings flew up as they might have from a plowed field, still shaped like the grounds of the cemetery, like its map, and wrinkled in the air.

And afterwards, at the house again, she numbly accepts more insults from Fay and waits out the slow departure of the Chisoms—taking Fay with them for a rest in Texas.

Part III is the longest of the four parts, both the story's journey through the underworld and the messenger of what the story learns there. It has four clear divisions. In the first, Laurel entertains four elderly ladies, friends of her parents, who raise a question so far unasked (among the signs of mastery in the story, one of the surest is the patience, the undefended gravity with which Miss Welty answers—or asks—all the reader's questions in her own time not his, and finally makes him admit her justice). The question is, why did Judge McKelva marry Fay?—"What happened to his judgment?" One of the ladies flatly states that Laurel's to blame; she should never have married but stayed home and tended her widowed father. Laurel makes no defense, barely speaks at all till the same lady weakens and begins "forgiving" Fay—

> "Although I guess when people don't *have* anything ... Live so *poorly*—"
> "That hasn't a thing to do with it," Laurel said ...

This new ruthlessness (a specific defeat of her own attempt to forgive Fay through the child Wendell) calms in the following scene—Laurel alone in her father's library. Here, because of a photograph, she thinks for the only time in our presence of her own marriage—"Her marriage had been of magical ease, of *ease*—of brevity and conclusion, and all belonging to Chicago and not here." But in the third scene—Laurel's contemporaries, her bridesmaids, at drinks—she bristles again, this time to defend her parents against affectionate joking—"Since when have you all thought my father and mother were just figures to make a good story?" Her friends retreat, claim "We weren't laughing at them. They weren't funny." (Laurel accepts the clarification; only at the end, if faced again with "They weren't funny" might she offer correction, huge amplification.) The fourth scene is longest, strangest, the crisis—from which Laurel, the story, all Miss Welty's earlier onlookers and surely most readers emerge shaken, cleared, altered. On her last night in Mount Salus before returning to Chicago and before Fay's return, Laurel comes home from dinner with friends to find a bird flying loose indoors, a chimney swift. She is seized at once by an old fear of birds (we are not reminded till the following morning that a bird in the house means bad luck ahead), and in panic shuts herself into her parents' bedroom—now Fay's—against its flight. Here, alone and silent except for sounds of wind and rain, among her parents' relics, she endures her vision— of their life, hers, the world's. Her initial step is to calm herself, to examine the sources of her recent angers, her present terror—

> What am I in danger of, she wondered, her heart pounding. Am I not safe from *myself*?
> Even if you have kept silent for the sake of the dead, you cannot rest in your silence, as the dead rest. She listened to the wind, the rain, the blundering, frantic bird, and wanted to cry out, as the nurse cried out to her, "Abuse! Abuse!"

What she first defines as the "facts" are these—that her helpless father had been assailed and killed by his own senseless, self-absorbed young wife and that she—his only child—was powerless to save him but can now at least protect his memory. Protect—and flush her own bitterness—by exacting justice from Fay, extracting from Fay an admission of her guilt. Yet Laurel knows at once that Fay, challenged, would only be baffled, sealed in genuine blind innocence. Balked in advance then by invincible ignorance, is Laurel to be paralyzed in permanent bitterness? She can be, she thinks, released and consoled by at last telling someone—the facts, the names. But tell whom? Her own mother, long since dead. To tell her mother though—should that ever be possible—would be an abuse more terrible than Fay's. Laurel can only go on telling herself and thereby through her perpetual judging become a new culprit, another more knowing Fay. That is—and can go on being—"the horror." At that moment, desperate with rage and forced silence, she makes the only physical movement open (the bird still has her trapped in the room). She retreats into an adjoining small room. It had been her own nursery, where she'd slept near her parents; then the sewing room; now a closet where Fay has hidden Laurel's mother's desk. Here, memory begins—a long monologue (yet always in third person) which bears Laurel back through her parents' lives, her life with them. (The structure and method of these fifteen pages at first seem loose, old-fashioned. No attempt is made through syntax or ellipsis to mimic the voice or speed of Laurel's mind, to convince us that we literally overhear her thoughts. Yet the process of memory proceeds with such ferocious emotional logic to an end so far beyond Laurel's imagined needs or desires—Laurel's and ours—that we are at last convinced, as shaken as she.) The memories begin warmly—here are things they touched, relics of their love, a family desk, a small stone boat carved with her father's initials, his letters to her mother (which Laurel will not read, even now), a photograph of them in full unthreatened youth. In the flood of affection, Laurel begins to move from her old stance of onlooker to a conviction of having shared her parents' lives, been a corner of their love. She continues backward through memories of summers in the West Virginia mountains with her mother's family. (Both her parents' families were originally Virginian; and it would be possible—therefore someone will do it—to construct a kind of snob-machine with these genealogies: Virginians are finer than Mississippians are finer than Texans. The story says no such thing; only "This is what happened"—Miss Welty's own mother was from West Virginia, her father from Ohio.) Those summers, recalled, seem made of two strands—her mother's laughing immersion in family love and her own childish bafflement: tell me how much and why they love you, your mother and brothers. This early bafflement is focused for Laurel in her first sight of her grandmother's pigeons. Without claiming a mechanical connection which Miss Welty clearly does not intend, it is worth noting that this sight is the beginning (so far as we know) of Laurel's present personal distance, her stunned passivity in the face of the Chisoms feeding on one another—

> ... Laurel had kept the pigeons under eye in their pigeon house and had already seen a pair of them sticking their beaks down each other's throats, gagging each other, eating out of each other's craws, swallowing down all over again what had been swallowed before: They were taking turns ... They convinced her that they could not escape each other and could not be escaped from. So when the pigeons flew down, she tried to position herself behind her grandmother's stiff dark skirt, but her grandmother said again, "They're just hungry, like we are."

It was a knowledge and revulsion which her mother had seemed to lack— until her long final illness at least. The terms of that illness are not fully explained—Laurel's mother went blind, lay in bed for years, growing slowly more reckless and condemnatory, more keen-sighted in her observation of husband and daughter as they hovered beside her helpless. As the illness had extended through five years (just after Laurel's widowhood) and as Laurel now recalls it, her mother had at last endured the awful knowledge in its simple killing progression—that we feed on others till they fail us, through their understandable inability to spare us pain and death but, worse, through the exhaustion of loyalty, courage, memory. In the pit of her illness, Laurel's mother had said to the Judge standing by her—

> "Why did I marry a coward?" ... Later still, she began to say—and her voice never weakened, never harshened; it was her spirit speaking in the wrong words—"All you do is hurt me. I wish I might know what it is I've done. Why is it necessary to punish me like this and not tell me why?"

Then she had sunk silent toward her death, with only one last message to Laurel—"You could have saved your mother's life. But you stood by and wouldn't intervene. I despair for you." In the teeth of such judgment, Laurel's father—the optimist—had married Fay; had chosen to submit again to need, and been killed for his weakness. What had been betrayed—what her mother like a drugged prophetess had seen and condemned before the event—was not his first love but his first wife's *knowledge*, the dignity and achievement of her unanswerable vision. Fay's the answer to nothing. Then can love be?—Answer to what? Death and your own final lack of attention

doom you to disloyalty. You're killed for your cowardice. With that news, the
scene ends. Laurel sleeps.

> A flood of feeling descended on Laurel. She let the papers slide
> from her hand and put her head down on the open lid of the desk
> and wept in grief for love and for the dead.

—Grief surely *that* love had not saved but harrowed her parents, a love she
had not shared and now can never.

Part IV is a quick hard but by no means perfunctory coda. Laurel wakes
in early light, having slept at her mother's desk. Now unafraid, she leaves her
parents' room, sees the exhausted bird perched on a curtain. Mr. Deedy, the
blundering handyman, calls by to peddle spring chores. Laurel asks him in to
catch the bird. He declares it bad luck and scares it around from room to
room but only succeeds in making a nosey tour of the house. Then Missouri,
the maid, arrives and she and Laurel gingerly arrange the bird's escape in the
only passage of the story where the touch seems to me to press a little heavily,
uneasily—

> "It's a perfectly clear way out. Why won't it just fly free of its own
> accord?"
> "They just ain't got no sense like we have ... All birds got to fly,
> even them no-count dirty ones...."

Laurel burns her mother's papers, saving only the snapshots and the carved
stone boat. She calls herself a thief—the house and contents are Fay's now—
but she justifies herself—

> It was one of her ways to live—storing up to remember, putting
> aside to forget, then to find again—hiding and finding. Laurel
> thought it a modest game that people could play by themselves,
> and, of course, when that's too easy, against themselves. It was a
> game for the bereaved, and there wasn't much end to it.

Her calm seems complete, her departure foregone and unprotested; but in a
final look through kitchen cupboards, she finds her mother's breadboard—its
worn polished surface inexplicably gouged, scored and grimy. Her numb
peace vanishes, her rejection of revenge. She knows that, in some way, this is
Fay's work, Fay's ultimate murder of Laurel's mother, the house itself, that
she has "conspired with silence" and must finally shout both "Abuse!" and
"Love!" And indeed Fay arrives at this moment, her return from Texas timed

for Laurel's departure (the bridesmaids by now are waiting at the curb to drive Laurel to Jackson). Laurel challenges Fay with the ruined breadboard—

> "It's just an old board, isn't it?" cried Fay.
> "She made the best bread in Mount Salus!"
> "All right! Who cares? She's not making it now."
> "Oh, my mother could see exactly what you were going to do!"

Laurel has judged at last, in rage, and in rage has discovered the order of experience, the mysterious justice of time and understanding, her mother's final accurate desperation—

> Her mother had suffered every symptom of having been betrayed, and it was not until she had died, had been dead long enough to lie in danger of being forgotten and the protests of memory came due, that Fay had ever tripped in. It was not until then, perhaps, that her father himself had ever dreamed of a Fay. For Fay was Becky's own dread ... Suppose every time her father went on a business trip ... there had been a Fay.

So memory itself is no longer safe, no "game for the bereaved." The past is never safe because it is never past, not while a single mind remembers. Laurel requires revenge. She accuses Fay of desecrating the house, but in vain—as she'd known the night before, Fay does not understand and will not ever, least of all from Laurel (she had used the board for cracking nuts). Fay can only resort to calling Laurel "crazy," to hurtful revelation, an anecdote of Laurel's mother's last wildness—throwing a bedside bell at a visitor. Laurel raises the breadboard to threaten Fay. Fay has the courage of her ignorance, stands and scornfully reminds Laurel that her friends are waiting outside— "You're supposed to be leaving." Then Fay goes on to claim she'd intended reconciliation, had returned in time for that—"... we all need to make some allowance for the cranks ..." Laurel abandons the weapon, one more piece of Fay's inheritance, and hurries to leave, escorted away by her own bridesmaids.

I have summarized at such length because it's my experience, both as reviewed writer and teacher, that even a trained reader (especially trained readers) cannot be relied on to follow the action, the linked narrative, of any long story, especially of a story whose action is interior. (Ask ten trained readers what happens in *Heart of Darkness*—not what are the symbols or controlling metaphors but, simply, who does what to whom and why? Who knows what at the end? *Then* you'll see some darkness.) Also because to summarize *The Optimist's Daughter* is to demonstrate how perfectly the meaning inheres in the form and radiates from it. Nothing is applied from outside or wrenched; the natural speed of the radiation—action into meaning—is never accelerated (with the possible exception of the trapped bird's escape); and no voice cries "Help!" at its lethal rays—lethal to illusion, temporary need.

But the length of a summary has left me little space to discuss important details—to mention only two: first, the language (which in its stripped iron efficiency, its avoidance of simile and metaphor, bears almost no resemblance to the slow dissolving impressionism, relativism, of the stories in *The Bride of the Innisfallen*; that was a language for describing what things are *not*, for intensifying mystery; this is a language for stating facts) and, second, the story's apparent lack of concern with Mississippi's major news at the time of the story—the civil rights revolution. Its apparent absence is as complete as that of the Napoleonic wars from Jane Austen. And for the same reason, surely—it is not what this story is about. When Judge McKelva's old law partner says of him at the funeral, "Fairest, most impartial, sweetest man in the whole Mississippi Bar," no irony seems intended nor can honestly be extracted. (I've stressed *apparent* absence because any story which so ruthlessly examines blindness is "about" all the forms of blindness; and if any reader is unprepared to accept the fact that in all societies at all times good and evil coexist in all men and can, under certain conditions of immense complexity, be compartmentalized, quarantined from one another within the same heart, then this story's not for him. So much the worse for him—neither will most art be.)

What I cannot skimp is my prior suggestion that the puzzlement or contented suspension of onlookers in Miss Welty's earlier fiction vanishes in *The Optimist's Daughter*, that the end clarifies. The stance of the onlooker—forced on him and/or chosen—is confirmed as the human stance which can hope for understanding, simple survival. The aims of participation are union, consolation, continuance—doomed. Laurel (who might well be the adult of the girl in "A Memory" or even of Laura in *Delta Wedding*) might so easily have left us with a last word fierce as her mother's. She might have said, "Show me a victor, an *actor* even." Or worse, she might have laughed.

For there is at the end, each time I've reached it, a complicated sense of joy. Simple exhilaration in the courage and skill of the artist, quite separate from the tragic burden of the action. Joy that a piece of credible life has been displayed to us fully and, in the act, fully explained (I take Laurel's understanding to be also the author's and ours; there can be no second meaning, no resort to attempts to discredit Laurel's vision). And then perhaps most troubling and most appeasing, the sense that Laurel's final emotion is joy, that she is now an "optimist" of a sort her father never knew (if not as she drives away from her home, then tomorrow, back at work)—that the onlooker's gifts, the crank's, have proved at last the strongest of human endowments (vision, distance, stamina—the courage of all three); that had there been any ear to listen, Laurel would almost surely have laughed, abandoning her weapon (as Milton's God laughs at the ignorance and ruin of Satan, only God has hearers—the Son and His angels). For Laurel has been both victim and judge—who goes beyond both into pure creation (only she has discovered the pattern of their lives—her parents', Fay's, the Chisoms', her friends', her own) and then comprehension, which is always comic. All patterns are comic—snow crystal or galaxy in Andromeda or family history—because the universe is patterned, therefore ordered and ruled, therefore incapable of ultimate tragedy (interim tragedy is comprised in the order but cannot be the end; and if it should be—universal pain—then that too is comic, by definition, to its only onlooker). God's vision is comic, Alpha and Omega.

NOTE

1. From *Shenandoah* 20 (Spring 1969): 58–73. Copyright 1969 by Washington and Lee University. Reprinted with permission of the editor. An updated version of this review appears in Price's *Things Themselves: Essays and Scenes* (N.Y.: Atheneum, 1972), 114–38.

FRANZISKA GYGAX

The Optimist's Daughter:
A Woman's Memory

MEMORY AND TIME

In her novel following *Losing Battles* Eudora Welty returns to the narrative mode of conveying mainly interior events through her characters. In her most recent autobiographical book, *One Writer's Beginnings*,[1] she describes this "inward journey that leads us through time":

> As we discover, we remember; remembering, we discover; and most intensely do we experience this when our separate journeys converge. Our living experience at those meeting points is one of the charged dramatic fields of fiction. (*OWB*, p. 102)

This statement leads Welty to a passage from *The Optimist's Daughter* in which the protagonist Laurel Hand *remembers* the moment when she and her husband saw the confluence of the Ohio and Mississippi rivers. Confluence "exists as a reality and a symbol in one" (*OWB*, p. 102); it connotes all our inward journeys coming together, and, as Welty concludes her autobiographical work, "the greatest confluence of all is that which makes up the human memory—the individual human memory" (*OWB*, p. 104). In our memory our experiences—normally submitted to a sequential order—can be grasped at one and the same moment. Through

From *Serious Daring From Within: Female Narrative Strategies in Eudora Welty's Novels.* © 1990 by Franziska Gygax.

remembering we realize our being alive, and since we can only remember something that has passed already, time is the most essential element linked with memory. Talking about time in fiction, Welty refers to Faulkner's famous statement that "[m]emory believes before knowing remembers,"[2] and she also insists on the inevitable need of remembering one's past: "Remembering is done through the blood, it is a bequeathment.... It is also a life's work."[3] It is only logical that Welty also mentions Faulkner's *The Sound and the Fury*, in which time is different for the three first-person narrators and their respective stories; thus, Faulkner presents "three different worlds of memory."[4]

In Nabokov's novel *Ada, or Ardor: A Family Chronicle* the memoirist of the book defines time and memory as interrelated: "Time is but memory in the making."[5] Everything that is already belongs to the past when we remember it, and it is always experienced differently according to the person who remembers. In *The Optimist's Daughter* the reader is confronted with the world of a middle-aged woman's memory. As the title explicitly says, she is also a daughter, and I suggest that she has reminiscences specifically linked with a female world. Considering the fact that time is traditionally related to paternal thinking in terms of the "genealogical imperative,"[6] the woman's memories might express a specific relationship to Father Time. The concept of linear time follows the patriarchal pattern in Western culture, which consists of "the prestige of the father over the son."[7] Thus, the line of time is conceived of as something that is directed towards an aim and also reflects an authority (father–son).[8]

In *Time and the Novel*, Patricia Tobin describes how the twentieth-century novel in particular tries to subvert the linear dominance by disrupting the chronology of time and to get rid of the "genealogical imperative." Among her examples is Gabriel Garcia Marquez's *One Hundred Years of Solitude*, which is characterized by a return "to myth, to nature, to magic, to the mother."[9] With the disappearance of the father (the murder of the father) the patrilinear narrative is no longer given.

I shall not set out to determine whether Welty's *The Optimist's Daughter* has a specific function in this tendency to displace the father, but I shall concentrate on the aspects of time and memory in a woman writer's creation of a female character. Julia Kristeva quotes James Joyce's "Father's time, mother's species" to emphasize that *woman* is more frequently linked with "the space generating and forming the human species" than with time. But she points out that the history of civilization shows "two types of temporality (cyclical and monumental) ... traditionally linked to female subjectivity.[10] In *The Optimist's Daughter* the female protagonist is the one who remembers and who relates to time more than any of the other characters. It is therefore pertinent to raise the question whether time is transformed into a female sphere and if so, how this transformation manifests itself.

Like time, memory, too, can have a specific function for *woman*. Mary Daly mentions memory as a device for women to tell the truth about their lives.[11] She refers to Virginia Woolf, who, as a writer, was very consciously aware of the power of memory:

> She was/is a Muse, singing other women into conscious Memory, a Soothsayer whose creative pursuit of the past overcame impotence and paralysis, actualizing potency. Intuitively she knew that the passive potency to hear/see/receive knowledge of the Background is interconnected with active potency to Name, for "it is only by putting it into words that I make it [reality] whole."[12]

Woolf's insistence on the existential importance of memory draws our attention to Welty's statement that remembering is essential for staying alive. For both writers the process of writing "actualizes Memory in an especially potent way."[13] It is probably not coincidental that Virginia Woolf is a "precursor" for Welty with respect to memory; as Welty herself states, Woolf "was the one who opened the door."[14] Indeed, reading Welty's works one is often reminded of Woolf's psychological presentation of characters.[15] One of the themes of *The Optimist's Daughter* also appears in Woolf's *To the Lighthouse*. Michael Kreyling, dedicating a whole chapter to a comparison of these two novels, especially emphasizes the "idea of distance, whether the distance is created by the passing of time or by the gulf between the self and the public role, self and society, self and loved one, and self and the truth."[16]

While I mention Virginia Woolf in connection with memory, I must also refer to the importance of the mother–daughter relationship, which plays a crucial role in Welty's novel. It is again in *To the Lighthouse* that Woolf explores aspects of this essential female realm. Both Welty's and Woolf's novels are examples of a women writers' tradition: "the excavation of buried plots in women's texts has revealed an enduring, if recessive, narrative concern with the story of mothers and daughters."[17] Therefore I shall especially focus on this mother–daughter narrative and compare it to the description of the father–daughter relationship. As the title indicates, the book is also about a father, the optimist, and his daughter. Although "optimist," in English, could also refer to a woman, the reference to the father becomes clear after a few pages of reading. Yet, as the following chapters will elucidate, the "buried plot" of the mother–daughter story could suggest a different title of the book since it lies at the core of the book.

LAUREL HAND: THE DAUGHTER OF AN OPTIMIST

Laurel McKelva Hand's father, Judge McKelva, has eye trouble, and therefore undergoes an examination in New Orleans where his daughter meets him. He tells his doctor friend that there is "something wrong with [his] *eyes*."[18] This very first dialogue of the book expresses an anxiety about not seeing well. This deficiency of sight already indicates a problem in perceiving one's surroundings. It does not concern Judge McKelva exclusively, but he is the most obvious example of a blind man, both literally and figuratively. His second marriage to Fay, a woman who does not show much understanding of his sufferings and who has an entirely different social background, seems to be an escape from his loneliness after the death of his first wife, Becky.

Not only is McKelva's eyesight waning, his "*memory* had slipped" (p. 5) too, as he himself states, when he did not remember that one should not prune a climber before it blooms. He noticed his eye trouble for the first time after pruning roses and therefore assumed that he hurt himself. Yet, the eye specialist assures him that "what happened didn't happen to the outside of his eye, it happened to the inside" (p. 7). This reference to a damaged retina enhances the suggestion of his not having the right vision of things. The retina, sensitive to light, is described as having "slipped" (p. 7),[19] and as a consequence McKelva believes that he sees behind him (cf. p. 5). This impression of seeing behind him is exclusively symbolic because, from a physiological point of view, such an incident is impossible. The bird reflectors McKelva mentions might have evoked an afterimage. His vision is not only impaired with respect to focusing, but also with respect to getting to the kernel of things, that is, the outward as well as the inward look remains dimmed. After McKelva has undergone eye surgery he is forced to lie totally still. Before the operation he has declared that he is an optimist in reply to the doctor's warning that the operation would not be "a hundred per cent predictable" (p. 10). Yet, during the time of convalescence he develops a less optimistic attitude towards his illness. Laurel, sitting at his bedside, is the observer and indirect recorder of his state of mind: immobile, he no longer shows the curiosity typical of his character and hardly speaks to her or to his wife. Laurel realizes that "what occupied his full mind was time itself; time passing: he was concentrating" (p. 19). McKelva's concern for time is also expressed in his first question in the morning about the exact time. In *Delta Wedding* it is also Laura's father who always wants to know what time it is (cf.

DW, p. 231). It is indeed "Father's time" that characterizes McKelva's relationship to his surroundings, including his daughter. Laurel is susceptible to her father's preoccupations with time and even sets "her inner chronology with his, more or less as if they needed to keep in step for a long walk ahead of them" (pp. 19–20). She seems to accept her father's pace, recognizing that she cannot influence or alter his concept of time. This insight is crucial, because her father during the long time of her mother's illness always tried to make his wife believe that she might get well soon, thus not accepting the different pace of the dying woman. This information is only given towards the end of the book, when Laurel relives the time of her mother's dying. Laurel's behavior at her father's deathbed must be conceived in relation to her memories of her mother's illness and her father's attitude at his wife's deathbed.

Laurel's mother also suffered from an eye illness, indicated only in some vague and rather mysterious references such as "it's like Mother's" or "the eye was just a part of it" (p. 9). The beginning of her eye trouble was a "little cataract" (p. 145), which was operated on, but Becky's eyesight deteriorated all the same, and she eventually lost it completely. Retrospectively, Laurel realizes how her father could not meet Becky's expectations: he could not accept his wife's illness and therefore "he apparently needed guidance in order to see the tragic" (p. 145). The comfort and hope he bestowed upon his wife contrasted with the actual state of Becky's mental and physical condition. When she desired to be brought back to her beloved mountains in West Virginia, he immediately promised to take her there. Laurel describes his offer as "the first worthless promise that had ever lain between them" (p. 149). Becky, realizing that her husband could not face the fact of her mortality, called him a coward and liar, and we are told that this accusation made him become an optimist (cf. p. 150). Thus, his optimism derives from an inability to accept his wife's approaching death. The narrator does not hesitate to tell us the sheer truth about the relationship between this couple: "It was betrayal on betrayal" (p. 150) because McKelva caused Becky's desperation by not acknowledging her desperation.

Becky died without speaking a word, lonely and "keeping everything to herself, in exile and humiliation" (p. 151); in this respect her husband follows her mode of resignation because he, too, stops communicating. Laurel is aware of his concentration and she even tries to help him to go along with "time." She comforts him once by assuring him that he will soon be able to wear his spectacles, but she immediately recognizes the potential insincerity of her statement.[20] Thus, Laurel is aware of her father's actual condition and does not deceive him by false promises.

The recollection of her mother's deathbed only occurs after her father's death, that is, the memories are not narrated at the time of her father's dying or immediately after his death. Only after the funeral can Laurel explore the true nature of her memories regarding her parents, and at a moment of epiphany, a recognition of the ambivalent character of her parents' relationship, she is capable of facing her mother's ordeal retrospectively.

Laurel's reminiscing is significantly triggered by the book titles she peruses when she enters her father's library. The library is—and always was—his domain. The room is described from Laurel's point of view by a third-person narrator with access to Laurel's memories. The perspective of the daughter in her father's library focuses on the portraits of her father's father and grandfather, her father's great-grandfather's desk, with the papers he had kept when he was mayor of Mount Salus, and with numerous files and folders. All these items strongly reflect a male spirit. The traditionally male realm is enforced by references to law-books or even a telescope (we recall Loch's viewing through the telescope, which I identified as typically male in contrast to Cassie's more encompassing "view"). This male atmosphere sharply contrasts with the description of "the woman's room" of Laurel's mother, with which the reader is confronted when Laurel enters her mother's sewing room.

Laurel's memories about her father unveil other characteristics mostly pertinent to men who are intellectually absorbed by their exacting work: such men, although experts in their fields, often have a narrow view with regard to human relationships. Looking out of the window Laurel perceives her long-time neighbor, the town teacher Miss Adele Courtland, who, as Laurel now realizes, waves toward the window as she used to when she hoped to catch a glance from Judge McKelva looking out the window. Laurel is certain that her father never saw the woman who quietly loved him. The reference to impaired vision is again both literal and figurative; McKelva, trying his best to serve his town as a judge, does not even recognize his neighbor's feelings towards him. He only sees what fits into his daily pattern of correct procedure. We have observed the same incapacity to adjust his vision when Becky is mortally ill. Laurel's insight into her father's oblivion regarding his surroundings seems possible only now that she can reminisce with a critical stance. Her exact viewing of her father's room enables her to understand her father's past life more accurately, too.

Approaching the desk, Laurel at first hesitates, but then opens every drawer to look for the letters her mother had written to her husband when they were separated. Confronted with completely empty drawers, she realizes that her father had never kept any letters. He had been careful to erase all written traces of a past moment in correspondence, whereas her mother had kept all of her husband's letters. Laurel, with obvious disappointment, must accept that "there was nothing of her mother here for Fay to find, or for herself to retrieve" (p. 123). The distance between Laurel and her father, which already began to grow at the hospital, now seems to be a more delicate problem to surmount. Michael Kreyling states that "Laurel contends with the issues of distance in human relationships, with memory, and with faith in human life";[21] only the right connections may help to bring together, that is, to achieve a confluence of the single aspects of life. The catalyst of such a process is the right vision.[22] There is a compelling need to try and grasp the sense-making links of one's history, of one's past, present, and future. For Laurel, who used to idealize her parents and her dead husband, a new in*sight* is necessary. Now, confronted with her father's death, she begins a new phase of her life: after her parents' and her husband's deaths she seems to have torn the last thread with her idealized past. She is bound to rely entirely on her memory in order to relive past moments.

Exploring her father's library after his death is an attempt to relive some of her and her father's past through its material evidence. But instead of discovering some token of the past, Laurel must realize that there is indeed nothing left in the library except the books, which make her recall the voices of her parents reading them aloud. But these memories relate to both father and *mother*. Ironically enough, the only trace Laurel finds is Fay's nail polish, which she is eager to clean off her father's desk. Thus, Laurel leaves her father's room without having discovered any material traces. Not even her memory can bring back to her the relationship with her father. Having entered the library in order to find some sign of the past, Laurel must rub off a sign of the present. As at her father's deathbed, she cannot make the right connection. The visit to her mother's room, the sewing room, discloses more missing links with the past and to Laurel's history. Here, her memory unveils much more than with her father.

At the outset of this chapter I mentioned the traditional concept of Father Time, the patrilinear line in a narrative, and its possible replacement; in our novel, Laurel's relation to time can no longer be called paternal because her father, the person she tries to get back to while in his library, does not appear as the central figure in Laurel's memories. Memory, which makes past moments come back and singles them out according to their significance, seems to turn against the father, that is, the recollections of her father do not appear to be as important as one would expect after the outset of the novel. The symbolic impact of the empty drawers furthermore illustrates how limited Laurel's power of memory is with regard to her father. "The optimist's daughter" is bereft of her father once again after she has literally lost him at the hospital. Her memory does not equally participate in reviving her father as it does when Laurel explores her mother's story.

Welty's intensive narrative concern with a mother–daughter relationship pushes the father into the background. Although the title of the novel suggests an inspection of a father–daughter relationship, we must acknowledge that the issue of relationship is transferred to the mother. As in *Losing Battles*, in which the dead Julia Mortimer exerts an essential influence, Laurel's mother is vividly present in the book although she has already been dead for almost twelve years when the action of the novel begins. Laurel's mother is not only a "silently" influential protagonist like Julia Mortimer, she is also the mother of the actual protagonist, through whose memory she becomes tangible for the reader. Unlike her father, Laurel's mother is made alive again just because of the peculiarity of the mother–daughter relationship. Indeed, "the buried plot" of the mother–daughter relationship (cf. above) is unveiled just after the father has been buried. The power of his daughter's memory with respect to his life is restricted, whereas it evokes life when concerned with the mother. His daughter's memory has a limited power with respect to his life, whereas it is potent enough to be the motor of an extended narration of the mother's life.

LAUREL: A MOTHER'S DAUGHTER

In her notable and weighty essay on the development of women's identity and the specificity of the mother–daughter relationship, Jane Flax comes to the conclusion that a woman's difficulty in becoming autonomous and independent derives from the intricate relationship with her mother.[23] This relationship influences the development of a woman's core identity and renders it problematic because the girl cannot separate her own identity from her mother's. The necessary process of differentiation[24] is threatened. Jane Flax states the main reasons for the impediment to differentiation: in patriarchal society children are looked after by their mothers, while their fathers usually work and are tied to the public world. The girl,[25] identifying with the mother because of her sex, faces a dilemma if she wants to leave the familial world: should she stay with her mother who nurtures her and to whom she feels tied, or be autonomous like a man and leave her mother (often feeling guilty thereby)?

This fragmentary outline of a psychological problem with which daughters are confronted helps us to grasp some of the aspects of the mother–daughter relationship between Becky and Laurel. As I have mentioned above, this relationship is depicted retrospectively and always from the daughter's point of view. Thus, the effects of the daughter's unconscious experiences dating from the preoedipal period[26] are also inherent in this presentation. The memory shaping Laurel's thoughts and feelings about her mother is already characterized by a very strong tie to her mother just because of the traditional mother role Becky obviously had.

The long, crucial passage dealing with Laurel's relationship to her mother is significantly introduced by Laurel's entering her mother's sewing room. Her contact with her dead mother, which is presented in great detail to us by the narrator, takes place in a realm traditionally attributed to a woman's sphere. The room connecting her father's library with the sewing room is, as the narrator calls it, "her father's and mother's room" (p. 129). It not only connects the two realms of Laurel's parents, it is—on a narratological level—also the link between the passages dealing with the respective memories about her parents. This connecting room now belongs to Fay, towards whom Laurel bears ill feelings because of Fay's assault on her sick father. Laurel does not enter this room deliberately; a bird, being caught in the house, frightens her and makes her escape into it and shut the door. "'Bird in de house mean death'" (*DW*, p. 159), the family's black servant in *Delta Wedding* observes, a remark Troy repeats to his family. In *The Optimist's Daughter* a carpenter, who wants to help Laurel release the bird, calls it a "sign o' bad luck" (p. 164). Certainly, the trapped chimney swift is symbolically related to Laurel's dead parents, but it refers more specifically to Laurel's attitude to the past: like the bird, who cannot get out of the house,[27] Laurel cannot leave this room because she is too frightened of the bird. In other words, she cannot (yet) bear to face her memories, which are "vulnerable to the living moment" (p. 179). The process of Laurel's recognition and insight begins in this room, where she has locked herself in and where she dares to question her remorseful attitude towards Fay.

Laurel desperately feels the need to tell her dead mother about Fay's attempt to shake her husband the night of his death. Laurel's urge to tell her mother is emphasized by the repeating of "mother" (cf. p. 132). Yet, she soon realizes her morally despicable attitude. This desire nevertheless illustrates how intensely Laurel feels the need to confide in her mother in order to be comforted like a little girl. At this moment of great anxiety she hears the chimney swift bang against the door. Horrified, Laurel recoils and enters the sewing room, which opens out of her parents' room.

The sewing room not only represents a women's realm, it also serves as a refuge for Laurel. Significantly, this room is associated with "firelight and warmth—that was what her memory gave her" (p. 133). Indeed, Laurel's reminiscences connected with this particular room refer to essential childhood experiences such as being lifted out of her bed or sitting on the floor collecting scraps of her mother's cloth. The description of the mother and her daughter together in this room evokes a close, comforting atmosphere.[28] Similarly, in *Delta Wedding* Laura remembers her mother, who made a doll for her; in both cases the action of the mother's sewing is conceived of as a soothing, loving contribution. Therefore, it is understandable that Laurel does not hesitate to approach her mother's secretary (which was moved to this sewing room) as she did before she looked through her father's desk. Moreover, Laurel remembers that her mother's "privacy was keyless" (p. 134); thus, she does not need a key to open her mother's desk. Metaphorically, the strong tie between mother and daughter is not loosened by impeding forces.

Unlike Judge McKelva, who immediately disposed of the letters sent to him, Becky kept all her letters.[29] Laurel realizes that "her mother had stored things according to their time and place ... not by ABC" (p. 135), with the exception of the letters from her father. Her "mother's time" is closely linked to place; the same correlation is stated by Eudora Welty in her essay "Some Notes on Time in Fiction."[30] Welty acknowledges that place has a quality that human beings can grasp, "it has shape, size, boundaries" whereas time is difficult to comprehend because it is "like the wind of the abstract,"[31] and its pace, which we cannot control, makes it even more inconceivable.[32]

As mentioned above, Laurel's father seemed obsessed with time while he had to lie still; he concentrated in order to sharpen his awareness of time. Dying, he perhaps recognized that "we are mortal: this is time's deepest meaning,"[33] but this insight dawns upon him only at the end of his life.[34] The scene in the sewing room with Laurel remembering how she and her mother visited her mother's home in West Virginia[35] exposes a different relation to time. It is Laurel's way of remembering that creates an awareness of time specifically related to a woman's world. The reader is confronted with a retrospective view of Laurel as a girl through a third-person narrator. The memories described mostly include impressions, feelings, or direct speeches of Laurel, her mother, and grandmother. The emphasis on these three female characters creates the impression of an almost matriarchal (microcosmic) world, although there are "the boys" (as Becky's brothers are called) who entertain their sister. The following passage is an example of how both the language and the situation reflect a female view:

> Bird dogs went streaking the upslanted pasture through the sweet long grass that swept them as high as their noses. While it was still day on top of the mountain, the light still warm on the cheek, the valley was dyed blue under them. While one of the "boys" was coming up, his white shirt would shine for a long time almost without moving in her sight, like Venus in the sky of Mount

Salus, while grandmother, mother, and little girl sat, outlasting the light, waiting for him to climb home. (p. 139)

The unity the three females represent is contrasted with the one "boy" who approaches them. The landscape is in harmony with the three figures sitting in the grass and they perceive the male intruder as a female star set against the sky.[36] We come across a similar portrayal of the male intruder into a female world when Judge McKelva arrives to fetch them home. Interestingly enough, this passage precedes a description of unity between Becky and her nature surroundings from Laurel's point of view:

Sometimes the top of the mountain was higher than the flying birds. Sometimes even clouds lay down the hill, hiding the treetops farther down. The highest house, the deepest well, the tuning of the strings; sleep in the clouds; Queen's Shoals; the fastest conversations on earth—no wonder her mother needed nothing else!

Eventually her father would come for them—he would be called "Mr. McKelva"; and they would go home on the train. (p. 141)

The distance between the idyllic, harmonious scene and McKelva is already expressed by the formal address "Mr. McKelva." The contrast between the nature descriptions and the husband is enhanced because of their predominantly female imagery: "the deepest well," "the clouds," and particularly "Queen's Shoals"[37] evoke associations with a female body. Ellen Moers quotes Freud's "complicated topography of the female genital parts ... often represented as *landscapes*"[38] in her exploration of female literary landscapes. Indeed, both passages quoted above also contain images connoting the female body. Moreover, on a figurative level, the male genitals (the treetops)[39] are hidden by the soft, comfortable, round womb represented by the clouds. The female landscape according to Freud, and as Ellen Moers has come across it in many writings by women, is "external, accessible, prominent, uneven terrain, not a hidden passageway or chamber."[40] The female landscape, especially created in connection with Becky, that the reader is confronted with is filtered, we should remember, through Laurel's memory. Although the voice is not Becky's or Laurel's but still the third-person narrator's, the descriptions are presented from Laurel's point of view (the most obvious, linguistic sign of this is the frequent use of "*her* mother"; my emphasis). This narrative perspective including both the mother and the daughter strengthens and enhances the bond between the two.

Laurel's reminiscences about her mother in West Virginia are triggered by her looking at some old photographs of her parents taken at Becky's home, which, as she proudly remembers, were developed by her mother herself. I believe it is not a coincidence that Laurel looks at snapshots "created" by her mother because seeing and remembering are intertwined. We recall Eudora Welty's own snapshot album, *One Time, One Place*, where she states this interrelation in a more general context:

> If exposure is essential, still more so is the reflection. Insight doesn't happen often on the click of the moment, like a lucky snapshot, but comes in its own time and more slowly and from nowhere but within.[41]

The kind of reflection that Welty emphasizes is pertinent to Laurel's attitude towards her past: remembering her and especially also her mother's past she manages to "see" more clearly. The process of gaining insight is indeed slower, as Welty points out, and it does not happen according to a person's wish. Laurel's intense occupation with her mother's past gives evidence of the particular and complex bond between mother and daughter.

Besides the mother–daughter relationship there are various references to the grandmother. Giving an account of the days spent in West Virginia, the narrator all of a sudden reports the death of Becky's mother, which came unexpectedly. The description of Becky's grief vividly conveys a daughter's mournfulness.[42] Laurel recalls "the first time she had ever heard anyone cry uncontrollably except herself" (p. 142), which intensifies the presentation of the mother's grief because it is observed by her own daughter (who, one day, will equally mourn her mother). The fact that the reader is confronted with the deaths of both mothers reinforces the supremacy of the mother–daughter relationship in this novel. Commenting on *The Optimist's Daughter* in an interview Eudora Welty stated that "the mother was the one who influenced both Laurel and her father. So they both referred back to her."[43] I suggest that it is predominantly Laurel who "refers back" to her mother and less so her father because his memories of his first wife are hardly mentioned.

At fifteen Becky had to travel to Baltimore with her sick father, the first part of the trip on a raft in order to get down the river. He died at the hospital, and Becky had to return home with the coffin. This tragic experience is remembered by Laurel in connection with her mother's own ordeal of sickness. Reminiscing about her mother's father and her own she comes to the conclusion that "neither of us saved our fathers" (p. 144). Although Laurel comprehends that in the end nobody can be saved by anybody, this statement not only rings of self-reproach, it also implies an ever-returning cycle for daughters. The letters Laurel finds in the last pigeonhole of her mother's desk are a further link in the essential chain between mother and daughter: these letters were sent to Laurel's mother by her own mother after Becky had left West Virginia. The written evidence of this close bond is represented precisely by the rereading of these letters by the granddaughter.[44] Writing and reading letters, addressed to daughters, is a (written) expression of the matrilinear narrative line discernible throughout the novel. Laurel's mother's and grandmother's written texts are the material evidences of the matrilinear narrative.

In *Losing Battles* the written word is also connected with an influential female character: we recall the schoolteacher Julia Mortimer, remembered by the community mainly because she has given (written) expression to her wishes after her death. The profession of schoolteacher is pertinent to such female characters: Becky was a devoted schoolteacher herself before marrying Judge McKelva. Miss Eckhart in *The Golden Apples* is a further example of a prominent schoolteacher in Welty's novels, although Miss Eckhart is less successful than Julia Mortimer at exercising influence on her pupils.[45] These schoolteachers do not resemble the poor and badly paid Victorian governesses who occupied "an ambiguous and ill-defined no-woman's land"[46] and whose dismal existences have been depicted especially by nineteenth-century women novelists. These Weltian schoolteachers are self-supporting women and, to some extent, have power over the next generation. The description of Becky McKelva as both schoolteacher and mother conveys the belief in writing and books that also leaves its imprint on her daughter. Furthermore, her daughter is named after the state flower of West Virginia (the big laurel), her beloved mother country; thus, the mother names her daughter according to *her* history.

Books play an equally important role during Becky's long illness, and Laurel's memory returns to the hours she spent at her mother's bedside hearing Becky recite whole parts of her mother's favorite *McGuffey's Fifth Reader*. A part of a poem is printed in the book (p. 147); it is the part that Laurel hears in her mind while remembering her mother's recitation. The poem is Robert Southey's "The Cataract of Lodore." It is pertinent to the context of the novel for two reasons: first, the reference to cataract, denoting both the waterfall and the clouding of the eye's lens, thus also referring to a dimmed vision, which plays such an essential role in this book. Second, the poem with its nursery rhyme form is meant to be read to children and thus represents a further sign of the closeness and dependence between mother and little girl. Furthermore, the poem printed on the page contrasts sharply with the empty desk of Laurel's father. In her mother's room Laurel both finds and reads her mother's letters, and also "listens" to a poem spoken by her mother.

Laurel's memory is stirred once again by a written document: in one of her grandmother's letters addressed to her mother she finds a reference to herself as a little girl. Her grandmother mentions one of her pigeons, which she would like to send Laurel for her birthday. The pigeons and their typical way of regurgitating and feeding the already swallowed food to other pigeons evoked a feeling of terror and disgust when Laurel once observed this procedure at her grandmother's home:

> But Laurel had kept the pigeons under eye in their pigeon house and had already seen a pair of them sticking their beaks down each other's throats, gagging each other, eating out of each other's craws, swallowing down all over again what had been swallowed before: they were taking turns. The first time, she hoped they might never do it again, but they did it again next day while the other pigeons copied them. They convinced her that they could not escape each other and could not themselves be escaped. (p. 140)

This description is considered to be a key passage by some critics[47] because it reflects human needs and the difficulty in being dependent on each other. In connection with the grandmother's letter Louise Westling remarks that "the grandmother understands her granddaughter's fastidiousness about human commitments and wishes to involve her in the grotesque give-and-take of close human involvement illustrated by the pigeons' feeding off each other."[48] Laurel's intense reaction resembles Laura's when she is pushed into the water by her cousin and confronted with a knowledge that frightens her. Both girls undergo a kind of initiation rite that threatens their innocent minds. On a narratological level, the image of the pigeons with its implication of the cycle, indicated both by the regurgitation and the feeding of the young, also emphasizes the matrilinear narrative line. This aspect of matrilineage is further reinforced by the association of the pigeon/dove with Aphrodite, goddess of fertility. She is often described as accompanied by doves (and sparrows).[49]

The letter with the implicit reference to the little girl's fear and repulsion is finally the catalyst for Laurel's awareness that she has never really faced her grief about her husband's early death. Her husband, Phil Hand,[50] who was killed in World War II, has hardly been mentioned before this crucial passage. Noticing a photograph of her and Phil on her father's desk, she dismisses her memories: "Her marriage had been of magical ease, of *ease*—of brevity and conclusion and all belonging to Chicago and not here" (p. 121).[51] Only now, confronted with her own, her mother's, her grandmother's, and her father's grief, is Laurel ready to heed her sorrowful feelings towards her dead husband: "Now all she had found had found her" (p. 154). Laurel recognizes that she has preserved Phil in her memory as something untouchable, "sealed away," but "now, by her own hands, the past had been raised up" (p. 154). She even dares to raise the fear-inspiring question about a possible end of their marriage—if Phil had lived—and face the idea of an imperfect marriage with its implied anxiety and worries. The storm raging outside accompanies the storm taking place inside her, and she virtually has a vision of her dead husband. Lily Briscoe's last words in *To the Lighthouse*, "I have had my vision," are equally true for Laurel.

After her epiphany Laurel has a dream in which she is riding over a bridge on a train together with her husband. Once again awake, she recalls her real trip with Phil, travelling from Chicago to Mount Salus. In her memory she visualizes the confluence of the two rivers, the Ohio and the Mississippi. Now, Laurel no longer clings to the impervious past but to memory, which "is the somnambulist" (p. 179) and through which "all that is remembered joins, and lives—the old and the young, the past and the present, the living and the dead" (*OWB*, p. 104). Similarly, Virgie Rainey recognizes that "all the opposites on earth were close together" (*GA*, p. 234).

The passage about the confluence of the two rivers is, as mentioned at the beginning of this chapter, crucial for Eudora Welty's concept of memory and time. Her decision to include this passage at the end of her autobiographical book emphasizes the significance of memory and time. The additional comment after the quotation in *One Writer's Beginnings* establishes the connection between memory and time explicitly and with specific reference to the writer's involvement: "My own [memory] is the treasure most dearly regarded by me, in my life and in my work as a writer. Here time, also, is subject to confluence" (*OWB*, p. 104). The moment of memory makes confluence possible, but memory also makes it pass again: it is not static, but changing and moving.

Laurel's attitude towards her father's second wife, Fay, whom she meets after the crucial night, is a proof of her newly acquired insight that memory is not bound to possessions but is free and liable to continuity. By leaving her mother's beloved breadboard, which Phil made, to Fay, who is a person of the future,[52] she frees herself from the past and its memorabilia because she has more than enough of it in her memory. The numerous moments of memory, mainly triggered by her mother's own past, now make such a vision come true. Her memories can still frighten her, but she will not be trapped; the bird caught in the house is similarly freed by Laurel herself.

Woman's time and woman's memory are presented as the main sources of genuine vision in *The Optimist's Daughter*. The mother is the focus for the daughter in order to look backwards. It is not coincidental that Eudora Welty writes about mother–daughter relationships. Ellen Moers mentions many women writers who write

> about the motherhood of their mothers or grandmothers, not, certainly, their own. Cather and Stein never married; Virginia Woolf remained childless by design....
>
> They wrote of the power and grandeur of motherhood with an air of finality, as if what they were describing would never come again; as if there would never more be any mothers.... These are mothers who "make of the moment something permanent," as Lily Briscoe says of Mrs. Ramsay in *To the Lighthouse*: they are women who say "Life stand still here."[53]

Yet, Moers also points out that, especially with regard to Virginia Woolf, there is not only homage paid in these mother portraits, there are "resentment, envy, the pain of betrayal, the cry of protest"[54] and descriptions of boredom in drawing rooms, at long dining tables, or in practical housework. In his comparison between *The Optimist's Daughter* and *To the Lighthouse*, Michael Kreyling comes to a different conclusion:

> The events and images of the novel [*The Optimist's Daughter*] are simple, homemade, yet charged with the possibility of a miraculous richness, or the threat of tinny emptiness. These are the same kinds of mundane, daily events out of which Virginia Woolf produces miracles.[55]

Indeed, the "simple, homemade" events refer to a woman's sphere, but they can often be the reasons for great anger and frustration, besides being the sources of "power and grandeur" or "miracles."

For Laurel her mother's room, her secretary, and the letters represent realms from which she can draw power and comfort, but again faced with her mother's death she must also endure moments of great pain and anxiety.[56] Memory to her has become the means to grasp the essence of time, that is, to recognize that there is past *and* memory, and that the former "can never be awakened," whereas the latter is "vulnerable to the living moment" and therefore lives. As "an optimist's daughter" she had to turn to her mother's time in order to find genuine memory. The "creative pursuit of the past" has made her "re-vision"[57] a successful one.

The book, focusing on "remembrance of things past," is a contribution to the literature of matrilineage. Although this novel is not mentioned among the hundreds of examples of mother–daughter portraits collected in *The Lost Tradition: Mothers and Daughters in Literature*,[58] it certainly belongs to this lost tradition. Moreover, the portrait of the protagonist's mother undermines the father portrait with its implications of male heroism[59] because the father is just the opposite of a hero (which Laurel recognizes immediately). On the contrary, the mother is the one "who *might* have done that" (dare to stand up against a mob, p. 80). Laurel, as her mother's daughter, has rediscovered this (potential) strength by remembering and by naming this female past, this "women's time."

NOTES

1. *One Writer's Beginnings* (Cambridge, Mass., and London: Harvard University Press, 1984). All page references in the text refer to this edition.

2. "Some Notes on Time in Fiction," in *The Eye of the Story*, p. 171. Originally published in the *Mississippi Quarterly* 26, No. 4 (Fall 1973), 483–492. For the quotation by Faulkner see *Light in August* (London: Chatto & Windus, 1960), p. 111.

3. Ibid.

4. Ibid., p. 169.

5. Vladimir Nabokov, *Ada, or Ardor: A Family Chronicle* (New York: McGraw-Hill, 1969), p. 559. Patricia Drechsel Tobin refers to this novel in her study *Time and the Novel: The Genealogical Imperative* (Princeton, NJ.: Princeton University Press, 1978). See Chapter 5, pp. 133–163.

6. Tobin, *Time and the Novel*, p. 5. Cf. also the emblematic presentation of time as a male figure with wings, for example, in *Pericles, Prince of Tyre* IV. Chorus 47, or *The Winter's Tale*, IV. 1. 4. Moreover, in Greek mythology Cronus is the male god who devoured his children. See also Ovid, *Metamorphoses*, XV, 234–235: "tempus edax rerum." In one of her poems, Adrienne Rich ironically refers to the male concept of time: "Sigh no more, ladies. / Time is male / and in his cups drinks to the fair." In "Snapshots of a Daughter-in-Law," in *Poems: Selected and New 1950–1974* (New York: W. W. Norton, 1975), p. 50.

7. Tobin, *Time and the Novel*, p. 12.

8. I rely on Tobin, who states that time in fictional narratives is similar to real-life experience of time. She mentions philosophical explanations of the linearity of thought and language structure. See ibid., pp. 18–20.

9. Ibid., p. 163.

10. Kristeva, "Women's Time," 15–17. Kristeva does not give the reference to the Joyce quotation. After my painstaking search, Joyce scholar Fritz Senn finally informed me that the phrase is from *Finnegans Wake*, but not as Kristeva quotes it. The correct phrase goes: "Father Times and Mother Species" (*Finnegans Wake* [London: Faber and Faber, 1939], p. 600). Interestingly enough, Kristeva refers to Cronus as he appears in Hesiod's mythology as an example of monumental temporality (p. 16). I see Cronus as a further example of the masculine principle of time: he devours his own children because he is afraid that they might usurp his power. With respect to Kristeva's emphasis on space as far

as women are concerned, see also Pitavy-Souques's point in "Le Sud: territoire des femmes?" *Revue Française d'Etudes Américaines* 10 (February 1985), 38. Pitavy-Souques speaks of "spatialisation du temps" with regard to the cycle of the year mainly represented in *Losing Battles* through the moon, a tree, and the celebration.

11. Mary Daly, *Pure Lust: Elemental Feminist Philosophy* (London: The Women's Press, 1984), p. 172.

12. Ibid., p. 173. The quotation in the last sentence given by Daly is from Virginia Woolf, *Moments of Being*, ed. Jeanne Schulkind (New York: Harcourt Brace Jovanovich, 1976), p. 72.

13. Ibid. Commenting on female, identity and writing, Judith Kegan Gardiner states that many women writers "feel that women remember what men choose to forget. If memory operates in the service of identity maintenance differently in the two sexes, it will appear differently in literature by women" ("On Female Identity and Writing by Women," in Abel, *Writing and Sexual Difference*, p. 188).

14. Kuehl, "The Art of Fiction XLVII," in Prenshaw, *Conversations*, p. 75. Eudora Welty emphasizes that she was especially fascinated by *To the Lighthouse* and reread the novel several times.

15. Cf. also Heinrich Straumann, *American Literature in the Twentieth Century* (London: Arrow Books, 1962), rev. ed., p. 163. Straumann mentions the similarity between Woolf and Welty (even before *The Optimist's Daughter* was published).

16. Kreyling, *Achievement of Order*, p. 153.

17. Abel, "Narrative Structure(s) and Female Development," in Abel et al., *The Voyage In*, p. 163.

18. *The Optimist's Daughter* (New York: Harcourt Brace Jovanovich, 1972), p. 4. All page numbers refer to this edition and are given in the text. A story with the same title was published in the *New Yorker* in 1969 (*New Yorker*, March 15). For a comparison between the story and the novel see Helen Hurt Tiegreen, "Mothers, Daughters, and One Writer's Revisions," *Mississippi Quarterly* 39, No. 4 (Fall 1986), special Eudora Welty issue, 605–626, or Kreyling, *Achievement of Order*, pp. 171–172.

19. It is interesting to note that for both memory and retina the verb "slipped" is used.

20. Although the fear of expressing "false hope" (p. 29) is explicitly stated by the third-person narrator and not by Laurel herself in either direct speech or indirect interior monologue, I read it as Laurel's own recognition because we mostly see through Laurel's eyes. Moreover, the conditional "it might be false hope" is closer to Laurel's wavering feelings.

21. Kreyling, *Achievement of Order*, p. 154.

22. In connection with Woolf's *To the Lighthouse* Kreyling also refers to the importance of seeing, "a light-house, for instance" (*Achievement of Order*, p. 155).

23. Flax, "Mother–Daughter Relationships" in Eisenstein and Jardine, *The Future of Difference* (Boston: G. K. Hall, 1980), p. 23.

24. For a definition of differentiation see Nancy Chodorow, "Gender, Relation, and Difference in Psychoanalytic Perspective," in ibid., pp. 5–6.

25. Flax criticizes Freud for not fully examining the pre-Oedipal period, which, as Flax explains, is crucial for the development of gender difference. See ibid., pp. 22–26.

26. In Woolf's novel, *Mrs. Dalloway*, the pre-Oedipal period also plays an important role. See Abel, "Narrative Structure(s) and Female Development," in Abel et al., *The Voyage In*, p. 164.

27. For detailed discussion of the bird imagery and especially of the chimney swift see Marilyn Arnold's article "Images of Memory in Eudora Welty's *The Optimist's Daughter*,"

Southern Literary Journal 14 (Spring 1982), 29–31, 34–37. Prenshaw states that Laurel "invites death into the house" ("Woman's World, Man's Place," in Dollarhide and Abadie, *A Form of Thanks*, p. 70).

28. See also Westling, *Sacred Groves and Ravaged Gardens*, p. 106.

29. In *One Writer's Beginnings* Welty speaks of her own mother as "that great keeper, my mother" (p. 75) who kept all the letters, including the ones written by her and sent to Welty's father. In the novel emphasis is laid on the fact that the father destroyed his letters.

30. *The Eye of the Story*, p. 163.

31. Ibid., pp. 163–164.

32. Welty continues to explain that "the novelist lives on closer terms with time than he does with place" (ibid., p. 164) because time determines the course of the novel (ibid., p. 167).

33. Ibid., p. 168.

34. Dealing with time in *The Optimist's Daughter*, Heide Seele also refers to McKelva's growing awareness of time in *Eudora Welty's "The Optimist's Daughter*," p. 53.

35. Eudora Welty's own mother was from West Virginia. See *One Writer's Beginnings*, p. 50. For the specific influence of West Virginia in Welty's work, see Barbara Wilkie Tedford, "West Virginia Touches in Eudora Welty's Fiction," *Southern Literary Journal* 18, No. 2 (Spring 1986), 40–52.

36. Westling also quotes this passage as an example of a typically female landscape (*Sacred Groves and Ravaged Gardens*, p. 106). Westling refers to Ellen Moers's *Literary Women*, which lists such female landscapes by various women writers (Moers, *Literary Women*, pp. 254–264).

37. Although the name "Queen's Shoals" is a real name (cf. *OWB*, p. 54), I consider "Queen's Shoals" to be one of those names given by women writers that Moers regards as "sexually suggestive" (Moers, *Literary Women*, p. 255).

38. Ibid., p. 254.

39. According to Freud, trees, as well as sticks, umbrellas, etc., connote the male sexual organ (quoted by Moers, ibid., p. 252).

40. Ibid., p. 257.

41. *One Time, One Place* (New York: Random House, 1971), p. 8.

42. In a collection of poems exclusively on mother–daughter relationships, a great number of poems deals with the daughters' sorrows at the deaths of their mothers (Lynn Lifshin, *Tangled Vines: A Collection of Mother and Daughter Poems* [Boston: Beacon Press, 1978]). See especially the poems by Erica Jong ("Mother," pp. 49–52), Honor Moore (from the play *Mourning Pictures*, p. 82), and Adrienne Rich ("A Woman Mourned by Daughters," pp. 83–84).

43. Martha van Noppen, "A Conversation with Eudora Welty," in Prenshaw, *Conversations*, pp. 241–242.

44. See Welty's memory of her own grandmother's letters to her mother, *One Writer's Beginnings*, pp. 55–56.

45. Welty comments on the differences between Miss Eckhart and Julia Mortimer: "Miss Eckhart was a very mysterious character. Julia Mortimer was much more straightforward and dedicated and thinking of the people as somebody she wanted to help. Miss Eckhart was a very strange person" (Jo Brans, "Struggling against the Plaid: An Interview with Eudora Welty," in Prenshaw, *Conversations*, p. 304). See also her comment on Miss Eckhart in *OWB*, p. 102.

46. Françoise Basch, *Relative Creatures: Victorian Women in Society and Novel 1837–67*, trans. A. Rudolf (London, 1974), p. 112.

47. Cf. Devlin, *Eudora Welty's Chronicle*, p. 180; Kreyling, *Achievement of Order*, p. 169; Westling, *Sacred Groves and Ravaged Gardens*, p. 107; Seele, *Eudora Welty's "The Optimist's Daughter,"* p. 119. Cf. also Welty's own comment in an interview, Martha van Noppen, *Conversations*, p. 241.

48. Westling, *Sacred Groves and Ravaged Gardens*, p. 107.

49. See Robert Graves, *The Greek Myths* (Harmondsworth, England: Penguin Books, 1955), vol. 1, pp. 49–50.

50. The name "Hand" emphasizes Phil's "large, good hands" (p. 161) and his talent at designing and making things.

51. This statement is put in parentheses (cf. p. 121); they enforce Laurel's tendency to shrug her feelings off with respect to her dead husband.

52. For a more detailed discussion of Fay, see for example Daniel Thomas Young, "Social Forms and Social Order: Eudora Welty's *The Optimist's Daughter*," in *The Past in the Present: A Thematic Study of Modern Southern Fiction* (Baton Rouge and London: Louisiana State University Press, 1981), pp. 87–115, Devlin, *Eudora Welty's Chronicle*, pp. 181–182, or MacKethan, *The Dream of Arcady*, pp. 203–204.

53. Moers, *Literary Women*, p. 236. Like Gertrude Stein or Willa Cather, Eudora Welty never married or had children. The reference to the quotation by Woolf is *To the Lighthouse* (Harmondsworth, England: Penguin Books, 1964), p. 183.

54. Ibid., p. 237.

55. Kreyling, *Achievement of Order*, p. 154.

56. See also Westling's comment that writing this novel "apparently gave her [Welty] a way of confronting her mother's death and accepting her grief, a process reflected in Laurel Hand's painful reassessment of her mother's character" (*Sacred Groves and Ravaged Gardens*, p. 45).

57. Adrienne Rich uses this term in her essay "When We Dead Awaken: Writing as Re-Vision," in *On Lies, Secrets, and Silence*; see especially p. 35.

58. *The Lost Tradition: Mothers and Daughters in Literature*, ed. Cathy N. Davidson and E. M. Broner (New York: Frederick Ungar Publishing, 1980).

59. Of course, the father figure is not necessarily presented as a heroic figure. Here, the father's heroism suggests the traditionally male concept of courage, bravery, aggression, etc. For examples of father figures who no longer fulfill the heroic deed, see the chapter "Faulkner's Sons of the Fathers," in MacKethan, *The Dream of Arcady*, pp. 153–180, especially pp. 154–155. Manning points out that the speech delivered by a friend at McKelva's funeral is a false tale about "romantic acts of heroism," as Laurel immediately recognizes (*With Ears Opening*, p. 171).

DENIS DONOGHUE

Eudora Welty's Sense of Place

I

In "A Worn Path"—the final story in *A Curtain of Green and Other Stories* (1941)—Eudora Welty tells of an old black woman, Phoenix Jackson, who lives "away back off the Old Natchez Trace." On "a bright frozen day in the early morning" one December she sets out to walk the long and only partly worn path to Natchez.[1] If you count small things and don't insist on catastrophes, much happens to her. Her skirt gets caught in a thorny bush, she negotiates a log thrown across a creek, and she imagines that a boy gives her a slice of marble cake. She gets through a barbed wire fence, comes on a scarecrow, meets a wagon track, finds a well and drinks from it, fends off a black dog only to fall into a ditch, gets a lifting hand from a hunter, pockets a nickel the hunter has dropped, and arrives at Natchez. There she asks a woman to lace up her shoes, finds the doctor's office, gets the bottle of medicine her grandson needs, accepts a nickel in Christmas charity from the nurse's attendant, decides to spend it on a paper windmill for her grandson, and sets off back the way she came. On the path to Natchez she had talked to herself and to the world: "Out of my way, all you foxes, owls, beetles, jack rabbits, coons and wild animals! ... Keep out from under these feet, little bob-whites" (*Stories*, 171). She observed that a hill was pine going up, oak

From *Place in American Fiction*. H.L. Weatherby and George Core, eds. © 2004 by The Curators of the University of Missouri.

going down. A field of old cotton led to one of dead corn and then to a maze where the path lost itself. Phoenix Jackson walked on, talking "in the voice of argument old people keep to use with themselves" (*Stories*, 172). She doesn't expect the world to reply. Trees, hills, dogs, the sun, the creek have their places, but none of Phoenix Jackson's feelings assumes that the world should respond to her in kind. She does not stop to turn the things that surround her into a landscape or to think of them in that capacity. Everything she meets is just whatever it happens to be. The worn path becomes a presence, even a force to us, but not to Phoenix Jackson. If she had anything as improbable as a philosophy, it would be untroubled Realism. Her consciousness is barely distinguishable from her will. Getting to Natchez engages every form of her energy. She is incurious about anything else the world contains.

Eudora Welty is like Phoenix Jackson in only one respect. Place is immensely a value to her, but she does not assume that when she looks at the natural world it will look fondly back at her. She knows trees, flowers, and birds with remarkable familiarity and has the sensibility of an adept, which she attributes to Audubon in "A Still Moment," but she does not look for a neo-Wordsworthian relation between the world and the mind that contemplates it. Her fiction, like her photographs, is devoted to the people she sees and their relation to the places where they live and work, but she does not separate the places from the people or hold the landscapes up for separate attention. It is as if she read T. S. Eliot's *After Strange Gods* and took heed of his animadversions on the subject of landscape. Eliot had Hardy in view, a writer he disliked for "self-absorption," and it is possible that his dislike sent him into harsh generalization:

> In consequence of his self-absorption, [Hardy] makes a great deal of landscape; for landscape is a passive creature which lends itself to an author's mood. Landscape is fitted too for the purposes of an author who is interested not at all in men's minds, but only in their emotions; and perhaps only in men as vehicles for emotions.[2]

Welty does not think that a landscape should be susceptible to a character's mood or that a character is justified in seeking among trees, flowers, swamps, and rivers an intuition of a shared life. Pantheism does not seem to attract her. Relations occupy her mind, but she does not presume on their hospitality or go beyond reasonable limits of affiliation.

Otherwise put: Welty is not a symbolist, according to our standard definition of symbolism. But I am impelled by Guy Davenport's "That Faire

Field of Enna" to think that we must distinguish, especially in reading Welty, two versions of Symbolism. The first is sufficiently indicated by reference to Thomas Carlyle, Gerard de Nerval, Stéphane Mallarmé, Arthur Symons, and the early William Butler Yeats. We find it in Mallarmé's program, "pour ne garder de rien que la suggestion" (to retain only the suggestion). It is also well apprehended in *The Symbolist Movement in Literature*, where Symons writes of "a literature in which the visible world is no longer a reality, and the unseen world no longer a dream." And in "The Symbolism of Poetry" where Yeats writes: "The purpose of rhythm, it has always seemed to me, is to prolong the moment of contemplation, the moment when we are both asleep and awake, which is the one moment of creation, by hushing us with an alluring monotony, while it holds us waking by variety, to keep us in that state of perhaps real trance, in which the mind liberated from the pressure of the will is unfolded in symbols."[3]

It is not surprising that Davenport gives a severe account of these symbols and the literature in which they are favored. He is an Objectivist on principle and thinks that "the artist shows the world as if meaning were inherent in its particulars." He has no interest in exchanging particulars for essences:

> Psychology in the study of dreams defined the symbol as essentially opaque, a confusion rather than an epiphany of meaning. The darker the symbol, the richer it was thought to be, and ambiguity became a virtue in literature. James may be partly responsible, but then James posited for our pleasure in such things an ambiguity that is true of experience (we do not know each other's inner dark of soul, nor what is written in letters locked in a cupboard, nor what people see when they say they've seen a ghost). The symbols of the French *symbolistes* and their school from Oslo to Salerno, from Dublin to Budapest, were not properly symbols at all, but enigmas derived from the German doctrine of elective affinities among things and from Fourier and Swedenborg. These symbols so-called in the sensibilities of Baudelaire and Mallarmé became an abstract art, paralleling the disappearance of intelligible images in the painting of Malevich and Kandinsky a generation later. You cannot interpret a *symboliste* symbol, you can only contemplate it, like a transcendentalist brooding on the word *nature*.[4]

Not that Davenport is willing to give up symbols, but he proposes to change their character and to redeem them for a better tradition—

Objectivism—by making them intelligible. He wants a symbol to be such that he can come to the end of it and know what he has come to the end of. He finds authority and precedent in Ezra Pound, James Joyce, Louis Zukofsky, sundry Objectivists, and (though he doesn't quite say so) Eudora Welty. But mainly Joyce:

> For the first time since Dante, symbols became transparent on Joyce's pages ... Joyce, who rethought everything, rethought symbolism. It must first of all be organic, not arbitrary or fanciful. It must be logical, resonant, transparent, bright. From Flaubert he had learned that a true symbol must be found in an image that belongs to the narrative. The parrot Loulou in *Un Coeur simple* acts symbolically to make us feel the devotion, loneliness, ecstasy, and inviolable simplicity of Felicité.... In Joyce a rolled-up newspaper with the words *Gold Cup* and *Sceptre* among its racing news becomes a symbolic blossom around which two men, symbolic bees, forage. This is a deeper symbolism than more apparent ones in operation at the same time: Odysseus among the Lotus Eaters, a spiritually lost Jew longing to return to Israel ("and the desert shall blossom like the rose"), a man psychologically a drone to his queen-bee wife, a man named Flower enacting the suffering of a saint named Flower (Anthony) and his temptations; and on and on. Joyce's symbols are labyrinths of meaning, but they are logical, and they expand meaning. They are, as mediaeval grammarians said, *involucra*— seed husks asking to be peeled.[5]

The distinction between the two Symbolisms, whatever we call them—soft and hard, opaque and translucent, occult and intelligible, Romantic and Classic, Yeats and Joyce—bears on one's reading of Welty. She is classical in her affections. Her symbols are not dissociated, they are images that "belong to the narrative." It follows, as a quality and not as a defect, that they are not endless in purport. In the last pages of *The Optimist's Daughter* a bird, a swift, gets out of the chimney in the McKelva home at Mount Salus and flies from room to room. Laurel tries to catch it and set it free. An itinerant handyman, Mr. Cheek—"Bird in the house? ... Sign o' bad luck, ain't it?" (*Novels*, 982)—tries to help, but he's no good. In the end, using two baskets, Laurel gets hold of the bird and releases it: "The bird was away. In the air it was nothing but a pair of wings—she saw no body any more, no tail, just a tilting crescent being drawn back into the sky" (*Novels*, 985). Readers are not invited to be as superstitious as Mr.

Cheek. It is enough if we reflect that Laurel, too, is trying to get out of the house intact, now that it belongs to the dreadful Fay, her deceased father's second wife. Laurel quarrels with Fay, insisting on saying what she has to say. Then she leaves the house, consigning to memory every experience she cares for: "The memory can be hurt, time and again—but in that may lie its final mercy. As long as it's vulnerable to the living moment, it lives for us, and while it lives, and while we are able, we can give it up its due" (*Novels*, 992).

The relation between Laurel and the bird is local and bounded. Because it is an intelligible relation, it is limited as if on principle, and we do it sufficient justice by going through to the end of it. Interpretation is enough; unlimited divination is not required. Nor was it required, a few pages earlier, when Laurel recalled taking the train with her husband, Phil, from Chicago to Mount Salus and seeing "the long, ragged, pencil-faint line of birds within the crystal of the zenith, flying in a V of their own, following the same course down." There is no need to go into a swoon of reverie. The propriety of the image can be intuited without fuss: "All they could see was sky, water, birds, light, and confluence. It was the whole morning world" (*Novels*, 979). Interpretation starts a flight of analogy, and when the intelligibility of the analogy has been apprehended, the flight is brought to an end. We are still in the morning world. To say that the symbol is transparent is to say that it begins and, when its interpretation has been rationally fulfilled, ends.

Yeats, at least in his *symbolist* phase, would have regarded Welty's birds as merely allegorical and her method as a device for saying things that "could be said as well, or better, in another way." He despised the allegorical form of meaning, as in Tintoretto's *Origin of the Milky Way*, which impels us to say: "That woman there is Juno, and the milk out of her breast is making the Milky Way." When you have said that, you have given the meaning of the picture, and "the fine painting, which has added so much irrelevant beauty, has not told it better." But in neo-French Symbolism, according to Yeats, there are no such iconographies, no occasions to gratify one's hermeneutic zeal by saying that *that* stands for *this*:

> If you liberate a person or a landscape from the bonds of
> motives and their actions, causes and their effects, and from all
> bonds but the bonds of your love, it will change under your
> eyes, and become a symbol of an infinite emotion, a perfected
> emotion, a part of the Divine Essence; for we love nothing but
> the perfect, and our dreams make all things perfect, that we
> may love them.[6]

Welty might retort: "I love nothing but the imperfect, and my imagination shows all things imperfect, so I love them because they are not infinite." If there is a penumbra around her images—to call them that for the moment—no vagueness attends them but a sense of their participation in a recalled mythology. Davenport calls it mirage:

> She arranges images so that we see them in sharpest focus and simultaneously as a ghost of reality. When, for instance, a child is rescued from an on-coming train in *Delta Wedding*, we are made to see (if our imagination has its eyes open) the black, fuming chariot of Dis swooping down on Persephone picking flowers. The scene is not exactly a symbolic enactment; it is a mirage of it.[7]

Welty's procedure differs in that respect from the more elaborate correspondences of Joyce's *Ulysses* because Joyce's procedure keeps the Homeric mirage going for the whole book, at least intermittently, while Welty's is occasional and optional. When Maureen, in *Delta Wedding*, gets her foot caught on the trestle and Uncle George tries to set it loose and fails, the Yellow Dog bears down on them and the engineer only barely stops the train in time. It is optional whether or not you think of Persephone and Dis. An occasional mirage gives you warrant for thinking that the local image is not unique; there have been such imperfections before. One's sense of life is amplified without losing the immediate force of the image.

Yeats called such correspondences "emblems" rather than "symbols," without being consistent in maintaining the distinction. Emblems get their meaning "by a traditional and not by a natural right."[8] We get our symbols from the natural world—the sun, the moon, rivers, caves, swans— but our emblems from tradition, the history of cultures, literature, philosophy—as Yeats's poems and essays feature Junzo Sato's sword, Milton's lonely tower, Plato's cave. But there is no need to cultivate one at the expense of the other, though Paul de Man argues in *The Rhetoric of Romanticism* that each entails its own philosophical disposition. It seems to me that Yeats resorted to nature and to culture betimes, opportunistically; at a given moment he may have felt that one of these values was more reliable than the other. Sometimes he used a symbol as if it were primarily an emblem. The first stanza of "Coole Park and Ballylee, 1931" ends: "What's water but the generated soul?"—not because nature and mind have collaborated to effect that kinship but because Porphyry did it in *On the Cave of the Nymphs*.

II

If we think of Welty's commitment to images, emblems, and the art of mirage, we see that it also governs her sense of place. She asks of a place only that it be itself and know itself in that being. Her places are not mere contexts of human and natural actions but, to begin with, they are places, not states of soul given an external form. All the better if a place acquires a certain force of presence corresponding to presence of mind and a quiet determination not to yield up its secrets to the first interrogation. The hill country of northeast Mississippi, where *Losing Battles* is set, has social but not sensitive bearing. What has happened to it is geological, but not teleological: mostly what has happened to it has been done by the people who have lived there, stretching back further than the historians can see. Welty comes to her sense of place not primordially but, as Davenport has shown, mythologically. These myths were local and immediate to the people who first heard them, but to us they are timeless, indicating patterns of experience we regard as nearly universal rather than regional. In Welty's hands they have the effect of making it appear not to matter much that her stories are set in one century rather than another. Time is important to them, but only so far as it has taken geographical and social lineaments.

It follows that it is not necessary to make a strict distinction, while reading Welty's fiction, between the values of space and time. Alexander von Humboldt pointed out that "in classical antiquity the earliest historians made little attempt to separate the description of lands from the narration of events the scene of which was in the areas described: for a long time physical geography and history appear attractively intermingled." The geographer Carl Ortwin Sauer has noted that "the literature of geography in the sense of chorology ["the study of the areal or habitat differentiation of the earth"] begins with parts of the earliest sagas and myths, vivid as they are with the sense of place and of man's contest with nature."[9] Herodotus is at once historian and geographer. There is no need to be strict in these designations unless we are willing to see the structures become sinister.

Modern preoccupation with time, as in Henri Bergson and Marcel Proust, has made us think that time and space are ideological rivals, and that each enforces a corresponding politics. Philosophers of space are thought to have a totalitarian impulse, concealed or not, while philosophers of time are deemed to be democrats. The dispute between Joseph Frank and Frank Kermode some years ago about "spatial form" seemed at any moment ready to turn rough with allegations of political bad faith. You could still start a row by proclaiming the merits of Wilhelm

Wörringer's *Abstraction and Empathy*, Wyndham Lewis's *Time and Western Man*, and Pound's *Cantos* against choice philosophers of Time. But the disputants ought to acknowledge that one can denounce, as Samuel Beckett does in his book on Proust, "the poisonous ingenuity of Time in the science of affliction" without thinking that such ingenuity can be deflected by spatial analogies. Beckett thought that Proust wrote as he lived—in time. In that respect he was a Romantic, an Impressionist: "By his impressionism I mean his non-logical statement of phenomena in the order and exactitude of their perception, before they have been distorted into intelligibility in order to be forced into a chain of cause and effect." An artist who might be called classical, on the other hand, assumes "omniscience and omnipotence" and "raises himself artificially out of Time in order to give relief to his chronology and causality to his development."[10]

But to claim that Welty equably acknowledges space and place is not as innocent as it sounds, though she has not been drawn into a dispute on the lines of Frank versus Kermode. If she had to choose between Time and Space as values, I think she would choose Space, and if pushed further into the choice she might invoke places as devices against time. But generally she avoids the choice. Without claiming the authority of Herodotus, Humboldt, and Sauer, she makes space and place subsume the historical time in which her people, houses, and habitats have become what they are. She is acutely aware of the time it takes to become anything worthwhile. It follows that she writes with notable tenderness of families, traditions, old wisdoms, houses that have survived; and writes severely of things that have had not taken enough time to be remembered or worth remembering. We are expected to be alert to these intimations. When Laurel looks at Dr. Courtland—"Laurel looked for a moment into the experienced face, so entirely guileless. The Mississippi country that lay behind him was all in it" (*Novels*, 887)—we are expected to take the force and momentum of that Mississippi country and to know or guess whatever Laurel and Eudora Welty know of that country and its measure of experience and guilelessness. Fay's coming from Madrid, Texas, is to begin with no rebuke to Texas—not till it emerges that every word she speaks to Laurel about her family is a lie and that she is white trash, wherever she comes from. But any second wife would need to be an angel to survive comparison with Judge McKelva's Becky and, in Laurel's memory of it, the West Virginia that Becky came from:

> The first time Laurel could remember arriving in West Virginia
> instead of just finding herself there, her mother and she had got
> down from the train in early morning and stood, after it had

gone, by themselves on a steep rock, all of the world that they could see in the mist being their rock and its own iron bell on a post with its rope hanging down. Her mother gave the rope a pull and at its sound, almost at the moment of it, large and close to them appeared a gray boat with two of the boys at the oars. At their very feet had been the river. The boat came breasting out of the mist, and in they stepped. (*Novels*, 968)

No wonder the narrator comments, making Laurel's sense of life explicit: "All new things in life were meant to come like that."

Perhaps it is too much. Davenport, who will not hear an evil word about Eudora Welty, utters a sharp one—"wail"—when his mind turns to her silent politics. He permits himself some misgiving about her social discriminations, which are mostly discriminations of place and tone. With Fay McKelva in mind, along with Bonnie Dee Peacock from *The Ponder Heart*, he maintains:

> Miss Welty has been fascinated before by these rapacious, weak-witted, pathologically selfish daughters of the dispossessed, and likes to bring them in sharp contrast with the decrepit chivalry and good manners of Mississippi gentry. The result, however complex and sensitive Miss Welty's handling of the misalliance, comes close to being a wail that an older order is being replaced by one that is by contrast barbarous and without transition.[11]

Some of these social distinctions are effected by standard means—exhibited vulgarity, lies, crassness, dreadful conversations, misbehavior at weddings, wakes, and funerals where good manners are expected—but often the rapacious, weak-witted, selfish people are shown living in places as obnoxious as their morals.

III

Eudora Welty has written of the sense of place in three essays, "Place in Fiction," "Some Notes on River Country," and "Writing and Analyzing a Story." The sentiment common to the three involves a feeling for locality and a corresponding feeling, amounting to a prejudice, against anything that makes light of its value. Welty is even ready to disapprove of fairy stories because "once upon a time" is not this time, that place; and she relegates the historical novel to the pathos of being just another fairy tale. "Fiction is properly at work on the here and now, or the past made here and now; for in novels *we* have to be there" (*Eye*, 117). To understand a character in a story, we must see him in relation to his place, "we must see him set to scale in his proper world to know his size" (*Eye*, 122). Place defines a character by confining him to his place. A story would be another story if its setting were changed. "Imagine *Swann's Way* laid in London, or *The Magic Mountain* in Spain, or *Green Mansions* in the Black Forest." Further:

> The very notion of moving a novel brings ruder havoc to the mind and affections than would a century's alteration in its time. It is only too easy to conceive that a bomb that could destroy all trace of places as we know them, in life and through books, could also destroy all feelings as we know them, so irretrievably and so happily are recognition, memory, history, valor, love, all the instincts of poetry and praise, worship and endeavor, bound up in place. From the dawn of man's imagination, place has enshrined the spirit; as soon as man stopped wandering and stood still and looked about him, he found a god in that place; and from then on, that was where the god abided and spoke from if ever he spoke. (*Eye*, 122–23)

In "Some Notes on River Country" Welty is so attentive to each genius loci that she nearly sets place against time, provided it is a social place, rich in density and texture:

> A place that ever was lived in is like a fire that never goes out. It flares up, it smolders for a time, it is fanned or smothered by circumstance, but its being is intact, forever fluttering within it, the result of some original ignition. Sometimes it gives out glory, sometimes its little light must be sought out to be seen, small and tender as a candle flame, but as certain. (*Eye*, 286)

It is not entirely true: there are lost places. In Ireland, a community called Ballykilcline no longer exists that was a living place before the Famine of 1847. But it is touching that Welty has made a claim for the perpetual flame of a place, knowing that in her love of this value she sins a little by excess. A few pages later it turns out that her authority in the excess is the Natchez tribe who attributed the decline in their numbers to "the fact that the fire had once been allowed to go out and that a profane fire burned now in its place" (*Eye*, 295).

But the highest claim for the value of place is made in "Place in Fiction," where Welty makes something like a moral distinction between place and people:

Hemingway in our time has sought out the formless and ruthless territories of the world, archaic ones often, where there are bullfight arenas, theatres of hunting and war, places with a primitive, or formidable, stripped-down character, with implacable codes, with inscrutable justices and inevitable retributions. But whatever the scene of his work, it is the *places* that never are hostile. People give pain, are callous and insensitive, empty and cruel, carrying with them no pasts as they promise no futures. But place heals the hurt, soothes the outrage, fills the terrible vacuum that these human beings make. It heals actively, and the response is given consciously, with the ardent care and explicitness, respect and delight of a lover, when fishing streams or naming over streets becomes almost something of the lover's secret language—as the careful conversations between characters in Hemingway bear hints of the secret language of hate. The response to place has the added intensity that comes with the place's not being native or taken for granted, but found, chosen; thereby is the rest more heavily repudiated. (*Eye*, 131–32)

It is a theory of pastoral. Place offers even cruel people the paradigm of a new beginning, in which they learn a language not the vernacular, not native but chosen, a lover's secret idiom. It is as if a place not only forgave the outrages committed on its land but existed in order to do so, making forgiveness its reason for being as it is. In "The Rock," Wallace Stevens writes of "a cure of the ground and of ourselves," and of

an illusion so desired

That the green leaves came and covered the high rock,
That the lilacs came and bloomed, like a blindness cleaned,
Exclaiming bright sight, as it was satisfied,

In a birth of sight.[12]

I am sure that Welty thinks of place not in the abstract but in its particularity, of places in which the ground is cured and rocks are covered with green leaves because of someone's desire that they should be so covered. These places are for some of us nothing but their names—China Grove, Dexter,

Dulcie, Farr's Ginn, Larkin's Hill, Beulah, Morgana, Bigbee. If they heal the
hurt and soothe the outrage, we have only Welty's word for it, and her
photographs, but these are enough for belief and conviction.

IV

To do so much, a place must not only have qualities, it must be—or
become—a character, according to one's conceit of it. It may not speak for
itself, but it must seem to be present, however silently, in many
conversations. So it is in "No Place for You, My Love," which was first
published in the *New Yorker* in 1952 and then reprinted in *The Bride of
Innisfallen and Other Stories* (1955).

The scene is, to begin with, New Orleans. A businessman, married,
from Syracuse meets a woman at a luncheon party in Galatoire's. She is from
Toledo, Ohio, and is probably involved in a love affair with a married man.
We don't know any names. The man from Syracuse invites the woman from
Toledo to take a drive with him—it is a Sunday in July—in his rented Ford
convertible. They drive south and keep going, not stopping even when they
have crossed the Mississippi on a ferryboat. There is still more South. They
see a graveyard, a church, a priest removing his vestments from a clothes
hanger, an old man walking south, a shack with a beer sign on it, "Baba's
Place." They go into Baba's Place, and the man orders a beer and a ham
sandwich. There are men playing cards; a dog, asleep; a goose waddling
about. Someone plays the jukebox. The man and the woman dance. After a
while they leave and drive back. There is little conversation. The journey is
mostly heat, mosquitoes, moths, gnats, the speed of the car. Approaching
New Orleans, he stops the car and kisses her. Nothing is said. They drive on
till they reach the city and he drops her off at her hotel. They shake hands.
He says "Forgive," knowing that she expects it of him. She goes into the
hotel lobby, "and he thought a figure in the lobby strolled to meet her." The
story ends: "As he drove the little Ford safely to its garage, he remembered
for the first time in years when he was young and brash, a student in New
York, and the shriek and horror and unholy smother of the subway had its
original meaning for him as the lilt and expectation of love" (*Stories*, 579–80).

Welty has written of "No Place for You, My Love" in "Writing and
Analyzing a Story." I have little to add to her account of it, except to bring
together a motif in the story and another one in the commentary which she
has separated. In the story, the man is thinking:

> Had she felt a wish for someone else to be riding with them?
> He thought it was more likely that she would wish for her

husband if she had one (his wife's voice) than for the lover in whom he believed. Whatever people liked to think, situations (if not scenes) were usually three-way—there was somebody else always. The one who didn't—couldn't—understand the two made the formidable third. (*Stories*, 568)

"Who is the third who walks always beside you?" Eliot asks in "The Waste Land." Welty's story has nothing more to say about the third, but in the commentary she notes another image of it. She has been explaining that in the first version of the story she had sealed the woman—a southerner at that stage—inside her own world and given the story over to her. She decided that she must get outside the woman's mind by making her a woman from the Midwest and by inventing a new character, "a man whom I brought into the story to *be* a stranger." She must keep out of his mind, too. Soon she came to see that the real point of view was neither the woman nor the man but the journey itself, south and back again:

> That country—that once-submerged, strange land of "south from South"—which had so stamped itself upon my imagination put in an unmistakable claim now as the very image of the story's predicament. It pointed out to me at the same time where the real point of view belonged. Once I'd escaped those characters' minds, I saw it was outside them—suspended, hung in the air between two people, fished alive from the surrounding scene. (*Eye*, 111)

The logic of the structure of the story now presented itself, and the scene of the little drama became an agent of it, more than a context for it:

> As I wrote further into the story, something more real, more essential, than the characters were on their own was revealing itself. In effect, though the characters numbered only two, there had come to be a sort of third character along on the ride—the presence of a relationship between the two.... This third character's role was that of hypnosis—it was what a relationship *can do*, be it however brief, tentative, potential, happy or sinister, ordinary or extraordinary. I wanted to suggest that its being took shape as the strange, compulsive journey itself, was palpable as its climate and mood, the heat of the day—but was its spirit too, a spirit that held territory, that which is seen fleeting past by two

vulnerable people who might seize hands on the run. (*Eye*, 111–12)

At the end of the commentary, Welty sees her two characters, man and woman, become one—and that one is the place of their predicament. "The vain courting of imperviousness in the face of exposure," she says, "is this little story's plot." The characters attempt it "as a mutual feat," while admitting nothing to each other "except the wicked heat and its comical inconvenience." Nevertheless "it happens that they go along aware, from moment to moment, as one: as my third character, the straining, hallucinatory eyes and ears, the roused-up sentient being of that place" (*Eye*, 113).

Does the place heal the hurt, soothe the outrage, promise man and woman the imperviousness they courted beyond exposure? That would be too much to hope for from this south of South. There are no pastoral consolations in this story. Welty does not yield to those "good Americans" who feel obliged, as Irving Howe said, to show "unconsidered respect" for "nature." She does not imply that "a special wisdom is to be found, and found only, among tight-lipped farmers, village whittlers, and small-town eccentrics."[13] Or among the cardplayers in Baba's Place. The landscape does not provide even local gratifications. But the journey south and back again is imagined as taking on the quality—"roused-up sentient being"—of the imperfect man and woman it subsumes.

NOTES

1. Welty, *Stories, Essays, and Memoir*, ed. Richard Ford and Michael Kreyling (New York: Library of America, 1998), 171. All quotations from Welty's fiction are taken from this volume and from *Complete Novels*, ed. Richard Ford and Michael Kreyling (New York: Library of America, 1998). Subsequent parenthetical references are to these editions.

2. Eliot, *After Strange Gods: A Primer of Modern Heresy* (London: Faber and Faber, 1934), 55.

3. Mallarmé, *Oeuvres Complètes* (Paris: Pleiade, 1945), 365; Symons, *The Symbolist Movement in Literature*, ed. Richard Ellmann (London: Constable, 1911), 4; W. B. Yeats, *Essays and Introductions* (London: Macmillan, 1961), 159.

4. Davenport, "That Faire Field of Enna," in *The Geography of the Imagination* (San Francisco: North Point Press, 1981), 269, 262.

5. Ibid., 262–63.

6. Yeats, *Essays and Introductions*, 147, 148, 148–49.

7. Davenport, "That Faire Field," 262.

8. Yeats, *Essays and Introductions*, 147.

9. Von Humboldt, *Kosmos* (Stuttgart and Tubingen, 1845), 1:64–65; Sauer, *Land and Life*, ed. John Leighly (Berkeley: University of California Press, 1965), 316–17 (von Humboldt quoted on 318, n. 5).

10. Beckett, *Proust* (London: John Calder, 1965), 15, 86, 81.

11. Davenport, "That Faire Field," 268.

12. Stevens, *Collected Poems* (London: Faber and Faber, 1955), 526–27.

13. Howe, *Selected Writings, 1950–1990* (San Diego: Harcourt Brace Jovanovich, 1990), 181.

Chronology

1909	April 13, Eudora Alice Welty is born in Jackson, Mississippi to Mary Chestina Andrews Welty and Christian Webb Welty.
1925	Welty graduates from Central High School, Jackson.
1925–1927	Attends Mississippi State College for Women, Columbus.
1927–1929	Attends University of Wisconsin, Madison; B.A. with a major in English.
1930–1931	Studies advertising at Columbia Graduate School of Business, New York City.
1931–1934	Welty's father, Christian, dies; Welty returns to Jackson to live. Works part-time for local radio station; takes freelance jobs as newspaper correspondent and publicist.
1935–1936	Works as publicity agent for the Works Progress Administration (WPA) in Mississippi.
1936	Publishes "Death of a Traveling Salesman" in *Manuscript*; exhibits photographs in one-woman show in Lugene Gallery, New York City.
1937	Publishes "A Piece of News" and "A Memory" in the *Southern Review*.
1939	Meets Katherine Anne Porter.
1940	Diarmuid Russell becomes Welty's literary agent; Welty attends Bread Loaf Writer's Conference.

1941	Spends summer at Yaddo Writers' Colony; *A Curtain of Green* is published, with introduction by Katherine Anne Porter; wins O. Henry Award, second prize, for "A Worn Path."
1942	*The Robber Bridegroom* is published; wins O. Henry first prize for "The Wide Net;" is awarded Guggenheim Fellowship.
1943	*The Wide Net and Other Stories* is published; wins O. Henry Award, first prize for "Livvie Is Back."
1944	Welty wins an American Academy of Arts and Letters award for $1,000; she moves to New York and works for six months for *New York Times Book Review*.
1946	*Delta Wedding* is published; Welty stays five months in San Francisco visiting John Robinson.
1947	Gives lecture "The Reading and Writing of Short Stories" at writers' conference, University of Washington, Seattle; August–November, returns to San Francisco.
1949	*The Golden Apples* is published; wins Guggenheim Fellowship; travels to Europe: France, Italy, England, Ireland. Meets Elizabeth Bowen.
1951	Welty visits England, and stays with Elizabeth Bowen in Ireland.
1952	Is elected to National Institute of Arts and Letters.
1954	*The Ponder Heart* and *Selected Stories* (Modern Library edition) are published; July–October, Welty returns to Europe; gives lecture "Place in Fiction," at Cambridge University; receives honorary LL.D. degree from the University of Wisconsin.
1955	*The Bride of the Innisfallen* is published—last book for 15 years; receives William Dean Howells Medal of the Academy of Arts and Letters for *The Ponder Heart*.
1956	Attends Broadway opening of Chodorov-Fields production of *The Ponder Heart* in February; show runs until late June; receives honorary LL.D. from Smith College.
1958–1961	Receives the Lucy Donnelley Fellowship Award from Bryn Mawr College; is made an Honorary Consultant of the Library of Congress; Welty's mother and brother fall ill— her brother Walter dies in January 1959.
1964	Publishes *The Shoe Bird*, a book for children; accepts teaching post at Millsaps College.

1966	Mary Welty (mother) dies in January; Welty's brother Edward dies a few days later.
1968	O. Henry first prize for "The Demonstrators."
1969	"The Optimist's Daughter" is published in *The New Yorker.*
1970	*Losing Battles* is published; Welty is awarded the Edward McDowell Medal.
1971	*One Time, One Place: Mississippi in the Depression, A Snapshot Album* is published with an introduction by Welty; Welty is named to American Academy of Arts and Letters.
1972	*The Optimist's Daughter* is published; Welty wins the National Institute of Arts and Letters Gold Medal for the Novel; She is appointed to a six year term on the National Council for the Arts.
1973	Welty wins the Pulitzer Prize for *The Optimist's Daughter*; Diarmuid Russell dies.
1978	*The Eye of the Story: Selected Essays and Reviews* is published.
1979	Travels to England for artist-in-residence program at University College, Oxford.
1980	The *Collected Stories of Eudora Welty* is published.
1981	Welty is awarded the National Medal of Literature and Medal of Freedom.
1983	Delivers the William E. Massey lectures at Harvard University in April.
1984	Publishes autobiography, *One Writer's Beginnings*; wins Modern Language Association Commonwealth Award.
1985	Wins the American Association of University Women Achievement Award.
1986	Jackson Public Library is named in honor of Eudora Welty; is awarded the National Medal of Arts.
1987	Is named Chevalier de L'ordre des Arts et Lettres (France).
1989	*Photographs* is published; portrait of Welty is added to National Portrait Gallery of the Smithsonian Institution.
1991	*The Norton Book for Friendship*, ed. Eudora Welty and Ronald A. Sharp, is published; is awarded the National Book Foundation Medal, the Helmerich Distinguished Author Award, the Cleanth Brooks Medal (Southern Letters); the Eudora Welty Society is organized.
1992	Awarded the Frankel Prize by the National Endowment for the Humanities.

1993	Receives PEN/Malamud Award (excellence in the short story); honorary doctorate, University of Dijon (France).
1994	*A Writer's Eye: Collected Book Reviews*, ed. Pearl Amelia McHaney, is published.
1995	Eudora Welty Writers' Center is established by Mississippi legislature on site of Welty's childhood home, 741 N. Congress St. in Jackson.
1996	Inducted into France's Legion of Honor.
1998	*Eudora Welty: Complete Novels* and *Eudora Welty: Stories, Essays, and Memoir* are published as part of Library of America series.
2001	Eudora Welty Dies on July 23.

Contributors

HAROLD BLOOM is Sterling Professor of the Humanities at Yale University. He is the author of 30 books, including *Shelley's Mythmaking* (1959), *The Visionary Company* (1961), *Blake's Apocalypse* (1963), *Yeats* (1970), *A Map of Misreading* (1975), *Kabbalah and Criticism* (1975), *Agon: Toward a Theory of Revisionism* (1982), *The American Religion* (1992), *The Western Canon* (1994), and *Omens of Millennium: The Gnosis of Angels, Dreams, and Resurrection* (1996). *The Anxiety of Influence* (1973) sets forth Professor Bloom's provocative theory of the literary relationships between the great writers and their predecessors. His most recent books include *Shakespeare: The Invention of the Human* (1998), a 1998 National Book Award finalist, *How to Read and Why* (2000), *Genius: A Mosaic of One Hundred Exemplary Creative Minds* (2002), *Hamlet: Poem Unlimited* (2003), *Where Shall Wisdom Be Found?* (2004), and *Jesus and Yahweh: The Names Divine* (2005). In 1999, Professor Bloom received the prestigious American Academy of Arts and Letters Gold Medal for Criticism. He has also received the International Prize of Catalonia, the Alfonso Reyes Prize of Mexico, and the Hans Christian Andersen Bicentennial Prize of Denmark.

PEGGY WHITMAN PRENSHAW is Fred C. Frey Professor of Southern Studies in the English department at Louisiana State University. She has edited collections of interviews with Welty and Elizabeth Spencer, as well as several volumes of essays on Welty and other women writers.

KENNETH BEARDEN is a professor at Butte College in California.

DEAN BETHEA is associate professor of English at Centenary College in New Jersey.

CHARLES E. MAY is professor emeritus at California State University, Long Beach. He has written extensively on the short story, and among his publications are *The New Short Story Theories* and *The Short Story: The Reality of Artifice*.

American novelist, poet, critic, and teacher ROBERT PENN WARREN became the first poet laureate of the United States in 1986. Warren's best-known novel is *All The King's Men* (1946), which was awarded the Pulitzer Prize in 1947. Warren was awarded the Pulitzer Prize for poetry twice, in 1957 for *Promises*, and 1979 for *Now and Then*.

WARREN FRENCH is professor emeritus of English at Indiana University-Purdue University, Indianapolis. He is the author of *John Steinbeck, John Steinbeck's Fiction Revisited*, and editor of *A Companion to The Grapes of Wrath*.

SUZANNE MARRS is professor of English at Millsaps College in Jackson, Mississippi, and has served as Welty Scholar at the Mississippi Department of Archives and History. She is the author of *The Welty Collection* and *One Writer's Imagination: The Fiction of Eudora Welty*, and is co-editor of *Eudora Welty and Politics: Did the Writer Crusade?*

ELIZABETH BOWEN was an Anglo-Irish novelist and short story writer. She was the author of many novels, short story collections, and essays.

MARILYN ARNOLD is an established writer of fiction and nonfiction. She has written many articles on Eudora Welty and Willa Cather, and is the author of the novel *Minding Mama*.

RUTH M. VANDE KIEFT was a friend of Welty's who followed her career for a quarter of a century. She is the author of several books on Eudora Welty.

SALLY WOLFF KING is associate dean of Emory College. She teaches Southern literature and Native American literature. She is the author of *Talking About William Faulkner*, and the coeditor of *Southern Mothers: Fact and Fiction in Southern Women's Writing*, as well as numerous articles on southern literature.

REYNOLDS PRICE is James B. Duke Professor of English at Duke University. A distinguished novelist, poet, dramatist, and essayist, he is the author of 25 books, among the most recent of which are *The Collected Stories*

(1993), *A Whole New Life*, and *The Promise of Rest* (1995). His work has been translated into 16 languages.

FRANZISKA GYGAX is professor of English at the Universität Basel in Switzerland. Her main interests include gender studies, queer studies, modernism, and the theory of autobiography. Among her publications are *Serious Daring from Within: Female Narrative Strategies in Eudora Welty's Novels* and *Gender and Genre in Gertrude Stein*.

DENIS DONOGHUE is Henry James Professor of English at New York University. His books include *Words Alone, Connoisseurs of Chaos, Ferocious Alphabets, We Irish, The Practice of Reading*, and *Speaking of Beauty*.

Bibliography

Bearden, Kenneth. "Monkeying Around: Welty's 'Powerhouse,' Blues-Jazz, and the Signifying Connection. *Southern Literary Journal* 31, no. 2 (Spring 1999): 65–79.

Bethea, Dean. "Phoenix Has No Coat: Historicity, Eschatology, and Sins of Omission in Eudora Welty's 'A Worn Path'." *International Fiction Review* 28 (2001): 32–41.

Binding, Paul. "Mississippi and Eudora Welty." In *Separate Country: A Literary Journey Through the American South.* New York/London: Paddington Press, Ltd., 1979. 131–148.

Bloom, Harold, ed. *Major Short Story Writers: Eudora Welty.* New York: Chelsea House, 1999.

Bowen, Elizabeth. "The Golden Apples." In *Seven Winters: Memories of a Dublin Childhood & Afterthought: Pieces on Writing,* ed. Elizabeth Bowen. New York: Alfred A. Knopf, 1962. 215–218.

Brantley, Will. *Feminine Sense in Southern Memoir: Smith, Glasgow, Welty, Hellman, Porter, and Hurston.* Jackson: University Press of Mississippi, 1993.

Bryant, J. A., Jr. *Eudora Welty.* Minneapolis: University of Minnesota Press, 1968.

Carson, Barbara H. *Eudora Welty: Two Pictures at Once in Her Frame.* Troy, NY: Whitston, 1992.

Chalmers, Rebecca. "Untangling the Wide Net: Welty and Readership." *Southern Literary Journal* 35, no. 2 (Spring 2003): 89–106.

Chouard, Geraldine. "Ties That Bind: The Poetics of Anger in 'Why I Live at the P.O.'" *Southern Quarterly* 39, no. 3 (Spring 2001): 34–50.

Costello, Brandon. "Swimming Free of the Matriarchy: Sexual Baptism and Female Individuality in Eudora Welty's *The Golden Apples.*" *Southern Literary Journal* 33, no.1 (Fall 2000): 82–93.

Desmond, John F., ed. *A Still Moment: Essays on the Art of Eudora Welty.* Metuchen, NJ: Scarecrow Press, 1979.

Devlin, Albert. *Eudora Welty's Chronicle: A Story of Mississippi Life.* Jackson: University Press of Mississippi, 1983.

———. *A Life in Literature.* Jackson: University Press of Mississippi, 1987.

Dollarhide, Louis, and Ann J. Abadie, eds. *Eudora Welty: A Form of Thanks.* Jackson: University Press of Mississippi, 1979.

Donoghue, Denis. "Eudora Welty's Sense of Place." *Place in American Fiction: Excursions and Explorations.* H.L. Weatherby and George Core, ed. Columbia, MO: University of Missouri Press, 2004. 133–146.

Eichelberger, Julia. *Prophets of Recognition: Ideology and the Individual in Novels by Ralph Ellison, Toni Morrison, Saul Bellow, and Eudora Welty.* Baton Rouge: Louisiana State University Press, 1999.

Evans, Elizabeth. *Eudora Welty.* New York: Ungar, 1981.

Ford, Sarah. "Rewriting Violence in Eudora Welty's *Losing Battles.*" *Mississippi Quarterly* 54 (Winter 2000–2001): 23–36.

Gretlund, Jan-Norby and Karl Westarp, eds. *The Late Novels of Eudora Welty.* Columbia, SC: University of South Carolina Press, 1998.

Gretlund, Jan-Norby. "ArchiTexture in Short Stories by Flannery O'Connor and Eudora Welty." *The Art of Brevity: Excursions in Short Fiction Theory and Analysis.* Per Winther, Jakob Lothe, and Hans H. Skei, ed. Columbia, SC: University of South Carolina Press, 2004. 151–161

Gygax, Franziska. *Serious Daring from Within: Narrative Strategies in Eudora Welty's Novels.* Westport, CT: Greenwood Press, 1990.

Harrison, Suzan. *Eudora Welty and Virginia Woolf: Gender, Genre, and Influence.* Baton Rouge: Louisiana State University Press, 1997.

Johnston, Carol Ann. *Eudora Welty: A Study of the Short Fiction.* New York: Twayne, 1997.

Kreyling, Michael. *Author and Agent: Eudora Welty and Diarmuid Russell.* New York: Farrar, Straus & Giroux, 1991.

MacKethan, Lucinda H. "Prodigal Daughters: The Journeys of Ellen Glasgow, Zora Neale Hurston and Eudora Welty." *Daughters of Time: Creating Women's Voice in Southern Story.* Athens, GA: University of Georgia Press, 1990. 37–63.

Manning, Carol S. *With Ears Opening Like Morning Glories: Eudora Welty and the Love of Storytelling.* Westport, CT: Greenwood Press, 1985.

———, ed. *The Female Tradition in Southern Literature.* Urbana: University of Illinois Press, 1993.

Mark, Rebecca. *The Dragon's Blood: Feminist Intertextuality in Eudora Welty's "The Golden Apples."* Jackson: University Press of Mississippi, 1994.

Marrs, Suzanne. *One Writer's Imagination: The Fiction of Eudora Welty.* Baton Rouge: Louisiana State University Press, 2002.

Martin, Matthew R. "Vision and Revelation in Eudora Welty's Fiction and Photography." *Southern Quarterly* 38, no. 4 (Summer 2000): 17–26.

McHaney, Pearl Amelia, ed. *Eudora Welty: The Contemporary Reviews.* Cambridge, UK; New York: Cambridge University Press, 2005.

McMillan, Sally. "Fairy Tales or Historical Records: Tales of the Natchez Trace in Eudora Welty's *The Robber Bridegroom.*" *Southern Studies* 10 (Spring-Summer 2003): 79–85.

Merricks, Correna Catlett. " 'What I Would Have Given Him He Liked Better to Steal': Sexual Violence in Eudora Welty's *The Robber Bridegroom.*" *Southern Studies* 12 (Fall-Winter 2005): 1–20.

Montgomery, Marion. *Eudora Welty and Walker Percy: The Concept of Home in Their Lives and Literature.* Jefferson, NC: McFarland & Co., 2004.

Mortimer, Gail L. *Daughter of the Swan: Love and Knowledge in Eudora Welty's Fiction.* Athens and London: University of Georgia Press, 1994.

Nissen, Axel. "Queer Welty, Camp Welty." *Mississippi Quarterly* 56 (Spring 2003): 209–229.

Oates, Joyce Carol. "Eudora's Web." *Contemporary Women Novelists: A Collection of Critical Essays.* Patricia Meyer Spacks, ed. Englewood Cliffs, NJ: Prentice-Hall, 1977. 167–172.

Pitavy-Souques, Daniele. " 'The Fictional Eye': Eudora Welty's Retranslation of the South." *South Atlantic Review* 65, no. 4 (Fall 2000): 90–113.

Pollack, Harriet, and Suzanne Marrs, eds. *Eudora Welty and Politics: Did the Writer Crusade?* Baton Rouge: Louisiana State University Press, 2001.

Prenshaw, Peggy Whitman, ed. *Conversations with Eudora Welty.* Jackson: University Press of Mississippi, 1984.

———, ed. *More Conversations with Eudora Welty.* Jackson: University Press of Mississippi, 1996.

———. *Eudora Welty: Critical Essays.* Jackson: University Press of Mississippi, 1979.

Price, Reynolds. "Finding Eudora." *Georgia Review* 53 (Spring 1999): 17–18.

Randisi, Jennifer Lynn. *A Tissue of Lies: Eudora Welty and the Southern Romance*. Washington, DC: University Press of America, 1982.

Schmidt, Peter. *The Heart of the Story: Eudora Welty's Short Fiction*. Jackson: University Press of Mississippi, 1991.

Trouard, Dawn. *The Eye of the Storyteller*. Kent, OH: Kent State University Press, 1989.

Turner, W. Craig and Lee Emling Harding, eds. *Critical Essays on Eudora Welty*. Boston: G.K. Hall & Co., 1989.

Vande Kieft, Ruth M. *Eudora Welty*. Boston: Twayne, 1987.

Waldron, Ann. *Eudora: A Writer's Life*. New York: Anchor Books, 1998.

Westling, Louise. *Eudora Welty*. Totowa, NJ: Barnes & Noble Books, 1988.

Weston, Ruth D. *Gothic Traditions and Narrative Techniques in the Fiction of Eudora Welty*. Baton Rouge: Louisiana State University Press, 1994.

Acknowledgments

"Welty's Transformations of the Public, the Private, and the Political" by Peggy Whitman Prenshaw. Reprinted by permission of Louisiana State University Press from *Eudora Welty and Politics: Did the Writer Crusade?* Eds. Harriet Pollack and Suzanne Marrs. Copyright © 2001 by Louisiana State University Press. Reprinted by permission.

"Monkeying Around: Welty's 'Powerhouse,' Blues-Jazz, and the Signifying Connection" by Kenneth Bearden. From *The Southern Literary Journal* Vol. 31, no. 2, 1999. © 1999 by the Department of English of the University of North Carolina at Chapel Hill. Used by permission of the University of North Carolina Press.

"Phoenix Has No Coat: Historicity, Eschatology, and Sins of Omission in Eudora Welty's 'A Worn Path'" by Dean Bethea. From *The International Fiction Review* 28, nos. 1 and 2 (2001): 32–41. © 2001 by International Fiction Association, Fredericton, N.B. Reprinted by permission.

"The Love and the Separateness in Miss Welty" by Robert Penn Warren. *Critical Essays on Eudora Welty.* Eds. W. Craig Turner and Lee Emling Harding. © 1989 by W. Craig Turner and Lee Emling Harding. Originally from *Kenyon Review* 6 (Spring 1944): 246–59. © 1958 by Robert Penn Warren. Reprinted by permission.

"Why Sister Lives at the P.O." by Charles E. May. From *Short Stories for Students*, vol. 10. Originally published in *The Critical Response to Eudora Welty,*

Every effort has been made to contact the owners of copyrighted material and secure copyright permission. Articles appearing in this volume generally appear much as they did in their original publication with few or no editorial changes. Those interested in locating the original source will find bibliographic information in the bibliography and acknowledgments sections of this volume.

Index